Edinburgh Studies
in the English Language

Dedicated to

Hermann Pálsson

Professor of Icelandic at the University of Edinburgh

in the year of his retirement, 1988, when he completes 38 years as a member of the Department of English Language at the University of Edinburgh

Edinburgh Studies in the English Language

Edited by

JOHN M. ANDERSON
Reader in English Language

and

NORMAN MACLEOD
Senior Lecturer in English Language

UNIVERSITY OF EDINBURGH

JOHN DONALD PUBLISHERS LTD
EDINBURGH

ISBN 0 85976 165 7

Distributed in the United States of America and
Canada by Humanities Press Inc., Atlantic Highlands,
NJ 07716, USA

Phototypesetting by Quorn Selective Repro Ltd., Loughborough.
Printed in Great Britain by Bell & Bain Ltd., Glasgow.

PREFACE

This volume is the first of an occasional series devoted to studies of the English language, in both its current and earlier varieties. The editors of the present volume are also the general editors for the series; and they and other members of the Department of English Language at the University of Edinburgh — Alex Agutter, Derek Britton, Fran Colman, Bridget Cusack and Heinz Giegerich —make up the editorial board. The contributions to this first volume (all by members of the University of Edinburgh) range from studies of the syntax and phonology of Old English to like studies of the present-day language, specifically its Scottish variety, and to studies of the language of literary texts; and they thus illustrate three significant types of study within the field of English Language which continue to be prominent in teaching and research at Edinburgh — linguistically-informed study of earlier periods of the language, the empirical and data-based study of (among others) the *local* regional variety of the language, and the linguistically-based study of literary language for both interpretative and text-analytical ends.

The series *Edinburgh Studies in the English Language* is offered as a venue for the publication of research whose primary concern is the linguistic character of English. The aim of the series is to reaffirm the vigour of a field distinguished by the descriptive richness of its tradition, by the particular character of the materials which are its immediate concern, and by the more general theoretical proposals that have sprung from it. In seeking to fulfil this aim, each volume in the series will be focused, broadly or narrowly, on one particular aspect of the language in a particular period or over a span of time. But the thematic character projected for subsequent volumes will not preclude the publication of individual papers that are important in their own right.

Further details concerning the themes of volumes 2 and 3, and the arrangements for the submission of contributions, are given in the *Editorial Statement*.

John M. Anderson

Norman Macleod

EDITORIAL STATEMENT

Edinburgh Studies in the English Language is an occasional series of volumes devoted to the English language. The aim of the series is to add to our understanding of the history and structure of the language in all its contemporary and historical varieties. The volumes following this one will be primarily thematic, with individual themes being announced in advance. (The themes for volumes 2 and 3 are indicated below.) The specification of a theme for a particular volume will allow for some contributions to be by invitation, or for the raising of contributions to be assigned to a guest editor. But all interested scholars are encouraged to submit appropriate material for any particular volume. In all cases intended contributions will be submitted to two readers for evaluation. One of these will normally be a member of the editorial board, which consists of members of the English Language Department at the University of Edinburgh. In recommending papers for publication the editors will take particular account of the readers' reports, but the formal decision on final acceptance will rest with the board. It is editorial policy to include in each volume a list of readers consulted.

The announced themes should not be seen as thoroughly exclusive: the editors will consider papers on any aspect of the academic study of the English language, including Scots. They will particularly welcome the submission of papers concerned with earlier periods of English or its diachronic development. Wherever a paper concerned with literary material is offered for consideration, this should be as part of a study in stylistics or in text structure. There is no restriction on approach: any appropriate linguistic or philological framework will be acceptable, but in all cases the emphasis should be on the analysis of linguistic material, treated either for what it adds to our understanding of the history and structure of English or in connexion with some significant theoretical issue.

Manuscripts should be submitted in three copies, two of which should bear no indication of authorship or affiliation. Intending contributors are asked to comply with the *ESEL Stylesheet*, which is available upon request from the appended editorial address. Return of manuscripts can be guaranteed only if adequate provision for return mailing is also sent. All submissions will be briefly acknowledged on receipt, with an indication of when a decision on acceptability can be expected. This will normally be within two or three months.

The theme for volume two is *Evidence for Old English: Material and theoretical bases for reconstruction*, guest editor Fran Colman; that for volume three is *'Variability' in the history of English*. Outline descriptions of these themes are given below. Contributions intended for volume two should reach Fran Colman at the editorial address before the end of March 1989; the closing date for submissions to volume three will be the end of December 1989. The editors will also welcome suggestions concerning possible themes for subsequent issues.

Volume 2: *Evidence for Old English*

Volume 2 of *ESEL* will contain articles presenting a variety of theoretical interpretations of the materials which are the primary data for reconstructing Old English. These materials consist of manuscript orthography and runic and coin epigraphy; but these alone do not constitute evidence. This comes from interpretations of the available data within a theoretical framework (or frameworks). The volume will reflect the increased awareness on the part of philologists and linguists of the interdependence of the two branches of the same discipline: of the significance of linguistic theory in interpreting the philological material, and of the light that knowledge about Old English may cast on a wide area of linguistic concerns, such as possible language universals, the nature(s) of various linguistic changes, synchronic variation in present-day English, and so on.

Volume 3: *'Variability' in the History of English*

The proposed theme for volume 3 of *ESEL* can be summed up in a quotation (from Weinreich, Labov and Herzog's "Empirical Foundations for a Theory of Language Change") that might almost be regarded as a motto for the volume:

> Not all variability and heterogeneity in language structure involves change; but all change involves variability and heterogeneity.

A recognition of the diachronic significance of variability is now a feature of a good deal of work in the history of English — particularly, for example, among those known to us in Edinburgh as 'Northern Scholars'. The editors of *ESEL*, seeing such work as fruitfully combining the linguistic and philological traditions, invite contributions from scholars interested in treating variants and variation as evidence for developments in the history of English.

Editorial address: John Anderson and Norman Macleod
Department of English Language
University of Edinburgh
David Hume Tower
George Square
Edinburgh EH8 9JX
Scotland

CONTRIBUTORS

Alex Agutter, Lecturer, Department of English Language, University of Edinburgh.

John M. Anderson, Reader, Department of English Language, University of Edinburgh.

Fran Colman, Lecturer, Department of English Language, University of Edinburgh.

Norman Macleod, Senior Lecturer, Department of English Language, University of Edinburgh.

Jim Miller, Reader, Department of Linguistics, University of Edinburgh.

CONTENTS

1

THE TYPE OF OLD ENGLISH IMPERSONALS

John Anderson

I shall be concerned here to offer a typological characterisation of 'impersonal' clauses in Old English (OE), and thus of the verbs that appear in them.* (I ignore here non-verbal impersonals, which *mutatis mutandis* do not differ in type.) This characterisation is offered within the framework of a case grammer (CG), particularly as developed in Anderson 1971, 1977; Böhm 1982. I begin, therefore, with an introductory sketch (§1) of the constraints imposed on syntactic theory by that particular conception and of the consequence for typology. §2 is occupied with some more detailed exemplification of the notions introduced in §1. From §3 on we shall focus on the character of 'impersonals', particularly in relation to OE, but also in an attempt to arrive at a precise formulation of the notion 'impersonal' and its types.

1 Case Grammar and Contrast

I take it that the specifications which the grammar provides, in the form of lexical or dictionary entries, for individual predicates contain only information that is idiosyncratic, or CONTRASTIVE, i.e. not predictable from other properties. This is generally accepted and applied (at least in intent) in relation to the phonological content of dictionary entries; the (word, or lexical) phonology is concerned precisely with the filling in of redundancies, whether these involve the fully specifying of individual segments or the assignment of suprasegmental structure. (However, for a rather more radical interpretation of contrast in phonology than is usual see Anderson 1987a.) But clearly (given the above characterisation of lexical entries) the same considerations apply to the non-phonological content of lexical entries — as is, indeed, demanded by the STRUCTURAL ANALOGY assumption, which expects recurrence of formal properties in relation to distinct planes (see Anderson 1985a (also this vol); and, on syntax, Anderson 1987b). However, typically, this contrastiveness requirement is not consistently applied to the syntactic information embodied in lexical entries.

---

* Some of the material on which this study is based was presented at the University of Essex in May 1985. That presentation and subsequent contributions, personal and impersonal, from Roger Böhm, Fran Colman and Roger Lass have greatly influenced the form and substance of the present work; but its subject-matter (or lack of) remains my personal responsibility.

For instance, such entries usually incorporate strict subcategorisation frames in which LINEARITY is invoked. Thus, for example, the observation that *kiss* is a verb which takes a direct object will typically be expressed as in (1):

(1) $\begin{bmatrix} +V \\ \\ +[\text{------} NP] \end{bmatrix}$

where the environment bar indicates the linear position of instances of *kiss* vis-à-vis its object. However, this position is not an idiosyncratic property of *kiss*; *kiss* does not contrast with verbs that take a preceding object. Position of the object relative to its verb is predictable, redundant: it is filled in by the syntax. I am, indeed, aware of no evidence for invoking linearity in lexical entries. Predicates do not contrast in this respect; linearity is universally redundant.

CG embodies an even more restrictive view of contrastiveness in syntax. Not only linearity but also any clausal configurationality (notably, the presence of VP) and the assignment of grammatical relations (GRs), such as subject, are hypothesised to be non-contrastive. PREDICATES contrast in the number of (participant) ARGUMENTS they take (i.e. are subcategorised for), the semantic functions or case relations (CRs) contracted by these arguments and whether or not particular arguments are themselves predicates (as with *happy* in *John looks happy* as an argument of *look*) rather than (nominal) TERMS. More detailed selectional properties of predicates make reference to this information and not to linearity, configurationality or GRs. These latter are predictable from the contrastive information (which may be even further compacted — see e.g. Anderson 1977: §2.1–.3, forthcoming b — but I do not pursue this here).

Consider, for example, the (randomly selected) English sentence in (2):

(2)   The farmer killed the duckling

All that the strict subcategorisation frame for *kill* need contain is the information that it takes an agentive — ERG(ATIVE) in the terminology of Anderson 1977 — and an ABS(OLUTIVE) (neutral, 'theme') argument, as expressed in (3):

(3)   → erg, abs

where '→' can be interpreted as 'takes as an argument' — more generally, 'takes as a dependent' (cf. previous references on CG, as well as Colman this vol). In the unmarked instances, erg and abs are further assigned terms (roughly NPs). Further selectional restrictions (whatever their semantico-pragmatic status), such as the preference of *kill* for an animatoid abs argument (i.e. one regarded as (if) animate), are formulable with respect to such a frame.

The subject of the clause in which *kill* appears is selected in accordance with a hierarchy of CRs:

(4)   erg > erg + case > abs + case > abs

where '>' means 'outranks as potential subject' and where 'case' is any CR.

Subjecthood is assigned to the argument in a particular predication whose CR specification is furthest to the left in (4). A single argument may contract more than one CR, as indicated by the '+' in (4), and as illustrated by the subject in (5):

(5)   The farmer left

which is simultaneously erg, as denoting the source of the action, and abs, denoting the entity affected. The full hierarchy need not concern us here (for discussion and motivation see e.g. Anderson 1977, 1979a,b). In the present instances ((2) and (5)) the erg argument is preferred as subject. As such, it appears in pre-verbal position; and the verb and the rest of its participants (if any) are grouped as a constituent (VP), with these arguments positioned to the right of the verb. *The duckling* in (2), as an abs argument which is denied subjecthood by the erg *the farmer*, has a privileged status among such arguments; it is a direct object, and as such immediately follows the verb, without (in the unmarked instance) adpositional marker. (On objecthood see further Anderson 1984a, and §2 below).

All of these properties (linearity, clausal configurationality, the distribution of GRs) are derivative of subcategorisation frames such as that in (3). And we can go on to offer specific proposals as to their precise derivative status. Anderson (1977), for instance, assumes a syntax with cyclic and post-cyclic components, and suggests that GRs are introduced cyclically, and that at least the linearisation of predicates and their arguments is also so introduced. This need not concern us immediately here — though I shall return specifically to the place of subject selection in §5 below. What is more important in the present context is the distinction drawn by CG between contrastive and redundant syntactic properties.

We can strengthen the CG hypothesis further by requiring that the set of contrastive properties constitute a small universal set. In particular, the CRs are so limited; Anderson (1971, 1977) suggests that the predicates in any language can be exhaustively specified as to the types of arguments they take with reference to only four CRs and combinations thereof: abs, erg, LOC(ATIVE) and ABL(ATIVE). These are invariant across languages; and, together with the distinction between arguments as predicates or not (terms), they supply the contrastive syntactic information in any lexical entry for a predicate.

This limits potential syntactic variation to the derivative properties. The phenomena we consider below involve primarily the assignment of GRs. I shall suggest that one language variable consists of whether or not GRs are assigned at all. Another is the nature of the GR(s) assigned: are they assigned in conformity with the hierarchy of (4) or otherwise determined? These distinctions form the basis for a language typology in this area. (Linearity is a partially distinct variable.)

Before turning to illustration of such variation, let me draw a distinction between two types of GR assignment which adds a further dimension to our typology. Subject assignment involves NEUTRALISATION of CRs: subjects may be ergs, as in (2), or abs (in the absence of erg):

(6)   The duckling died

or some combination of these with another CR or with each other (as with the subject of (5)). But assignment of GRs may also involved DIVERSIFICATION: thus, not all abs arguments are direct objects. According to Anderson 1977: 38, 278–9, 1984a, neither abs argument in (7):

(7)   The killer was that farmer

is a direct object, whereas that in (2) is. The post-verbal abs in (2) and (7) are diversified by the differential assignment of direct-object-hood.

CG limits relational variation between languages to neutralisation and diversification of the CRs. Let us refer to these as GRAMMATICALISATIONS of the CRs. Any typology of such variation requires the establishment of the limits of variation: what types of grammaticalisation are instantiated; does the occurrence of a particular type correlate with the presence of other syntactic properties (e.g. Is object formation always associated with subject formation?); do certain combinations of CRs favour or resist particular types of grammaticalisation (cf. e.g. Anderson 1984b); do certain classes of predicate (e.g. nominalisations) favour particular types of grammaticalisation (cf. Anderson 1985b, forthcoming a; and §2 below)? And along another dimension: do some language systems show less grammaticalisation of CRs than others — as is arguably the case in Dyirbal, where in the unmarked instances abs and erg are not neutralised, except that erg + abs is not distinguished derivatively from abs (Anderson 1979b: §2; and cf. §6 below)?

What follows is intended as a contribution to the elaboration of such a typology, as well as to the elucidation of a particular domain in the syntax of OE, in the form of an attempt to set out some of the characteristics of a particular type of grammaticalisation. Firstly, however, let me try to illustrate some types of grammaticalisation from a perhaps more familiar area.

2 Neutralisation and Diversification

Subject formation in Present-day English (henceforth PE) clauses illustrates one very common pattern of neutralisation. Subjecthood is assigned in accordance with the hierarchy of (4) above. Some apparent discrepancies in the assignment of subjecthood in this respect are to be accounted for otherwise.

For example, the fact that sentences like (8) in PE, with 'temporal' subject:

(8)   Tuesday saw the demise of the duckling

are not replicated in other apparently subject-forming languages (like German — Kirkwood 1970; Rohdenburg 1974) should not be taken as showing that English allows a wider range of subjects as far as their CRs are concerned; in particular, that it allows, counter-hierarchically, (temporal) locatives to be subjects, in preference to abs. Rather, PE allows greater extension to the notion 'acceptable argument of an erg', or in the present instance 'erg + loc' ('experiencer'). Notice that *see* is a verb that elsewhere takes an erg + loc and an abs argument (*The shepherdess saw the demise of the duckling*). (8) does not require a distinct subcategorisation frame; *Tuesday* is a (surrogate, if you like) erg + loc not countenanced in e.g. German. 'Temporals' are not available for subjecthood:

(9)   *Tuesday (was) killed the duckling by the farmer

unless they are interpreted as erg (case), as e.g. in (8), or are abs (*Tuesday lasted forever*). *Tuesday* in (8) does not contract the simple CR loc, as it does in (10):

(10)   The farmer killed the duckling on Tuesday

or, hypothetically, in (9). Subjecthood is not available to 'temporals' in a simple locative function, let alone a circumstantial function, as in (10). The limited accessibility to subjecthood of temporals is related to their capacity in PE for interpretation as erg (case).

The notion of subject applicable to languages like PE and German — and, I would claim, universally (where invoked) — is reconstructable uniformly with respect to selection in accordance with the hierarchy of (4). Conditions on subject selection do not vary, though particular constructions may be exempted (Anderson 1984b; and see further below). However, not all neutralisations of CRs are subject-forming, i.e. in conformity with the hierarchy of CRs. This is arguably the case with the selection of the so-called 'focus' argument in Tagalog (Anderson 1979b: §4), with respect to the selection of which erg has no special status. Whether we refer to neutralised relations selected in this way as subjects or not might be thought to be a 'merely' terminological matter. But such an equation not only violates the traditional understanding of the extension of the term 'subject' and the privileged position of 'agents' therein (cf. e.g. Atkinson, Kilby and Roca 1982: §6.2), but also obscures important typological differences between these two varieties of neutralisation: considerations to do e.g. with the presence of objects and the availability of passivation. Let me now illustrate this with some material from PE itself.

Predications which are realised in PE as NOMINALISATIONS, i.e. predications constituting a term in a superior predication, are also associated with a neutralised argument, as illustrated in (11):

(11.a)   the farmer's extermination of the duckling
    b)   the duckling's demise
    c)   the farmer's departure

where the ATTRIBUTIVE genitive arguments are respectively erg, abs and erg + abs. But such genitives are not selected in accordance with hierarchy (4). Notice that as well as (11.a) we can also have (12):

(12)   the duckling's extermination by the farmer

in which the abs argument is preferred as genitive over the erg. In clausal structures, such an argument is allowed subject position only in passives:

(13)   The duckling was killed by the farmer

where its occurrence as such is in conformity with the hierarchy of (4), in that it is the only term in a predication whose other argument is a predicate (*killed*) not available for subjecthood, whereas *the farmer* is part of a non-finite (subjectless) predication:

(14)   [The duckling was [killed by the farmer]]

(or it is circumstantial — Anderson 1977: §3.3). There is no evidence of such a structure in (12), however.

Notice too that even a subset of circumstantial locatives may be selected as genitives. Thus we have (15):

(15)   Tuesday's extermination of the duckling by the farmer

as well as (16):

(16.a)   the farmer's extermination of the duckling on Tuesday
   b)   the duckling's extermination by the farmer on Tuesday

(15) cannot be accounted for in the same way as (8), as being compatible with the hierarchy of CRs; such genitives are not limited to particular types of predicates but are generally available in nominalisations. (15) is genuinely counter-hierarchical, as is (12).

Attributive formation in PE nominalisations is a distinct kind of neutralisation from subject formation in clauses (for further discussion see again Anderson 1985b, forthcoming a). It is not bounded by the hierarchy (and it is not merely that certain kinds of nominalisation arguments are exempted — though this is also the case). And there is no evidence for passive or object formation. With respect to the latter, notice that, just as the erg argument in (12) and (15) is marked with the *by* generally associated with (unneutralised) erg, so the abs in (11.a) is marked with *of*, whose association with abs, rather than a GR such as object, is reinforced when we now turn to a further property of attributive formation.

Attributive formation also differs from subject formation in PE in being optional. Compare with (11.a) and (12) the form in (17):

(17)   (the) extermination of the duckling by the farmer

and with (11.b) that in (18):

(18)   (the) demise of the duckling

in which, in the absence of neutralisation, erg is realised as *by* and abs as *of*. Just as (12) does not show passive, so the abs in (11.a) is not differentiated from other abs by object assignment. Moreover, as is appropriate with an (unneutralised) argument that (like the neutralised one in (11.c)) is simultaneously erg and abs, we find in (19):

(19)   (the) departure by/of the farmer

marking with either *by* or *of*. In the (optional) absence of attributive formation, the distribution of prepositions reflects the CRs assigned to the appropriate arguments, as it does with the non-genitive arguments in nominalisations which show attributive formation.

Obligatory status for subject formation is not as such universally criterial (see below). But it does provide a further distinction between clausal subject formation and attributive formation in nominalisations in PE.

We should note here, incidentally, that the genitive in GERUND constructions in PE exhibits both a subject and a non-subject strategy. The non-subject neutralisation is exhibited in (20):

(20.a)   (the) killing of the duckling by the farmer
   b)   the farmer's killing of the duckling
   c)   the duckling's killing by the farmer
   d)   Tuesday's killing of the duckling by the farmer

(though the (c) variant is often at best marginal with *-ing*-forms). And the operation of subject formation is illustrated in (21):

(21.a)   the farmer's killing the duckling
   b)   the duckling's being killed by the farmer

where the latter show an object, in (a), which turns up as the passive subject in (b), which is clearly marked as a passive. There is no subject-forming example parallel to (20.d), of course. In the subject-forming sub-system the genitive *s* may optionally be lacking:

(22.a)   the farmer killing the duckling
   b)   the duckling being killed by the farmer

This dual pattern of neutralisation with gerunds has important consequences for the analysis of such constructions (which, in a sense, are either nominalisations or de-clausal); but I do not pursue this here.

The preceding examples illustrate two dimensions in the grammaticalisation of CRs: reference to the hierarchy vs. absence thereof, and optionality vs. obligatoriness. In both respects we have been concerned with neutralisations in the main. However, incidentally, illustrations of diversification have arisen. A comparison of (20.b) and (21.a) reveals that an abs may be realised either as an object (21) or not (20). I have already alluded to this diversificatory function of object formation above, with reference to (2) and (7). And in their case diversification takes place in a subject-forming system (rather than by virtue of a comparison between such and a sub-system lacking subjects). Absence vs. presence of subject formation also diversifies the realisation of erg in (13) vs. (2), where again the diversification is a product of partial neutralisation. A further example of diversification associated with partial neutralisation is provided by the OE phenomena to which we now turn. These phenomena are also relevant to the question (raised at the conclusion of the preceding section) of whether particular constructions, specified in terms of the configuration of arguments and CRs attributed to them, differ in their susceptibility or resistance to neutralisations.

3 OE Impersonals and Subject Formation

OE (and other, particularly Indo-European languages) is traditionally said to possess constructions termed 'impersonal' (see e.g. van der Gaaf 1904: ch.1; Mitchell 1985: §§1025–51). My characterisation of IMPERSONAL constructions is, however, rather more restrictive than either van der Gaaf's or Mitchell's. An impersonal construction is a clause (a) which lacks even an elliptical, reconstructable argument in the nominative case and (b) whose finite (and thus tensed) verb lacks person/number variation (it is invariably in the form of the 'third person singular'). Thus, (23):

(23)   ...norþan   sniwde
        'from the north' 'it-snowed'

is impersonal, whereas (24):

(24)   Hit sniwð
        'it' 'is-snowing'

is not. (24) is what I shall call SEMI-IMPERSONAL, in that it meets only criterion (b).

It seems to me misleading to lump these two construction types together, in that, for instance, it obscures a fundamental typological difference between OE and PE: whereas *sniwan* in OE can appear in either impersonal or semi-impersonal constructions, PE *snow* is limited to the semi-impersonal. PE has no impersonal constructions proper.

Notice, moreover, that Mitchell's (1985: 427) formulation ('an impersonal construction is one which has only the formal subject *hit* ... or which has no expressed subject and for which no subject other than the formal *hit* can be supplied') misleadingly suggests that any impersonal construction (in my sense) has a corresponding semi-impersonal one. However, as Mitchell himself observes later (§1032), following Wahlén 1925, impersonal constructions like (25):

(25)   Me   hingrode
        'I' + dat/acc 'hungered'

and (26):

(26)   ... him   ðæs   scamode
        'he/they' + dat 'that' + gen 'shamed'

are not matched in OE by semi-impersonals with 'formal *hit*'. 'Formal *hit*' is most frequent with participant-less constructions like (23/24); and semi-impersonals are available as an alternative with some single-participant verbs (Mitchell 1985: §1033), including verbs which take only a sentential argument. But Mitchell's definition obscures the restrictions on its distribution; impersonal constructions as a whole cannot be said to be matched by corresponding semi-impersonals. Indeed, 'formal *hit*' alternatives are typical of those constructions where otherwise no non-impersonal variant would be available: the predicate is argumentless or takes a sentential one.

Let us begin our examination of the properties of impersonals with the two-participant type illustrated by (26). These constitute Elmer's (1981) RUE class, as well as most PLEASE/DESIRE verbs. (We consider *lician* 'to-please', exceptional in this regard, in the section which follows.) Such a clause meets both criteria for impersonal status: there is no nominative argument, and a change in the person and/or number of neither argument leads to a change in the finite verb form. One of the arguments is in the dative case, the other is genitive. The first bears the CRs erg + loc ('experiencer'), as simultaneously instigator and location of the (internal) event; the other is abl (as (abstract) source). We can subcategorise *scamian* as in (27),

(27)   → erg + loc, abl

The case inflexions reflect this distribution of CRs: i.e. they are redundantly specified. And the neutralisation we associate with subject formation is absent in these realisations, as far as the testimony of case-marking and concord is concerned.

Some such verbs (e.g. *hreowan* 'to-pity') show either a dative or an accusative experiencer. Given the paucity of the evidence and the fact that dative and accusative are frequently not distinguished in OE (notably e.g. in non-third-person pronouns), it is difficult to determine the systematicity of such differences in the apparent behaviour of verbs (Mitchell 1985: §1027). So too with the alternation with some verbs between a genitive abl and a (increasingly frequent) prepositional. It may be, however, that at least some such verbs should be specified for idiosyncratic case marking. Van der Leek (1986), on the other hand, has argued that the dative/accusative alternation is systematic and semantically consistent: I do not pursue this here.

However, as noted, assignment of initial or even derived subjecthood to an argument in constructions like (26) containing a type-(27) verb does not seem to be warranted. Apart from the lack of morphological correlates, position in OE is indecisive. Thus, no conclusions concerning subjecthood can be drawn from the tendency to place the highly empathetic and frequently topical experiencer (particularly if pronominal) in initial position (Wahlén 1925: 10). However, we return to a more detailed examination of the evidence in §5 below.

That status as an 'impersonal verb' is dependent on the configuration of CRs rather than at least in part on the case inflexions is confirmed by the fact that 'experiencer' verbs which show a genitive argument that is not an abl are not impersonal in OE. Thus, *þearf* 'I-need' takes a 'virtual, unrealised' abs, which as such is usually marked by a ('partitive') genitive (Anderson 1985c), as in (28):

(28)   Ne   ðearf   he   nanes   þinges buton ...
       'not' 'need' 'he' + nom   'nothing' + gen 'except' ...

unless, of course, the abs is a predication:

(29)   He   ne   ðearf   na   faran   fram   stowe   to   stowe
       'he' 'not' 'need' 'not' 'go'   'from' 'place' 'to' 'place'

But (28) and (29) are both personal: the 'experiencer' is nominative. Despite the potential parallel in inflexional marking with *scamian* verbs, *þearf* does not appear in constructions like that in (26). The impersonal construction is not available to verbs subcategorised for 'experiencer' and abs, even when the abs comes to be marked by the genitive.

It is only later (in Middle English) that *þearf*, along with other such verbs, including the loanwords *lakken* and *wanten*, shows an impersonal construction as an alternative to (29):

(30)   Have   thou   y-nough,   thee   thar not pleyne thee
       'have' 'you' + nom 'enough' 'you' + dat/acc 'need' 'not' 'complain' 'you'

(van der Gaaf 1904: §183). I shall not pursue the consequences of this, partly in that it would involve a more detailed analysis of OE (and other) predicate types than can be provided within the scope of the present study. But it is perhaps worth remarking that it looks as if in the Middle English period the possibility of appearing in an impersonal construction was extended to verbs in which the 'experiencer' was erg + abl, rather than erg + loc, as with these verbs and also *aȝen* (OE *agan*) (van der Gaaf 1904: §§175–7).

We can conclude provisionally that (the arguments of) verbs subcategorised as in (27) can contract out of subject formation in OE. But such 'impersonal verbs' also appear in personal constructions, i.e. clauses which meet neither of the criteria put forward above. Let us note at this point a variant in which the experiencer argument is in the nominative and controls concord (as in (28/29):

(31)   Ic   ðæs   ne scamige
       'I' = nom   'that' + gen 'not' 'shame' + 1st sg

(cf. Mitchell 1985: §1038). We need not allow for this in terms of a separate subcategorisation frame, but rather, as with the PE nominalisation discussed in §2, in terms of the optionality of subject formation.

This optionality of subject formation extends to single-participant constructions like that in (25), with which we should compared (32):

(32)   [Iesus] cuoeð   ic   ðyrsto
              'says'   'I' + nom   'thirst' + 1st sg

With some verbs in such constructions (notably 'mental' ones), a 'formal *hit*' can rather be provided:

(33)   (Hit) me   of þincð
       'it' 'I' + dat/acc 'sorrow' + 3rd sg

just as with no-participant verbs. Again (cf. §2 above) optionality in assigning a GR (itself a neutralisation) creates a diversification in the realisation of a particular CR or CR combination.

The non-experiencer argument with verbs like *scamian* may also be predicational, either finite or infinitival. The construction may again be either impersonal:

(34)   Me   sceamaþ ðæt ic wædlige
       'I' + dat/acc 'shame' + 3rd sg 'that' 'I' 'am in want'

or personal:

(35)   Gif we   scomiaþ ðæt we   ... sprecan
       'if' 'we' + nom 'shame' + pl 'that' 'we'   ... 'speak'

(34) remains impersonal, as meeting the criteria introduced above. There is no motivation for regarding the subordinate clause as a subject, given this, and given its clearly non-subject status in (35), even apart from the lack of any positive evidence for its subjecthood. Indeed, clausal arguments in OE simply do not undergo subject formation.

Consider, for instance, a verb like *gelimpan* 'happen'. It appears in constructions with one participant, which, as an abs, if nominal, undergoes subject formation, as in (36):

(36)   Ða   sio   tid   gelomp
      'when' 'the' 'time' 'came to pass'

However, a clausal argument fails to subject-form and remains resolutely post-verbal, despite pre-V position being unmarked for subjects.

(37)   Gelomp   þæt an swiþe wis mon...
      'happened' 'that' 'a' 'very' 'wise' 'man'...

Such a construction may be supplied with a 'formal *hit*':

(38)   þa   gelamp hit þæt æt ðam gyftum...
      'then' 'happened' 'it' 'that' 'at' 'the' 'marriage'...

confirming the non-subject status of the subordinate clause in (38) and (37).

Mitchell, however, asserts (1985: §1039) that the presence of *hit* makes it 'impossible' to deny subjecthood to the subordinate clause in such examples as (38). This seems to be based on the assumption that the *hit* is somehow here 'in apposition' with the clause. Such a conclusion is perplexing, given that 'formal *hit*' otherwise does not entail 'apposition' (cf. (24)), and that no motivation is offered for an 'appositional' interpretation of the *hit* in examples like (38), which indeed seems to be at odds with the notion 'formal *hit*' and certainly is not required even by Mitchell's own definition of 'apposition' (1985: §1428). A more generally appropriate assumption is that 'formal *hit*' here is simply introduced by the same mechanism as elsewhere, as a 'default subject' (cf. §6 below), and that, as elsewhere, OE clauses are not subjects. This has, if nothing more, the virtue of absolving Mitchell of his self-induced 'terminological' difficulty as to whether to call the subordinate clause in (35), (37) and (38) a 'subject' or a 'causative object' — given the absence of motivations for according subjecthood to subordinate clauses. — Though that in (37/38) is scarcely a 'causative object' either!

(37) introduces another type of impersonal (Elmer's (1981) HAPPEN class), again unparalleled in PE (which has semi-impersonals only, of the type of (38)): an impersonal which lacks a subject by virtue of the failure of a clausal argument to assume subjecthood and the absence of another eligible argument. Let us now proceed to attempt a classification of impersonals in OE and the configurations of CRs with which they are associated.

4 Types of Impersonal in OE

We have encountered impersonals associated with several different sub-categorisation frames. Firstly, there are those which involve verbs without participants, as in (23). Constructions including such verbs may alternatively be provided with a 'formal *hit*' (24), and so be semi-impersonal. Similarly, verbs which take only an abs argument appear in impersonal constructions if the abs is predicational rather than a term (contrast (37) and (36)), unless once more the construction is supplied with a 'formal *hit*' (38). Impersonal/semi-impersonal status can thus be associated with the subcategorisation frames in (39):

(39)   → (abs → V)

i.e. absence of a participant or presence of a predicational (V rather than N) abs participant alone.

The specification in (39) also allows for (semi-)impersonal constructions with *beon/wesan* 'be' and *(ge)weorþan* 'become', as in *On sumera hit bið wearm* 'In summer it is warm' (Wahlén 1925: 12; Mitchell 1985: §1045), with an adjectival predicate as argument, or in *Da wæs sona æfter þon þæt smyltnes com cristenra tida* 'Then [it] was soon after that that the gentleness of Christian times came' (Mitchell 1985: §1046), with a clausal argument, as well as 'passives' with a single, predicational participant, such as *Sægd is þæt ...*' [It] is said that ...' (Mitchell 1985: §841).

Further, transitive verbs in OE which take a dative or genitive 'object', and are personal when active, appear in 'impersonal passives' rather than 'personal' — with the possible exception of the dative-'object' verb *fultumian* 'to-help' (Mitchell 1985: §851). Thus, with *ti(o)lan* 'to-provide', which takes a genitive 'object', we find examples such as (40):

(40)   Forðæm   se   ðe   his   ær   tide
        'therefore' 'he' 'who' 'himself' + gen 'before the time'

ne   tiolað   þonne   bið   his   on tid
'not' 'provides' 'then' 'will be' 'he' + gen 'at the time'
untilad
'unprovided'

(Mitchell 1985: §849), with no nominative argument for *beon*, which has only a predicate (*untilad*) as argument, with *his* as an argument of the latter. Clauses such as the main one in (40) (whatever their status: 'passive', derived adjectival construction, ...) also meet the criterion of (39) for impersonalhood: we have '*beon* → abs → V'.

Impersonal constructions are also associated, optionally, with verbs like *scamian*, which lack an agent (erg) but take an 'experiencer' (erg + loc) argument and a 'causal' source (abl), as expressed in the frame of (27). So too with verbs that take simply an 'experiencer', as *hingrian, þyrstan*:

(41)   → erg + loc

(cf. (25)). These suggestions concerning subcategorisation ((27) vs. (41)) require some comment.

It is the case both that verbs like *scamian* may appear in clauses lacking an overt 'cause' NP or clause (*me sceamaþ*) and that *þyrstan*, for example, may apparently show such an argument:

(42)   Ðeah   ðæt   folc   ðyrste   ðære   lare
        'though' 'that' 'people + acc/nom 'thirst' 'that knowledge' + gen/dat

But I take these to be extensions of the basic pattern in both instances: with *scamian* etc. the 'cause' is sometimes unspecified; with *þyrstan* etc. a 'cause' may optionally be present, such that we might substitute (43) for (41):

(43)   → erg + loc (abl)

However, the necessarily imperfect intuitions on which these are based have not been substantiated with e.g. statistics concerning the occurrence of such verbs with and without genitive arguments. So I should perhaps not press the distinction drawn here between *scamian* and *þyrstan* verbs: — but see below for a possible argument in support. 'More work is needed here', as Mitchell might say; but, I would imagine, with the help of a computer.

Similarly, some verbs of the type of *gelimpan* allow an optional 'experiencer':

(44)   → abs → V (erg + loc)

Consider, for example, (45):

(45.a)   Ðonne   hit   gebyrigan   mæg ...
          'when'   'it'   'happen'   'may' ...
     b)   ... ac him   gebyraþ   to standenne þa men
          'but' 'he/they' + dat 'behove' + 3rd sg 'to bury' 'the men'

in which (b) displays such an experiencer. We should then extend the frame in (39) with which such impersonals are associated as in (46):

(46)   → (abs → V) (erg + loc)

to allow for such a possibility.

The verb *þyncan* 'to-seem', for example, as well as taking an abs and an optional 'experiencer', as illustrated in (47):

(47)   Ða   ðæm   hearpere ða   ðuhte   ðæt   hine ...
       'when' 'the harper' + dat 'then' 'seemed'   'that'   'he' + acc ...

may show both a predicational and a term abs (as a result of raising — see e.g. Anderson 1984c: chs.4 and 6):

(48)   Ðynceþ   him   swiðe   leoht   sio byrðen ...
       'seemed' 'he/they' + dat   'very'   'light' 'the burden' ...

the predicate being adjectival (*leoht*). In accordance with the constraints we have observed (collapsed as (50) below), neither the predicational abs nor the erg + loc argument is eligible for subjecthood; however, the nominal abs (*sio byrðen*), as allowed by (4) (and the OE restrictions on sentential subjects), is available for subject formation. This means that we must interpret the occurrence of frames (27/43) and (46), which by themselves allow or require impersonal constructions, as indicating that the arguments specified therein are not eligible for subjecthood, but that their presence in a frame does not forbid the selection of another eligible argument which may be present, even though it is outranked in terms of (4) by one or other of the arguments to which subjecthood is prohibited. (For a rather different interpretation of (48), involving total absence of subject formation, cf. Anderson 1984b.)

The related verb *þencan* takes an obligatory erg + loc and a not necessarily sentential abs, and thus appears in a personal construction:

(49.a) nænig heora   þohte   ðæt   he ...
        'none of them' 'considered' 'that' 'he' ...
    b) Ða   þohton   hig   ðis word
        'then'   'considered' 'they' 'this word'

in which, indeed, the abs may be absent (*Weras þeahtedon and þohton* 'Men consulted and considered').

We can now characterise impersonal constructions in OE as being associated (optionally) with the subcategorisation frame in (43) (which conflates (27) with that for *þyrstan* etc.), or with that in (46). These might be collapsed as (50):

(50)   → (abs → V)$_a$ (erg + loc)$_b$ (abl)$_c$

where a and c are mutually exclusive, and the presence of a makes b necessarily optional; and, of course, in the presence of a subject formation is necessarily absent, whereas otherwise it is optional. Constructions which show only such an array of arguments are (optionally or obligatorily) impersonal. As noted above, the presence of a further argument which is eligible for subjecthood means that subject formation will apply, but only to it, whether it be erg or abs, and in accordance with hierarchy (4) if there is more than one such 'extra' argument. This formulation allows for all the possibilities we have considered, and, together with its conditions, defines the types of OE impersonals.

However, we should note finally with respect to verbs of the *scamian* type that a further personal variant is available, in addition to that exemplified in (31) and (35), with subject 'experiencer'. This is exemplified in (51) for the verb *ofhreowan* 'pity':

(51.a) Him   ofhreow   ðæs   mannes
       'he/they' + dat   'pitied' + 3rd sg   'the men' + gen

   b) Se mæssepreost ðæs monnes   ofhreow
      'the priest' + nom 'the man' + gen   'pitied' + 3rd sg

   c) Ða   ofhreow   ðam munece   ðæs hleoflian mægenleast
      'then' 'pitied' + 3rd sg 'the monk' + dat 'the leper's weakness' + nom

where (a) shows the impersonal construction and (b) one in which the 'experiencer' is subject, while in (c) the argument which appears as genitive in (a) and (b) is marked with the nominative. This (c) variant is associated with ascription to the nominative of the status of 'source of the action' rather than simply 'causative object': we have a full 'causative' interpretation. Thus, with animate referents the nominative argument can be associated with 'volition' (Fischer and van der Leek 1983). The nominative argument in (51.c) is, perhaps, accordingly erg rather than abl. And we should attribute to such a verb the subcategorisation frame in (52):

(52)   → erg + loc, abl/erg

rather than in (27). If erg is present, it will, in accordance with the hierarchy of (4), become subject of the clause; whereas in its absence and the presence of abl, erg + loc is optionally available for subject formation, in accordance with (50), giving either (51.a), without subject formation, or (b) (with).

Given the analysis of the internal structure of CRs proposed in Anderson 1973, 1977, viz. (53):

(53) abs   erg   loc   abl
                  place place
            source   source

the alternative expressed in (52) between abl and erg involves the optionality of the feature 'place' in the specification for the second argument. However, we shall find motivations below for attributing both erg and abl to the subjects of sentences like (51.c), as is indeed argued for by Anderson 1977: §1.3.2. If this is appropriate, we should substitute 'abl (erg)' for 'abl/erg' in (52).

The absence of a variant of the (51.c) type with *hingrian* verbs (Elmer 1981) supports their analysis as predicates differing from the *scamian* class; I suggested above that with the former the abl argument is merely optional. We can now say that the erg variant in (51.c) is available only to verbs which otherwise take an obligatory abl, i.e. *scamian* verbs. Notice too that verbs like *gelimpan*, with optional erg + loc, and abs rather than abl, lack both a (51.c) variant and a (b).

The preceding discussion of *hingrian* etc. has assumed, following Fischer and van der Leek (1983), that the genitive in (42) realises a 'cause' or abstract 'source' (abl). However, such an analysis is by no means incontestable. Genitives in OE also typically express 'unrealised absolutives' (Anderson 1985c). And it may be that we should associate such an interpretation with the genitive of (42) and the like. This does not, however, affect the delimitation of the set of impersonals, given that, in terms of the proposals of Anderson 1985c, 'unrealised absolutives' are derivatively abl by lexical rule. So too (*pace* van der Leek 1986) it is unnecessary to attribute to instances of *behofian* like *Ac se man* (nom) *behofað micclum gebeda* (gen) ('But the man needs greatly prayers') an underlying source (abl) argument: *gebeda* is an 'unrealised absolutive'; a causal interpretation of it is, indeed, in this case semantically clearly inappropriate.

A different pattern still is exhibited by *lician*. In the light of its isolation with respect to the impersonal verbs we have been considering, it is curious the extent to which many earlier accounts of the 'impersonals' concentrated their attention on it and its evolution (cf. e.g. Jespersen 1927: §11.2; Lightfoot 1979: §5.1 — though the former does at least eschew the term 'impersonal'). What is yet more curious about this, though, is that *lician*, when its arguments are terms, typically does not even occur in impersonal constructions (except in terms of Lightfoot's eccentric definition of such), and certainly not one of the 'standard' sort, illustrated by (51.a). Rather, it occurs in a personal contruction with 'experiencer' subject (*Ic licige*), or in one of the (51.c) type, as exemplified in (54):

(54)   He   me   wel   licaþ
        'he' + nom 'I' + dat/acc   'much'   'pleases'

(54) presumably has the argument structure of (51.c); it too is 'causative', as is evidenced by such 'volitional' examples as (55):

(55)   Æghwylc man   þurh goda dæda   Gode   lician sceal
        'every man'   'through good deeds' 'God' + dat 'please' 'ought'

Lician in (54/55) can therefore be specified as taking an erg + loc and an erg (or erg + abl) argument. The absence of an impersonal variant like (51.a) corresponding to this type is predicted by the schema of (50). (54/55) contain a simple erg (or erg + abl) whose presence requires subject formation and which itself assumes subjecthood.

Thus, whereas the redundancy rule of (56) seems to hold good for OE:

(56)   V → erg + loc, abl   ⇒   V → erg + loc, erg

as with *scamian* etc., the converse does not hold, as illustrated by *lician*.

Lician typically occurs in an impersonal construction only when it takes a predicate as argument rather than a term, as in (57):

(57) Ac   me   swa ðeah   no ne licade   on him   ðæt he ...
     'but' 'I' + dat/acc 'so' 'however' 'not' 'pleased' 'in him' 'that' 'he' ...

Here a sentential erg fails to subject-form (as with any sentential argument in OE), in which case neither does the erg + loc argument. This last type of impersonal, involving a predicational erg, is associated with a total block on subject-formation, even if other eligible arguments are present.

Anderson (1984b) does accord a non-subject-forming status to *lician*, in regarding the nominative argument as not a subject but an abs in a clause lacking subject formation, thus leaving the abs as the principal relation (cf. e.g. Anderson 1979b — and see §5 below), marked by the nominative and controlling concord. However, though this may be appropriate for (54) and similar examples in the languages discussed in that paper, such an interpretation is scarcely applicable to volitional examples like (55). However, it may be that *lician* in OE was both 'causative' and non-subject-forming. But the latter *lician* would then constitute the unique member of a class of verbs that takes erg + loc and abs but which does not undergo subject formation, with presence vs. absence of subject-formation being invisible.

Moreover, there is yet another (though not widely attested) construction involving *lician* to which a non-subject-forming interpretation seems to be appropriate. Examples like *... him gelicade hire þeawas ...* ('He was pleased with her behaviour'), with dative 'experiencer', third person singular verb and an abs argument ambivalent as a nominative/accusative, but presumably the latter in view of the lack of concord (plural abs, singular verb), are true impersonals, containing an abs, marked, as with non-subjective abs elsewhere, with an accusative, and an obligatory experiencer. Such a case array otherwise triggers subject-formation (cf. *þencan* in (49.a) or *lufian* 'to-love'). *(Ge)lician* must thus be marked as exceptional in this respect in the lexicon; i.e. as optionally failing to subject-form despite not satisfying (50). (Subject-formation gives *Ic licige* etc.) It is an exceptional impersonal, both in its case array and in its (associated) case marking.

I conclude this section with an illustration of the behaviour of *geweorþan* 'happen, become', which in taking a number of optional arguments, some combinations of which satisfy (50), appears in a range of constructions, personal and impersonal. Thus, we find:

(58.a) Wæs   onlic   bi   hig   geworden   swa bi   Zachariam
       'was' 'alike' 'with' 'them' 'happened' 'as' 'with' Z.
       gewearþ   and   bi   Elizabeþ his wife
       'happened'   'and' 'with' E.   'his wife'
       (no participants: impersonal)
    b) Hu   geweorþeþ   ðæt
       'how' 'happens'   'that'
       (abs → N: personal)

c)   Ealle   gesceafte   forhte   geweorþaþ
       'all'   'creatures'   'fearful'   'become'
       (abs → N, abs → V: personal)

d)   Ond   swa   wæs   geworden   þætte ...
       'and'   'so' 'was' 'happened' 'that' ...
       (abs → V: impersonal)

e)   Me   gewearþ
       'I' + dat/acc 'became (suited)'
       (erg + loc: impersonal)

f)   Hy   gewearþ   ðæt ...
       'they' + nom/acc 'became (was agreeable)'   'that' ...
       (erg + loc, abs → V: impersonal)

g)   Hu   gewearþ   þe   þæs
       'how' 'happened' 'you' + dat/acc   'that' + gen
       (erg + loc, abl: impersonal)

If we assume that (e) is a reduced form (with suppressed abl), then we can express the subcategorisation range of *geweorþan* as a combination of that for *þyncan* with that associated with *scamian*, with the latter being associated with impersonal realisations only (for further exemplification, see Hubbard 1918), and the former being shared with *weorþan* (on differences in interpretation between *weorþan* and *geweorþan* in such constructions see Klaeber 1919), together with the capacity to take (abs and) a simple loc (goal) argument (not illustrated here; but cf. again Klaeber 1919). Choice of personal vs. impersonal in (58) and choice of subject, where appropriate, are regulated by (50) and (4).

5 Subject Formation Reconsidered

In the preceding we have associated impersonalhood with absence of a nominative argument which controls concord on the verb. And I have described such clauses as lacking subjects. However, it is often suggested that there are other correlates of subjecthood: consider e.g. the sets of morphosyntactoc 'properties' discussed by Keenan (1976) and Andrews (1985). (No consistent semantic property can be associated with subjecthood.) Moreover, these properties may sometimes appear to be 'in conflict', in being in a particular language associated with different arguments. Now, some of these 'conflicts' are spurious, in that they involve 'properties' (such as 'control') which have been mistakenly attributed to 'subjects' rather than the appropriate CRs (Anderson 1977, 1979a,b, 1984b). But there is an interesting residue of 'conflicting' claims on subjecthood.

Consider, for example, the *there + be* construction in PE. In formal English control of concord, otherwise a property of 'subjects', is clearly exercised by the NP which follows *be*:

(59.a)   There is/*are a frog in the garden
   b)   There *is/are frogs in the garden

but the preverbal *there* 'behaves' otherwise as other 'subjects' do, in e.g. undergoing raising:

(60.a)   There seems to be a problem here
   b)   There seem to be problems here

and simply by occupying the linear position it does. (Since nominative case marking is not evident in such examples, and, anyway, is tending to be sensitive to factors other than subjecthood (*Who did you see?* — cf. Klima 1964), I leave it aside here.) Since, apart from anything else, one of the arguments concerned is a 'formal' element like OE *hit*, and thus presumably not part of the subcategorisation frame, and the frames in (59/60) are constant, the distribution of CRs does not seem to be relevant here.

However, this particular 'conflict' is quite compatible with an analysis which invokes an independently motivated organisational possibility: that a single rule may apply twice, once in the cycle and once post-cyclically. This is quite well established in the phonology (cf. e.g. Kiparsky 1982, 1985). On the basis of the structural analogy assumption (cf. again Anderson 1985a, 1987b) we would expect the possibility to be replicated in the syntax: structural properties claimed to be particular to each plane require to be justified as such. Thus the unmarked assumption is that on both planes (of phonology and syntax) a single rule may apply both cyclically and post-cyclically, subject of course to the different constraints associated with these distinct domains (see further below). I suggest that subject formation is such a rule.

Let us distinguish between subject selection, in accordance with the hierarchy (4), and subject formation. If subject formation occurs but, in marked instances, does not take place on the basis of a selection determined by (4), it must instead involve introduction of a specified 'formal', default subject, such as the *hit* of the semi-impersonals discussed in the preceding two chapters. With *sniwan* and *gelimpan* in OE subject formation may alternatively be totally absent, as in (23) and (37). In PE subject formation is obligatory and such a formal subject must be introduced when, for instance, a clause fails to undergo unmarked subject formation, as in (61):

(61)   It seems that this is familiar

Sentential abs arguments in PE do not undergo subject formation, unless they have undergone raising, as in (62):

(62.a)   That this is familiar seems likely
   b)   That this is familiar is likely

(on the assumption that *seem* and *be* are raising predicates). On the nature of this restriction see Anderson forthcoming b (which also discuss sentential ergs). Briefly, what is involved is that by virtue of raising the predication becomes a term in the upper clause and thus eligible for subject formation; see further, however, §7 below.

There, too, in PE seems to be such a 'formal' subject, one that like other subjects is eligible for raising (60). But it is only a CYCLIC SUBJECT, compatible with its eligibility for raising and with its unmarked position (determined, according to Anderson 1977: §3.6, at 'shallow structure', the output to the cyclic rules, on the basis of the cyclic subjecthood assignments) and with eligibility for inversion (which 'interchanges' an 'auxiliary' verb and a pre-verbal subject (*Does there seem to be a problem?*). POST-CYCLIC SUBJECT formation assigns subject status to the post-verbal abs in (59/60) in accordance with the hierarchy of (4), subjecthood being manifested by control of concord. That the same rule is involved here, despite differences of manifestation, is supported by the shared basis of selection, the hierarchy (4), and by an overlap in manifesting properties. Cyclic and post-cyclic subject in PE usually coincide, but attribution of cyclic subjecthood to *there* permits, indeed in its case requires, selection of a distinct post-cyclic subject, as in (59).

OE also seems to show ('the beginnings of') such a 'formal' use of *þær* (Mitchell 1985: §§1491–7), in which it occurs in unmarked subject positions (cf. below):

(63.a)   þær   wæs gidd ond gleo
       'there' 'was' 'song' 'and' 'music'

   b)   Gif ..., sie ðær   eac stæf mid   to wreðianne
       'if' ..., 'let be' 'there' 'also' 'staff' 'with' 'to' 'sustain'

though 'adverbial' *þær* could occupy the same positions. In this case the nominatives in such sentences would be only post-cyclic subjects. However, many alleged examples of 'formal' *þær* can be given a spatial interpretation. *Hit* (and possibly other items) occurs as an alternative to non-spatial *þær*:

(64)   Is   hit lytel   tweo   ðæt ...
      'is' 'it' 'little' 'doubt' 'that' ...

Moreover, no 'formal' item is necessary where in PE *there* would be obligatory, as shown by (65):

(65)   On ðam timan wæs   sum   þegen Drihten gehaten
      'in' 'that' 'period' 'was' 'a certain nobleman' D.   'called'
      on Norðhymbralande
      'in' 'Northumbria'

If (63) and (64) show a 'formal' cyclic subject and the nominatives are post-cyclic subjects only, then such an interpretation is appropriate to (65) also, with the difference that it lacks an overt 'formal' cyclic subject. (65) is 'cyclically impersonal', and only post-cyclically personal. We return to such construction types in §6 below. Meanwhile, let us take up again the OE impersonals considered in §§3–4 above.

I argued in the preceding two sections that the OE impersonals fail to show signs of subject formations. But the manifestations of subjecthood concerned (nominative marking and control of concord) we can associate with specifically post-cyclic subjects in OE. The question of whether such constructions have a cyclic subject remains open, on the basis of the evidence we have looked at.

As already noted (§3), position cannot be regarded as criterial for cyclic subjecthood in OE, given the possibility of all of SVX, XVSY, SXV, XSV (where S = subject, V = verb and X,Y = any other arguments in the clause) as clause orders. Certainly, one might argue for 'unmarked' positions for S (adjacent to V in main clauses, initial in subordinate?). But since initial position at least is presumably associated with the high topicality or empathisability of subjects, occurrence in such a position of erg + loc arguments of the kind we have been considering cannot be regarded as manifestation of a 'subject property'.

Anderson (1986: n.6), on the other hand, suggests, rather tentatively, that sentences like those in (66):

(66.a) Ða ongan hyne hyngrian
     'then' 'began' 'he' + acc 'to-hunger'

  b) Ðonne mæg hine scomian
     'then' 'can' 'he' + acc 'to feel shame'

  c) ... him sceal sceamian ætforan Gode
     'he/they' + dat 'must' 'to feel shame' 'before' 'God'

might be analysed as showing a dat/acc argument raised out of an impersonal construction to become ultimately cyclic subject of a raising verb (which class I take to include the 'pre-modals'). It is indeed difficult to imagine an alternative interpretation compatible with the syntax of raising verbs. For it is not just that the oblique NPs concerned occupy the 'unmarked' subject positions relative to the raising verb, which is at least suggestive (despite the qualifications concerning positional criteria noted above); these verbs are subject-taking verbs, and in such sentences as those in (66) the only candidates for this status are the adjacent oblique arguments. If, as seems to be appropriate, in OE and more generally, raising is formulated as taking a subject as raisee, then in this respect erg + loc arguments of impersonal verbs 'behave' as cyclic subjects.

An apparently similar argument based on control of deletions in coordinate structures is rather more suspect. As is well known, the omitted subject of the second clause in sentences like (67):(67)

Fred turned away from Mary and left immediately

can be construed as being identical only with the subject of the preceding clause, *Fred*, and not with *Mary* (or both). OE erg + loc arguments in impersonals also 'control subject deletion' in this way:

(68) Gode ofhreow þa and hraþe cwæþ to þam angle ...
     'God' + dat 'felt pity' 'then' 'and' 'swiftly' 'said' 'to the angel' ...

(noted e.g. by Bynon 1985). However, it is clear that 'control of deletion' was not so restricted in earlier periods of English, as has been well illustrated by Wolfe (1970). She noted, for example, instances like (69) from the works of Malory:

(69.a)   and then there was a masse songe afore hym, and brake hys faste
 b)   and kynge Mark rode ayenst hym, and smote eache other ful hard

where 'control' is exercised by non-subjective arguments, and in (b) by a combination of two arguments. In view of this, and in view in particular of the paucity of evidence concerning 'control of delection' in OE, the evidential value of (68) and the like with respect to the subject status of oblique arguments in impersonal constructions is rather doubtful.

I am also not aware of clearcut examples of omission of such an argument in circumstances otherwise restricted to subjects in OE. It thus seems that the uncovering of potential evidence from 'deletion' and its 'control' must await further investigation of this area in relation to earlier stages of English (as argued by Wolfe 1970).

Perhaps more hopeful-looking as a source of evidence for the cyclic status of the erg + loc arguments in which we are interested is the fact that 'the auxiliaries *beon/wesan* and *weorþan* are unexpectedly found with the second participle of *(ge)þyncan* "to seem"' (Mitchell 1985: §1049). OE 'personal' passives are found only with verbs that in the active take an 'accusative object' (with the possible exception noted above). If we take objecthood (particularly marked with an accusative) as implying assignment of subjecthood to another, erg (loc) participant in the same clause, then examples such as (70):

(70) hu nearowe ealle ða niðerlican gesceafta   him
   'how' 'constrained' 'all' 'the' 'low' 'creatures' 'he/they' + dat
   wæron geðuhte
   'were' 'seemed' + pl

might suggest an active in which *ða niðerlican gesceafta* is accusative and some other participant, *him* (the erg + loc argument) is subject. However, in active clauses the equivalent of *ða niðerlican gesceafta* does not appear in the accusative. Rather in the only personal clauses in which *þyncan* occurs, such an argument is nominative, as in (47) or (71):

(71) ðær him   foldwegas fægere þuhton
   'there' 'he/they' + dat 'earth-ways' 'beautiful' 'seemed' + pl

(Mitchell 1985: §1051). Moreover, (70) may simply illustrate the 'perfect with *beon/wesan/weorþan*' found with intransitive verbs, rather than constituting a 'passive'. (I do not understand Mitchell's dismissal of this interpretation on the basis of *þa wæs he geðuht ðam folce þæt he witega wære, and Iohannes Crist* 'Then he seemed to the people that he was a prophet and John Christ'.) It is therefore difficult to derive any support from these phenomena for the cyclic subjecthood of such erg + loc arguments (and cf. the discussion of (48) above).

We have, then, only a modicum of evidence for the cyclic subjecthood of the erg + loc arguments in impersonal constructions, and then only for erg + loc with *scamian* and *hingrian* verbs. However, I suggest that such an interpretation is not implausible, given what evidence there is, and on typological grounds. Other languages display lack of morphological marking for subjecthood and yet show evidence of cyclic subjects. This is characteristic of many 'ergative' languages (cf. e.g. Dixon 1979), for instance, such that case-marking and/or concord do not reflect subject-assignment, whereas eligibility for e.g. raising does. Even more striking in this respect are those languages in which cyclic (and post-cyclic) rules involve reference to both CRs and GRs in subordinate clauses (and generally, in the case of post-cyclic rules). (Recall (§1) that, given the cyclic (end-of-each-cycle) introduction of GRs, they are not available to the cyclic clause: see Anderson 1977, etc.) These languages thus provide evidence that cyclic subject formation does not obliterate the CRs of the argument involved; both kinds of relation remain available. A number of such instances are discussed by Böhm 1983.

In Niuean, for example, common nouns in basic transitive and intransitive clauses are marked distinctively as to whether they are erg (preposition *he*) or abs (*e*) (Böhm 1983: §3.3). So:

(72.a) Nofo   e   tagata   ia   i   Tuapa
        'live'   abs   'man'   'that' loc   T.

   b)   Ne   lagomatai   he   ekekafo   e   tama
        past 'help'   erg   'doctor'   abs   'child'

Here post-cyclic subject formation is not evidenced. As expected, the raised element in (73):

(73.a) Maeke   a   Pita   ke   nofo   i   Tuapa
        'possible'   abs   P.   sbj   'stay' loc   T.

   b)   To   maeke   e   ekekafo   ke   lagomatai   e   tame   ē
        future 'possible' abs   'doctor' sbj   'help'   abs   'child' 'this'

bears an abs marker, whatever its source; raising associates a lower argument with an upper abs. (The abs marker with proper nouns, as *Pita* in (73.a), is *a* rather than *e*.) However, the victims of these raisings are cyclic subjects, erg in (73.b) and abs in (a). This is the situation I have been suggesting may hold with respect to OE impersonals with (some) erg + loc participants: absence of post-cyclic subjects, presence of cyclic.

However, in Niuean, as Böhm, following Seiter (1978), goes on to point out (1983: 134–5), there is another raising possibility with transitives, namely that illustrated by (74):

(74) To   maeke   e   tama   ē   ke lagomatai he   ekekafo
      future 'possible' abs   'child' 'this' sbj 'help'   erg   'doctor'

Here the abs argument, rather than the subject erg in (73.b), is raised out of the lower clause. Böhm associates this with an equivalence in status between abs and subject. In non-subject-forming (sub-)systems abs has syntactically the same status as subject in systems with subjects. They are both PRINCIPAL relations, those most sensitive to syntactic 'processes', and uniquely eligible for raising (Anderson 1977: §3.5.7, 1978: 668, 1979b: 9). Raising in Niuean involves as victim an argument bearing a principal relation, either the derived principal (subject — 73.b) or the basic or initial (abs — (74)); in (73.a) these coincide.

Cyclic subject-formation thus leaves available to the syntax the character of the argument involved. This is in accordance with an independently motivated distinction between cyclic and post-cyclic rules.

Kiparksy (1982) and others have argued that cyclic rules in the phonology are subject to the STRICT CYCLE CONDITION (SCC), whereas post-cyclic are not. One would, once more, expect this situation to be replicated in the syntax, given the structural analogy assumption (cf. again Anderson forthcoming b). Kiparsky formulates the SCC as in (75):

(75) *The strict cycle condition*
    a. Cyclic rules apply only in derived environments
    b. A representation Φ is derived with respect to rule R in cycle j *iff* Φ meets the SD of R by virtue of (i) a combination of morphemes introduced by cycle j, or (ii) the application of a phonological rule in cycle j

Kiparsky (1985) points out that the SCC applies to structure-changing rules but not structure building; thus e.g. the rules which build lexical syllable structure are exempt.

With respect to the syntax, I interpret the SCC as requiring, crudely, that clause-bounded cyclic rules be non-structure-changing. There can therefore be, for example, no cyclic rule of dative movement (whose existence is undesirable on other grounds — see e.g. Anderson 1978; Faltz 1978) or of 'unaccusative' (cf. here Anderson 1980); whereas raising, though structure-changing, is clearly in conformity with the SCC. Post-cyclic subject formation is a neutralisation, thus structure-changing. But cyclic subject-formation, which is clause-bounded, cannot change structure, merely add it, if it is not to violate the SCC. The assignment of subjecthood or objecthood to an argument in the course of the application of the cyclic rules thus does not obliterate its CR. Accordingly, in Niuean both the CRs and the GRs are simultaneously available to the cyclic rule of raising. And in OE impersonals, if the erg + loc is in some instances a cyclic subject, this does not involve erasure of its CR assignments, which resist post-cyclic subject formation.

In many languages, however, the CRs of arguments which have been assigned subjecthood or objecthood in the cycle are not thereafter referred to by the syntax. This seems to be the case in PE, in which, for instance, raising applies to any immediately subordinate subject (whatever its CR) and the CR of a subject is not relevant to its position or case-marking or ability to control concord. Anderson (1977: ch. 3) attributes this to the neutralising function of (cyclic) subject formation in languages. They show 'full' subject formation; whereas Niuean, for example, displays only 'semi-subject-formation': the rule can be either structure-changing (PE) or structure-building (Niuean), as a linguistic variable. But such an interpretation of cyclic subject formation in PE and the like is incompatible with the SCC.

Rather, it would seem appropriate to relate this typological difference in part to a 'transparency' constraint. In languages or subsystems in which the CRs of subordinate clauses are invoked by the cyclic syntax, as in Niuean, post-cyclic subject formation is blocked (or at least cannot apply if all surface indication of the relevant CRs is thereby obscured); otherwise, it is optional, as with OE impersonal verbs, or obligatory, as in PE, or, perhaps, simply absent, as apparently in Tongan 'canonical transitives' (Böhn 1983: §3.1). One question of interest is whether or not this last class is indeed empty: is post-cyclic subject formation absent only if the CRs of subordinate clauses are relevant to the cyclic syntax?

6 Cyclic vs. Post-cyclic Subject Formation

I am aware of no evidence for associating either cyclic or post-cyclic subjecthood with sentential abs arguments in OE. Thus, (37) (as well as, of course, (23)) is both cyclically and post-cyclically subjectless. Erg + loc arguments with *scamian* etc. and *þyrstan* etc. apparently show cyclic subjecthood, but optionally lack post-cyclic subjecthood. It is also now even clearer that the definition of impersonal given in §3 is of only parochial interest. What we have been considering is constructions in which, at some stage, subjects are lacking (where in other circumstances they might be present). Absence of a nominative argument and of concord is only one reflexion of this. Sentential arguments will show lack of both whether they lack subject formation, as generally in OE, or are assigned subjecthood, as in PDE (76):

(76.a)   That Frances should fancy him surprises Jonathan
   b)   That Frances should fancy him seems likely

given that we associate subjecthood in PE with immediately pre-verbal position. Moreover, as I have just noted, it may be that sentences like (25) and (26) are only post-cyclically 'impersonal' — or, more appropriately, in view of the preceding, post-cyclically subjectless. And sentences may have distinct cyclic and post-cyclic subjects, as in the *there*-construction in PDE (or *þær*- in OE). It is also possible for constructions to lack cyclic subjects but to show post-cyclic: that is, there are what one might call 'cyclic impersonals'. — But it is again more generally appropriate to refer to these as cyclically subjectless, since any attempt to broaden our initial definition of impersonal to encompass them would amount to conceding just this: 'impersonals' are constructions which lack subjects at a particular stage in their derivation at which the appropriate assignment of subjecthood is otherwise available. (65) is, I suggest, an OE sentence which is cyclically but not post-cyclically subjectless. And Italian appears to be a language in which quite a number of construction types are cyclically but not post-cyclically subjectless.

Intransitive verbs in Italian, whether agentive or not, allow their abs argument to occur either pre- or post-verbally, as shown in (77):

(77.a) Dei profughi ungheresi   sono rimasti   nel paese
        'some' 'Hungarian refugees'   'remained'   'in the country'
   b)   Sono rimasti dei profughi ungheresi nel paese

and (78):

(78.a) Molti stranieri hanno lavorato in quella fabbrica
        'many' 'foreigners' 'worked'   'in' 'that' 'factory'
   b)   Hanno lavorato molti stranieri in quella fabbrica

(Perlmutter 1983). The abs in the (b) variants in (77) and (78) (the so-called 'impersonals') fails to raise. Contrast e.g. the sentences in (79):

(79.a) Dei profughi ungheresi sembrano   essere rimasti
        'some' 'Hungarian refugees' 'seem' + 3rd pl 'to have remained'
        nel   paese
        'in the country'
   b)   Sembrano essere rimasti dei profughi ungheresi nel paese

Despite controlling concord on *sembrare*, and despite infinitive formation on the lower verb (*essere*), *dei profughi ungheresi* in (79.b) occupies the same position as in (77.b), i.e. immediately after *rimasti*. So too in (80.b):

(80.a) Molti stranieri sembrano   avere lavorato in
        'many' 'foreigners' 'seem' + 3rd pl 'to have worked' 'in'
        quella fabbrica
        'that factory'
   b)   Sembrano avere lavorato molti stranieri in quella fabbrica

the erg + abs argument fails to raise. This suggests that these arguments are not cyclic subjects; in such sentence types cyclic subject formation is optional. As cyclic non-subjects, these abs arguments fail to occupy subject (immediately pre-verbal) position, as in the *there*-construction in PE (59/60). As a post-cyclic subject, however, the abs in (79/80.b) controls concord on the finite verb to which it is most immediately subordinate, as does the abs in (60).

Cyclic subject formation is also absent in sentences of the type of (51.c), as illustrated by (81):

(81.a) Molte   sinfonie   di Mozart   gli   piacciono
        'many' 'symphonies' 'of' M.   'to-him' 'please' + 3rd pl
   b)   Gli piacciono molte sinfonie di Mozart

(Perlmutter's (1983) 'inversion' construction), as well as in 'passives'. What all these constructions have in common is that the potential subject, i.e. the argument highest on the hierarchy of (4), is not a simple erg. (On the analysis of (51.c) and (81) whereby the relevant argument is simultaneously erg and abl, cf. again Anderson 1977: §1.3.1.) However, in all such sentences the eligible argument (in terms of (4)) is a post-cyclic subject, and thus determines concord, once more as in the English *there*-construction.

It seems, then, as if we might be able to identify (sub-)systems which show: both cyclic and post-cyclic subjecthood, either assigned in both instances to the same argument, as typically in PE, or distinctively apportioned, as in *there*-constructions; only cyclic subjecthood, as in the OE impersonals with *scamian* etc.; or only post-cyclic subjecthood, as in Italian 'impersonals', or in (65) and the like in OE. In some systems, both cyclic and post-cyclic subject formation are lacking: this is illustrated by those language (sub-)systems which are both syntactically and morphologically 'ergative' (cf. again Dixon 1979), the classic example of such being Dyirbal (Dixon 1972).

In Dyirbal, in most circumstances at least, the derived principal relation subject is not assigned. Instead cyclic and post-cyclic rules which would in subject-forming systems invoke subject refer to the basic principal, abs. Thus, not only does case-marking work on an 'ergative' basis:

(82.a) balan   dⱼugumbil   baniɲu
        classifier 'woman'   'is-coming'
   b) balan   dⱼugumbil   baŋgul yaɽangu   balgan
        classifier 'woman' classifier-erg 'man' + erg 'is-hitting'
        (= 'The man is hitting the woman')
   c) bayi   yaɽa baŋgun   dⱼugumbiɽu   balgan
        classifier 'man' classifier-erg 'woman' + erg 'is-hitting'
        (= 'The woman is hitting the man')

but, for example, deletion under equi applies to abs arguments rather than a grouping that suggests subjects selected in accordance with (4):

(83.a) ŋadⱼa dⱼiŋgaliɲu   biligu
        'I'   'am-running'   'for-climb' (= 'I am running in order to climb')
   b) balam   miraɲ   baŋgul yaɽaŋgu   dimbaɲu
        classifier 'beans' classifier-erg 'man' + erg 'brought'
        ŋinda   babili
        'you' 'for-scrape' (= 'The man brought beans for you to scrape')

The erg argument, *baŋgul yaɽaŋgu* in (b), is not eligible for omission under equi, unless it undergoes 'abs-assignment' and the subordinated verb is marked accordingly by a special affix. (See further e.g. Anderson 1977: §§3.5.5–.8, 1979b: §2.)

Finally, we can re-define semi-impersonals (such as (24), (33) or (38)) as showing not absence of subject formation but rather DISPLACED SUBJECT FORMATION. Subject formation in their case ignores the argument selected by hierarchy (4) and attributes subjecthood to a specified 'dummy' or 'formal' element, a 'default' subject. Displaced subject formation is initially cyclic, and it may or may not be 'confirmed' post-cyclically. That is, the 'formal' cyclic subject may or may not be post-cyclic subject: 'formal' *it* or *hit* is also post-cyclic subject; 'formal' *there* or *þær* is not.

7 After-thoughts

The account offered in the preceding of various types of 'impersonal' construction, including centrally those associated with OE, rests on the assumption that subject formation plays some role in the syntax of many languages. The CG analysis differs from others primarily in denying the relevance of subjecthood to initial structures (and to lexical entries): it is derived. On this assumption (motivated in §§1–2), I have argued that subject formation can apply both cyclically and post-cyclically, its cyclic application being subject to the SCC. Both cyclic and post-cyclic subject formation make reference to the hierarchy of (4), with assignment of subjecthood to a 'dummy' being a default option (displaced subject formation) associated with certain combinations of arguments and their CRs.

However, it is arguable that a more perspicuous account of this whole area emerges if we related various relevant syntactic phenomena directly to the hierarchy of CRs rather than interposing (cyclic) subjecthood, which can be regarded as epiphenomenal, at best a 'notational convenience'. Anderson (1984a: 49, n.2) defends the systematicity of such 'notational conveniences', as allowing distinct processes to refer to a single, recurrent entity. In a sense, the 'syllable' is also a 'notational convenience': each occurrence of it in a formulation could be replaced by the specification of a sequence of segments. But this would serve to disguise the systematicity with respect to the phonology of certain sequences, i.e. just those constituting such a unit. However, it seems to me that the status of 'subject' is rather different from this, at least with respect to the cyclic syntax.

Whereas reference to the syllable simplifies the formulation of rules both universally and in particular languages, reference to 'subject' is simply an indication that (4) is involved in the formulation of a particular rule. Since (4) is universally given, occurrence of 'subject' in a cyclic rule merely means 'victim selected in accordance with (4)'. On the other hand, post-cyclic subject formation does involve neutralisation; and since post-cyclic subjecthood may be realised differently in different languages, this might be taken to confer some independent systematicity on the notion 'post-cyclic subject'.

Thus, raising in PE selects as victim in the subordinate clause the highest argument defined by hierarchy (4); and it does exactly the same in OE (including the erg + loc in examples like (66) above). Post-cyclically in PE, (4) is again invoked with reference to the determination of concord, but here neutralisation is involved. Similarly, 'shallow structure' assignment of 'subject position' in PE creates a neutralisation, in that it entails suppression of the realisation of the CR of the argument placed in this position.

In OE, nominative assignment and control of concord, once more imposing neutralisation, are made post-cyclically. But certain combinations of arguments (those specified in (50)) are projected out of the hierarchy: they are not eligible. — However, as we have seen, this does not inhibit another argument, not included in (50), from being assigned nominative marking and control of concord, as in

(48): it, in the absence of the arguments projected out by (50), is hierarchically highest. In Italian, on the other hand, the entire hierarchy is (optionally) projected out cyclically in constructions lacking an argument which is simply erg. Only the post-cyclic neutralisations warrant the introduction of a distinct construct 'subject'.

We arrive at a construct that corresponds to the traditional view of 'grammatical subject' by invoking a conjunction of 'shallow structure subject' (the hierarchically highest argument in a sentence as it emerges from the cyclic rules) and 'post-cyclic subject' (as selected by the post-cyclic rules). In PE the former is manifested by position, the latter by concord. Usually these coincide to define a 'canonical subject'; but as in *there*-sentences, there may be a conflict (*there* not being available as a post-cyclic default). It is not clear that such a construct has any systematic status, however.

We may also note in passing that attributive formation in PE (recall §2 above) may similarly represent simply post-cyclic neutralisation rather than (also) formation of cyclically relevant GRs. However, I do not pursue this question here.

Freeing the syntax from cyclic subject formation has a number of descriptive advantages. Consider, for instance, the restriction on subject formation of sentential abs discussed in §5 above. They become subjects only if they have undergone raising and thus become a term in the upper clause, as in (62): cf. the deviant (61.b). However, if the victim of raising is a subject, then the sentential abs in (62) must already have become subject of the lower clause in order to undergo raising. This is clearly paradoxical, in these terms. And we do not find evidence for the subjecthood of sentential abs in the absence of raising:

(84)   *That I met the brother chanced

It therefore seems preferable to formulate raising in terms of direct reference to (4), with sentential abs not being excluded therefrom in PE. Whereas 'shallow structure subjecthood' (positioning) reflects a hierarchy that lacks sentential abs, such that that in (84) is excluded but (62) is allowed as having become a term via raising.

As in OE, neither a sentential abs nor its optional erg + loc co-argument is eligible for subjecthood, 'shallow' or post-cyclic. Contrast (85):

(85)   It seems to me that this is familiar

and (86):

(86.a)   *That this is familiar seems to me
    b)   *I seem that this is familiar

However, (87):

(87)   That this is familiar seems likely to me

illustrates that, as in OE (cf. (48)), the ineligibility of the erg + loc and the predicational abs *likely* to become subject does not exclude an abs term (such as *that this is familiar*, after raising, or *that* in *That seems likely to me*) from being assigned subjecthood.

Under the analysis developed in previous sections, 'formal' *there* and *it* are introduced cyclically as a result of displaced subject formation. One consequence of the assumption that subject formation is absent from the cycle is that the introduction of these 'formal' elements must be delayed until 'shallow structure', presumably as part of the positioning stipulation, as a default option either for predicates without eligible 'subjects' or for transitives without an eligible 'object' (more generally, predicates with a missing abs). Delayed introduction of *it/there* also means that infinitive formation does not pre-supposed raising (as already noted in the case of Italian), even in cases, such as (60) where raising is normally supposed. This imposes a significant constraint on the insertion of 'dummies', but again I do not pursue the issue here: for some relevant discussion cf. Anderson (forthcoming b).

The history of English subsequent to OE shows the obligatory integration of the erg + loc arguments projected out in accordance with (50) into 'shallow structure' and post-cyclic reference to the hierarchy made by positioning and concord control, and thus loss of variants such as (51.a): erg + loc arguments now fail to form 'subjects' only in the presence of another erg. Such a development is not unparalleled: see e.g. Cole *et al* 1978; Anderson 1984b. Sentential abs arguments are also integrated in certain circumstances, as exemplified by (62) above. Also, the introduction of the default 'dummies' *it/hit* and *there/þær* becomes obligatory rather than optional when other arguments are projected out. These developments contribute to the establishment of an obligatory status for subject in finite clauses in PE.

Over roughly the same period the inflexional system of English (including in particular morphological case-marking) has markedly diminished in expressive capacity. It is perhaps misleading, however, to attribute the loss of impersonals, even indirectly, to the reduction in morphological distinctions on nouns (cf. van der Gaaf 1904, Fischer and van der Leek 1983). Certainly, the loss of case-marking on nominal arguments of verbs destroys the distinctiveness of the constructions exemplified in (51). But the language has other devices to maintain such distinctions, some of which it does indeed employ in relations to predicates of similar types; for example, in distinguishing between (a) and (b) in (88):

(88.a)   That development benefits me
    b)   I benefit from that development

We lack the variant in (89):

(89)   *(It) benefits me from that development

But this cannot be attributed to lack of expressive potential in this area. Rather, the anomalousness of (89) comes from the elimination of the hierarchical exceptions projected out by (50); given that such erg + loc arguments are no longer exempt from 'subject formation', even the variant of (89) with a 'formal' subject is ruled out. How precisely this extension of 'subject formation' is related to inflexional loss (and the evolution of word order constraints) remains (to me) unclear.

REFERENCES

Anderson, John M. 1971. *The grammar of case: towards a localistic theory*. Cambridge: Cambridge University Press.
Anderson, John M. 1973. *An essay concerning aspect*. The Hague: Mouton.
Anderson, John M. 1977. *On case grammar: towards a theory of grammatical relations*. London: Croom Helm.
Anderson, John M. 1978. On the derivative status of grammatical relations. In Werner Abraham (ed.) *Valence, semantic case, and grammatical relations*, 661–94. Amsterdam: Benjamins.
Anderson, John M. 1979a. Subjecthood. *Hungarian Studies in English* 12. 121–38.
Anderson, John M. 1979b. On being without a subject. Bloomington: Indiana University Linguistics Club.
Anderson, John M. 1980. Anti-unaccusative, or: relational grammar is case grammar. *Revue roumaine de linguistique* 25. 193–225.
Anderson, John M. 1984a. Objecthood. In Frans Plank (ed.) *Objects: towards a theory of grammatical relations*, 29–54. New York and London: Academic Press.
Anderson, John M. 1984b. The natural history of dative sentences. In N. F. Blake and Charles Jones (eds.) *English historical linguistics: studies in development*, 241–78. (= *CECTAL Conference Papers Series, 3*.) Sheffield: University of Sheffield.
Anderson, John M. 1984c. *Case grammar and the lexicon*. (= *Occasional Papers in Linguistics and Language Learning*, 10.) Coleraine: University of Ulster.
Anderson, John M. 1985a. Structural analogy and dependency phonology. *Acta Linguistica Hafniensia* 20. 5–44.
Anderson, John M. 1985b. Case grammar, invariance and linguistic variation. *TESOL France News* 5,3. 6–11.
Anderson, John M. 1985c. The case system of Old English: a case for non-modularity. *Studia Linguistica* 39. 1–22.
Anderson, John M. 1986. A note on Old English impersonals. *Journal of Linguistics* 22. 167–77.
Anderson, John M. 1987a. The limits of linearity. In John M. Anderson and Jacques Durand (eds.) *Explorations in dependency phonology*, 199–220. Dordrecht: Foris.
Anderson, John M. 1987b. Structural analogy and case grammar. *Lingua* 70. 79–129.
Anderson, John M. forthcoming a. Invariance and linguistic variation: a case grammar characterisation. *Proceedings of the Elfter Fremdsprachen-Didaktiker-Kongreß*, Ludwigsburg, 7–9 October 1985.
Anderson, John M. forthcoming b. Extraposition as absence of subject-formation.
Andrews, Avery 1985. The major functions of the noun phrase. In Timothy Shopen (ed.) *Language typology and syntactic description, 1: clause structure*, 62–154. Cambridge: Cambridge University Press.
Atkinson, M., D. Kilby and I. Roca 1982. *Foundations of general linguistics*. London: Edward Arnold and Unwin.
Böhm, Roger 1982. *Topics in localist case grammar*. D.Phil. thesis, New University of Ulster.
Böhm, Roger 1983. Semi-subjects: evidence for split principals. *Acta Linguistica Hafniensia* 18. 117–53.

Bosworth-Toller = *An Anglo-Saxon dictionary based on the manuscript collections of the late Joseph Bosworth, edited and enlarged by T. Northcote Toller.* London: Oxford University Press.

Bynon, Theodora 1985. Historical syntax and the substance-structure dichotomy. Paper presented at the VIIth International Conference for Historical Linguistics, Pavia, 9–13 Sept 1985.

Cole, P. W., W. Harbert, G. Hermon and S. N. Sridhar 1978. On the acquisition of subjecthood. *Studies in the Linguistic Sciences* **8**. 42–71.

Dixon, Robert M. W. 1972. *The Dyirbal language of north Queensland.* Cambridge: Cambridge University Press.

Dixon, Robert M. W. 1979. Ergativity. *Language* **55**. 59–138.

Elmer, Willy 1981. *Diachronic grammar: the history of Old and Middle English subjectless constructions.* Tübingen: Niemeyer.

Faltz, Leonard M. 1978. On indirect objects in universal grammar. *Chicago Linguistic Society* **14**. 76–87.

Fischer, Olga C. M. and Frederike C. van der Leek 1983. The demise of the Old English impersonal construction. *Journal of Linguistics* **19**. 337–68.

van der Gaaf, W. 1904. *The transition from the impersonal to the personal construction in Middle English.* (= *Anglistische Forschungen*, 14.) Heidelberg: Carl Winter.

Hubbard, Frank G. 1918. *Beowulf* 1598, 1996, 2026; uses of the impersonal verb *geweorþan. Journal of English and Germanic Philology* **17**. 119–24.

Jespersen, Otto 1927. *A Modern English grammar*, part II: syntax, vol. 2. London: George Allen and Unwin, and Copenhagen: Ejnar Munksgaard.

Keenan, Edward L. 1976. Towards a universal definition of 'subject'. In C. N. Li (ed.) *Subject and topic*, 303–33. New York and London: Academic Press.

Kiparksy, Paul 1982. Lexical morphology and phonology. In *Linguistics in the morning calm*, 3–91. Seoul: Hanshin.

Kiparsky, Paul 1985. Some consequences of lexical phonology. *Phonology Yearbook* **2**. 85–138.

Kirkwood, H. W. 1970. On the thematic function and syntactic meanings of the grammatical subject in English. *Linguistische Berichte* **9**. 34–46.

Klaeber, F. 1918. Concerning the functions of Old English 'geweorþan' and the origin of German 'gewähren lassen'. *Journal of English and Germanic Philology* **19**. 250–71.

Klima, Edward S. 1964. Relatedness between grammatical systems. *Language* **40**. 1–20. Reprinted in David A. Reibel and Sanford A. Schane (eds.) *Modern studies in English*, 227–46. Englewood Cliffs, New Jersey: Prentice-Hall.

van der Leek, Frederike 1986. Case and argument status of NPs with respect to the verb. Paper presented to the Department of English Language, University of Edinburgh, March 1986.

Lightfoot, David W. 1979. *Principles of diachronic syntax.* Cambridge: Cambridge University Press.

Mitchell, Bruce 1985. *Old English syntax*, vol. I. Oxford: Oxford University Press.

Perlmutter, David M. 1983. Personal vs. impersonal constructions. *Natural Language and Linguistic Theory* **1**. 141–200.

Rohdenburg, Günter 1974. *Sekundäre Subjektivierung im Englischen und im Deutschen. (PAKS-Arbeits-bericht 8.)* Bielefeld: Cornelsen-Velhagen & Klasing.

Seiter, W. J. 1978. Subject/direct object raising in Niuean. *Berkeley Linguistic Society* **4**. 211–22.

Wahlén, N. 1925. *The Old English impersonalia*, part I: *impersonal constructions containing verbs of material import in the active voice.* Ph.D. thesis, University of Göteborg.

Wolfe, Patricia 1970. On the development of some deletion constraints in English. Paper presented at the Annual Meeting of the Linguistic Society of America, Washington, D.C., December 1970.

2
HEAVY ARGUMENTS IN OLD ENGLISH

Fran Colman

1 Introduction

It is well-known, and well-documented in handbooks of Old English (OE) (e.g. Quirk and Wrenn 1957: §144; Mitchell and Robinson 1982: §143 ff.; Mitchell 1985: ch. IX), that the predominant SVX pattern (in the present study X refers to any non-subjective argument of the verb; see §2 below for the terms 'argument', 'circumstantial' and 'participant') of Present-day English (PE) syntax did not pertain in so-called 'classical' OE of the ninth century (see §3 below for a summary of syntactic patterns evidenced in prose texts from this period.* PE may have SXV only in case the pre-verbal X is a circumstantial, and another X follows the verb: compare the sentence in (1):

(1)   She kindly sent us some photographs

where *kindly* is circumstantial (cf. Quirk and Greenbaum 1977: §7.4, on 'optional adverbs'), with the unacceptable one in (2):

(2)   *He here brought the table

where *here* is a participant, or in (3):

(3)   *He slowly ate

where *slowly* is a circumstantial but no X follows the verb (see also Anderson 1976). Prevailing SXV patterns for certain clause-types in ninth-century OE, especially in the light of putative SXV order for Indo-European (Lehman 1974; Vennemann 1974: 349) and for Proto Germanic (Hopper 1975; also Mitchell 1985: §3916), suggest that English has undergone a change in basic word-order: crucially, from SXV to SVX (and see Vennemann 1974: 351; Bean 1983: chs. 1 and 7). That such a change occurred is taken for granted in the present study, which aims not to present percentages of order-types to demonstrate a change, but to offer an account, based on analyses of selected OE data, for one possible motivation for the change.

---

*   John Anderson, University of Edinburgh, Roger Lass, University of Capetown, and Dr. Bruce Mitchell, University of Oxford, have been painstaking and patient in their comments on drafts of this study. My pig-headed ignoring of some suggestions will no doubt be to the detriment of the study and at my own (and the reader's) peril.

Explanations for this change in English word-order have been put forward, and others may be suggested, in the light of available OE data, in relation to various theories of language change; but in general these suffer from both lack of comparison with evidence from other languages and the inconclusive nature of some OE data.

Vennemann (1975) returns to (more) traditional concepts of a relationship between un-syncretised inflectional morphological expression and SXV word-order, according to which a change from SXV to SVX (via, for Vennemann, TVX, i.e. topic first and verb second; see also Vennemann 1974) goes along with, or results from, syncretism in expression, and eventual loss, of inflectional morphology. But an account of word-order change based mainly on inflectional morphology is rendered less convincing by data from languages which either maintain SXV order in the face of syncretism in expression of inflectional morphology (e.g. Carib: see Derbyshire 1981), or which evince a word-order change while maintaining a high degree of inflectional morphological expression (e.g. Makúsi, which has changed from SOV to OVS: see Derbyshire 1981). Furthermore, syncretism in expression of inflectional morphology may be expected to result in a fixed word-order, but not (despite Vennemann's (1975) rather weak argument for the ambiguity of SOV vs. OSV) a change in word-order (see Vincent 1976: 63): there is no reason to suppose that erosion of morphological expression must result directly in word-order change: English word-order, despite loss of expression of inflectional morphology, could just as well have remained as SXV. Bean (1983: 139) ends up agreeing with Vennemann (but without the TVX stage), but still does not 'explain' why a shift from SXV to SVX was necessary in English. Moreover, an account of word-order change in English based primarily on erosion of morphological expression implies that 'classical' (or early) OE (with, arguably, prevailing SXV) had a fully differentiating system of morphological expression (see e.g. Fries 1940). But the suggestion of reliance of early OE syntax on morphological expression may be considered exaggerated, given the not small degree of syncretism in the expression of case in even the earliest OE (see Gardner 1971: 77 ff.; Shannon 1974: 59).

Theories of 'after thought' syntax (see Hyman 1975; Dik 1978: esp. §6.2.5) may look tempting for an account of the change from SXV to SVX in late OE. Consider, for instance, (4):

(4) ac dæghwamlice man   ehte   yfel æfter
     'but' 'daily'   'one' 'commit' 3 sg pret   'evil' 'upon'
     oðrum   7 unriht   rærde   7
     'other' dat pl '&' 'wrong' acc 'raise' 3 sg pret '&'
     unlaga   manege ealles   to   wide
     'injustices' acc 'many' 'altogether' 'too' 'widely'
     geond   ealle þas ðeode
     'throughout' 'all' 'this' 'people' acc
     (Bethurum 1957: XX: 10–12)

where the verb *rærde* is preceded by the object *unriht*, but also followed by a coordinate complex object phrase. Compare also (5):

(5)   forðan   Aelmær hi   becyrde   þe
        'because' 'Aelmær' 'them' 'betray' 3 sg pret 'whom'
        se arcebiscop   Aelfeah   ær   generede
        'the' 'archbishop' 'Aelfheah' 'previously' 'save' 3 sg pret
        æt   his   life
        'with respect to' 'his' 'life' dat
        (Rositzke 1940: AD 1011).

But such examples in themselves provide no evidence of grammaticalisation of what might be considered as 'afterthought'. Further, other accounts are possible: for (4), given the presumed purpose of Wulfstan's sermons, and the skill of the author in constructing a written text that gives an impression of impromptu speech, we cannot rely on Wulfstan's prose as sole evidence of what may have been going on in OE syntax, but perhaps rather as evidence of marked usage in persuasive writing; (5) may well illustrate extraposition from the subject noun (*Aelmær*), rather than 'afterthought'. Not only are OE data ambiguous as to the possible role of afterthought, but evidence from Fijian appears to run counter to claims about processes of grammaticalisation of afterthought (Derbyshire 1981). For a summary of various other theories of word-order change see Bean 1983: ch. 2. On Campbell's (1970: 94) not very clearly defined notion of influence of verse patterns on OE prose, see Mitchell 1985: §3892, and also §3889 (see also Mitchell 1964: 119).

The present paper presents a preliminary exploration of an idea found in Vincent (1976): viz. the possible role of 'Heavy Noun Phrase Shift' in word-order change. The exploration of this idea (and its modification, see §2 below) is here presented in terms of Dependency Case Grammar, which allows formal expression of the basis for perceptual problems associated with SXV order (see §§2 and 4 below). Vincent's (1976) discussion, primarily of Latin, focuses on perceptual difficulties involved in the production and comprehension of multi-clause structures in an SXV (specifically, for Vincent, SOV) language. In such a language, any relative clause (except for those with transitive subject relatives) placed next to its referent in another clause, by centre-embedding, will result in a sentence with both finite verbs final. The more relative clauses, the more centre-embedding, the greater pile-up of sentence-final finite verbs. For instance, from Vincent (1976: 59):

(6)   Claudia   puerum   quem   Maria   amabat
        'Claudia' 'boy' acc   'whom' 'Maria' 'love' 3 sg pret
        laudavit
        'praise' 3 sg pret.

For examples of centre-embedding in OE see §3 below. On the difficulty of processing centre-embeddings see further Anderson (1976: 17 ff.; 1979: 10 ff.).

An SXV language may solve this perceptual problem by extraposition, e.g. from Vincent (1976: 60):

(7)   Mulierem   aspicio   quae pisces   vendit
        'woman' acc 'see' 1 sg pres 'who' 'fish' acc 'sell' 3 sg pres.

For examples of extraposition in OE see §§4.2.1.1 and 4.2.2.1 below. For OE it would appear that a noun clause or complement sentence is regularly extraposed, as in (8):

(8)   oð   þæt ic wille   seggan   þæt ic
        'until' 'that' 'I' 'want' 1 sg pres 'say' infin 'that' 'I'
        wite   buton   getweon   þaet þaet   me
        'know' 1 sg pres 'without' 'doubt'   'that' 'which' 'me' dat
        þincð   þæt ic wite
        'seem' 3 sg pres 'that' 'I' 'know' 1 sg pres
        (Bacquet 1962: 403),

where the complex object of *seggan*, viz. *þæt* ... end, occurs after the verb, and contains another extraposed clause, viz. *þæt ic wite*. But as Vincent (1976: 64) remarks for Latin: 'this rule [extraposition] was itself only saved from a number of ambiguity problems by the complex inflection of the noun and relative pronoun. If the effect of sound-change was essentially to destroy this morphological system ... then the perceptually pernicious effects of Extraposition from NP will be multiplied'. Given increasing syncretism in expression of inflectional morphology in OE (see above), and the predominant OE use of the indeclinable relative particle *þe*, it would seem that extraposition would be increasingly 'pernicious' in OE also. Even were this not the case, extraposition cannot, of itself, account for an overall change of SXV to SVX.

In a diachronic study of OE data, we find that not only do relative clauses move to the right of the main (finite) verb (on noun clauses see above): so, too, do non-clausal Xs (see §4 below), in the move towards predominant SVX order. Extraposition does not account for the occurrence of a post-verbal non-clausal X. Rather (or as well), we may invoke, as does Vincent (1976) for Latin, the notion of 'Heavy Noun Phrase Shift' (HNP shift: a term borrowed from Ross 1967), as the basis for one possible account of the change from SXV to SVX. In the Latin:

(9)   natura   homini   addidit   rationem
        'nature' 'man' dat 'add' 3 sg perf 'reason' acc
        qua   regerentur   appetitus
        'which' abl 'govern' pl pres pass 'appetite' nom pl

'nesting has been avoided by moving the whole complex NP, including the head noun, to the end of the sentence. As a consequence, surface SOV order had been given up in favour of SVO' (Vincent 1976: 62).

As presented by Vincent (1976), HNP shift involves movement of an argument of the verb, here the 'direct object', to the right of the verb. Once the SVO pattern is established by HNPs, and re-analysed as basic, then 'light' objects will follow, resulting in the predominant SVO order; and further, for OE at least, SVX order, since not only direct objects move to the right of the verb, but other arguments as well (see §§2 and 3 below).

2 Some Definitions

2.1 HNP SHIFT involves an NP which is a non-subjective argument of the verb: typically, a 'direct object', which may be classified in some way as 'heavy'.
2.2 NON-SUBJECTIVE ARGUMENT OF VERB applies to all constituents of a clause that belong, in traditional logic-based terms, to the predicate: i.e. all except for subject (and finite verb). Within a clause, arguments may function as PARTICIPANTS or CIRCUMSTANTIALS (see e.g. Matthews 1981: 124).

Participants may be defined as 'those putative case phrases [arguments] which are distinctive for a class of predicates' (Anderson 1977: 26–7). Thus a participant depends for its presence on a particular (lexical-semantic) class of verb; and in turn, helps to distinguish that verb as belonging to a particular class. So, for instance, the directional prepositional phrase (PP) in (10):

(10)   he went into the room

defines the verb *go* as not only agentive, but directional as well; cf. (11):

(11)   he swam in the pool

where *swim* is agentive but not directional or locational, and the PP is not a participant of the verb. Some PPs in PE will be participants, others will be circumstantials. But most adverbials, for instance (like some PPs), do not define a class of verb: e.g. instrumentals, such as the PP in (12):

(12)   I want to hit him with a hammer

or agentive adverbs, as in (13):

(13)   I hit him vituperatively

give no further definition of the verb, since instrumentals and agentives can collocate only with agentive verbs. So such adverbials will be circumstantials. Some place adverbs, such as *here, home*, and some prepositions, such as *through, down* etc., may function as goal adverbs and define the verb as directional (*come here; drive through*): such adverbs are therefore participants.

It must be confessed, though, that participant/circumstantial status is not always clear-cut: consider the ambiguous status of some PPs in OE: whether or not they represent expansions of an object NP, and therefore are part of the participant or not, may be open to question. Shannon (1964: 33), for instance, presents the PP in e.g. (14) and the second PP in (15) as 'parts of nominal phrases', but without justifying their inclusion as (parts of) participants rather than circumstantials:

(14)   his londes   ofer   al   his   rice
        'his' 'land' gen 'throughout' 'all' 'his' 'kingdom' acc

(15)   to   þæm   londum   on   þa   healfe muntes
        'to' 'those' 'land' dat pl 'on' 'that' 'side' 'mountain' gen.

HNP shift involves participants (cf. the inclusion of circumstantials also, in HA shift, below), since a direct object must be a participant of the verb.

2.3 DIRECT OBJECT: oft-cited potential object properties are outlined and questioned in Anderson (1984: 33 ff.); OE data would support Anderson's objections to the following possible criteria for defining object (specifically, 'direct' object):

2.3.1 Inflectional Accusative inflectional markers are usually associated with (direct) objecthood, but for OE:

— 'object' marking is not the only function of accusative inflectional markers: cf. e.g. adverbial *ealne weg* 'always, all the way', *ham* '(to) home' (see also Anderson, 1985);

— other case markers may express putative '(direct) object': e.g. the 'object' of *gyrnan* 'ask for' is marked for genitive, that of *fultumian* 'help', for dative (see also (100) below; Anderson, 1985);

— many 'accusative' forms have no case-markers: e.g. *weg, ham* (above; and see again Gardner 1971: 77 ff.; Shannon 1964: 59, on syncretism in expression of case in OE).

2.3.2 Configurational This proposed property of objects relies on assuming a close relation between verb and object: specifically, 'the uniqueness of object NPs as daughters of VP' (Anderson 1984: 37). To the extent to which (at least early) OE is an SXV language, configurational properties fail to identify objects, since there would seem to be little motivation for positing the category VP in such a language (again, see Anderson 1984: 37). XVS word-order in certain main clauses in OE (see §3 below) presents a further obstacle to isolation of VP: indeed, the subsequent shift in such clause-types to SVX can be seen as a move towards development of VP, along with the change of SXV (but this must be the topic of another paper ...; see, however, DeArmond 1984).

The analysis of an OE verb-final clause in (16) illustrates the difficulty of motivating consistent VP for OE (on dependency/case trees see §4 below):

Here the accusative-marked *hine* is the 'direct object'; but this has no intimate relationship with the verb *bræd*, being separated by the subject *man*, as well as the circumstantial *ða*.

2.3.3 Passivisation 'Objecthood in English is traditionally associated with passivization, such that it has been claimed, for example, that "the subject of a passive verb is what in the active would be an object" ' (Anderson 1984: 41). In addition to Anderson's counter-arguments to this criterion (p. 42) we may remark that OE lacks formal expression of passive: rather, what may be translated into a passive construction in PE may be expressed in OE by an active one: e.g. the clause in (16) above, where *man* represents the indefinite pronoun, may be rendered as 'he was then taken into the king's chamber' (see further Mitchell 1985: §747). According to handbooks on OE (e.g. Campbell 1959: §727; Mitchell and Robinson 1982: §89; Mitchell 1985: §§600.1 and 746), the form

diagram (16)

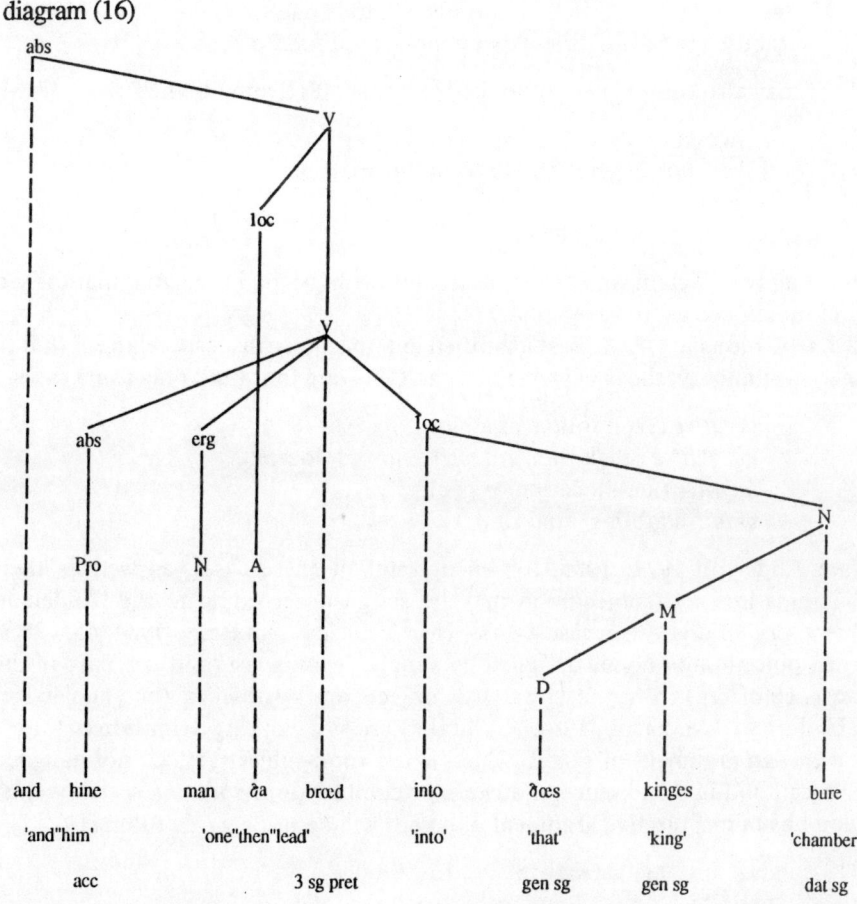

(Rositzke 1940: AD 1053)

hātte, related to *hatan* 'call', alone among OE verbs, is marked for passive, e.g. in *se munuc hatte Abbo* 'the monk was called Abbo' (Mitchell and Robinson 1982: §202). Now, certainly, there is a surface morphological difference between the form *hātte*, and both the present (*hætt* or *hāteþ*) or past (*hēt*) 3 sg. forms of *hatan*: but to build on this distinction a claim that OE had a passive voice (even for one verb) is to rely on the unfortunate consequences of 'translation': simply for the form *hātte* to be best rendered in PE by a structural use of passive (see above) is no argument for the existence of a structure best described as 'passive' in OE.

Past participles combined with *beon/wesan* 'be' and *weorþan* 'become' are commonly inflected in OE, suggesting adjectival function (Mitchell 1985: §§983 ff.; and the discussion in §§759 ff.): e.g. *getawode*, marked for plural, in (17) (from Mitchell 1985: §748):

(17) Eala þu biscop to bysmore synd
      'alas' 'you' 'bishop' 'shamefully' 'be' pres pl

getawode   þas   earman   landleoda
'abuse' pa part pl 'these' 'wretched' 'land-folk' pl.

They may also complement other verbs: e.g. in (18) (from Mitchell 1985: §748):

(18)   Soðlice ða   ðe   to   us   asende
       'truly' 'those' 'who' 'to' 'us' 'send' pa part pl
       becumað
       'become' pres pl.

It is highly uncertain whether constructions with 'be' had been grammaticalised and functioned as 'passive' in OE.

2.3.4   Objects in OE are best identified in terms of localist case relations (CRs), viz., in summary, those expressed by the following four (and only four) cases:

> *ergative* (erg): source of action,
> *absolutive* (abs): thing affected, moved, located,
> *locative* (loc): location or goal,
> *ablative* (abl): spatial source

(see Anderson 1977; 1985, for an account of these cases, as well as their combinations). If subjecthood may be assigned according to the 'Anderson hierarchy' of erg > erg, case, > abs, case > abs (see Anderson 1984: 45; 1985), then objecthood may be assigned by simply deleting erg (and erg, case in the absence of erg) from the hierarchy: 'objects are a subset of (non-subjective) absolutives' (Anderson, 1984: 40). I take here as a working definition of 'direct object' an argument of a verb which is abs (non-subjective: i.e., not assigned subjecthood in the absence of any erg or combinations with erg, see above). A non-abs non-subjective argument of a verb will be loc, e.g. the PP in (19):

(19)   and   his   haligan sawle   to   Godes
       'and' 'his' 'holy'   'soul' acc   'to' 'God' gen
       rice   asende
       'kingdom' dat 'send' 3 sg pret
       (Rositzke 1940: AD 1012),

or abl, e.g. the PP in (20):

(20)   and   him   man sealde   gislas
       'and' 'him' dat 'one' 'give' 3 sg pret 'hostage' acc pl
       of   ælcere scire
       'from' 'each' 'shire' dat
       (Rositzke 1940: AD 1013),

or a combination of loc and abl.

Having suggested a way of identifying direct objects in OE (borne out by analyses of data to follow), we now need to consider what could be meant by 'heavy', if we are to assess (at least provisionally) the role of HNP shift in OE word-order change.

2.4 The notion HEAVY NP has been defined as 'long and/or clause-containing' (Postal 1974: 83), but as Postal (1974: 83 n.1) remarks: 'this is very rough indeed. For instance, the presence of quantifiers is also sufficient ... And, as Ross notes, this is true even when the quantifiers are in adjectival forms like *whole* and *entire*'. What follows below attempts to define more precisely the types of weight which may accrue to an NP.

2.4.1 Lexical weight Word structure (WS), for any language, may be represented formally in square brackets, enclosing an abbreviated lexical entry (represented in capitals), plus morphological categories. Major word-class is indicated outside the brackets (see further Colman to appear). For instance, the WS for PE *men's* may be represented as in (21):

(21)
$$\begin{bmatrix} \text{MAN} \\ \text{pl} \\ \text{gen} \\ \text{mutative} \end{bmatrix}$$
N

Open-class words require a specific lexical entry (indicating the complex of idiosyncratic properties abbreviated by the capitalised elements) to distinguish those of the same major word-class, with the same morphological categories, from each other: compare the WS for PE *geese's* in (22):

(22)
$$\begin{bmatrix} \text{GOOSE} \\ \text{pl} \\ \text{gen} \\ \text{mutative} \end{bmatrix}$$
N

But closed-class words are lexically empty: that is, the WS of such a word may be represented formally by reference to only major word-class and morphological categories, e.g. for PE *him*, represented in (23):

(23)
$$\begin{bmatrix} \text{pro} \\ \text{masc} \\ \text{sg} \\ \text{III} \\ \text{oblique} \end{bmatrix}$$
N

No other word form in PE could be so characterised. Thus pronouns are lexically 'light' in relation to nouns, which have the 'weight' of a specific lexical entry. So, on this basis, a potential HNP will be nominal, rather than pronominal (see §§3 and 5 below on position of pronoun objects in OE), e.g. for OE *manna*, the WS in (24):

(24)
$$\begin{bmatrix} \text{MANN} \\ \text{masc} \\ \text{pl} \\ \text{gen} \\ \text{mutative} \end{bmatrix}$$

N

but for *hine*, that in (25):

(25)
$$\begin{bmatrix} \text{pro} \\ \text{masc} \\ \text{sg} \\ \text{III} \\ \text{acc} \end{bmatrix}$$

N

2.4.2 Constituent weight　An NP may be expanded in the following ways:
— determiners and modifiers (adjectives, possessives, quantifiers etc.), e.g. in OE as in (26):

(26)　Ac　　he　teah　　　　　ða　　forð　his
　　　'but' 'he' 'continue' 3 sg pret 'then' 'forth' 'his'
　　　ealdan　　　wrencas
　　　'former' 'treachery'　　acc pl
　　　(Rositzke 1940: AD 1003)

where the noun *wrencas* is modified by the possessive *his* and the adjective *ealdan*:
— other case-marked nouns, e.g. in OE as in (27):

(27)　and　man　　geutlagode　　þa　　Aelfgar　eorl
　　　'and' 'one' 'outlaw' 3 sg pret 'then' 'Aelfgar' 'earl' acc
　　　Leofrices　　sunu　　eorles
　　　'Leofric' gen 'son' acc 'earl' gen
　　　(Rositzke 1940: AD 1055)

where Aelfgar is modified by *eorl*, and this whole NP is modified appositively by *sunu*, modified by *Leofrices*, further modified appositively by *eorles*;
— prepositional phrases also thus indirectly participants of the verb, e.g. in OE as in (28):

(28)　and　　hi　　hæfdon　　　　þære burhware

'and' 'they' 'have' pl pret 'the' 'citizen'   gen pl
fultum   of   Lundene
'help' acc 'of' 'London' dat
(Rositzke 1940: AD 1016)

where *of London* modifies *þære burhware* (which in turn is a case-marked NP modifying *fultum*, see above);
— coordinated NPs, e.g. in OE as in (29) and (30):

(29)   ac   we ða   gyt   næfdon   þa
       'but' 'we' 'then' 'yet'   'not-have' pl pret 'the'
       gesælða   ne   þone wyrðscype
       'happiness' acc 'nor' 'the' 'honour' acc
       (Rositzke 1940: AD 1009)

(30)   and   betæhte   þa scipu   and
       'and' 'entrust' 3 sg pret 'the' 'ship' acc pl 'and'
       þa   gislas   Cnute   his suna
       'the' 'hostage' acc pl 'Cnut' dat 'his' 'son' dat
       (Rositzke 1940: AD 1013);
       — relative clauses, e.g. in OE as in (31):

(31)   se   cyning   het   ofslean   ealle
       'the' 'king' 'command' 3 sg pret 'slay' infin 'all' acc
       þa   Danish men   þe   on   Angelcynne
       'the' 'Danish' 'man' acc pl 'who' 'among' 'English-race' dat
       wæron
       'be' pl pret
       (Rositzke 1940: AD 1002)

where the relative clause modifies *men*. Note, too, that a relative clause may modify a pronoun (for OE see Mitchell 1985: §2249), thus lending constituent weight to the lexically light NP, e.g. in OE as in (32):

(32)   ðu   ðe   sitst   ofer   cherubin
       'you' nom sg 'who' 'sit' 3 sg pres 'above' 'cherubim'
       (Mitchell 1985: §2183).

2.4.3 The analysis of OE data that follows aims at a formal representation of the role of HNPs in word-order change in OE; but we shall see, too, that it is not only the weight of the abs participant of the verb (the 'heavy object') that may contribute to a shift from SXV; also significant is the occurrence and weight of phrases which are not necessarily participants of the verb. Therefore I shall re-define HNP shift as HEAVY ARGUMENT SHIFT (HA shift).

I would not want to claim HA shift as an exclusive factor in word-order change in late OE: various accounts (e.g. those cited in §1 above), which may be seen to have inherent drawbacks, may suffer also by virtue of representing claims for single 'causes' of change. Rather, we may see word-order change in English as a result of possibly several factors whose combined effects conspire in bringing about re-ordering in the surface syntax (see further §4 below on effects of tangling and their possible relation to morphological change). But certainly, a formal representation of OE clauses illustrates potential perceptual problems of SXV order in OE; and claims about the part such problems (and their possible solutions) might play in a shift away from SXV would be supported by Swinney's (1981: 208) claim that processes of sentence-comprehension involve 'left — to — right' segmentation of lexical candidates. Although Swinney's research focuses on lexical ambiguity, the findings are relevant to the notion of HAP as a factor in word-order change, by illustrating the psychological problems in a construction of the SXV type which has its head in final position.

3 Preliminaries to Presentation of OE Data

3.1   The data presented in §4 below are drawn from an eleventh-century prose text: specifically the *C Text* of the *OE Chronicle*, AD 1000–1066 (Rositze 1940). The selection of data for this study is necessarily restricted, but the findings may be borne out by comparison with other eleventh-century prose writings, e.g. other manuscripts of the *OE Chronicle*, and writings of Aelfric and Wulfstan. The latter, however, as carefully composed literary works, do not lend themselves to as ready an analysis as practicable for a brief study.

The eleventh-century data are seen as evidence of a stage in the diachronic change from early OE word-order to that of PE. The mixture of word-order patterns for each of various clause types we will find represented in the eleventh-century text suggests not that OE word-order was 'relatively free' (cf. discussion in Quirk and Wrenn 1957: §133; Wagner 1969: ch.1), but that a change from 'classical' OE patterns was underway by the eleventh century, and that English was already moving towards predominantly SVX order. Evidence for this move is continued in the later (twelfth-century) prose of the *Peterborough Chronicle*: see Mitchell's (1964: 144) remarks on Clark's (1958) claims for the modernity of the prose in the *Peterborough Chronicle*: 'the language is changing to Modern English, but it has not changed ... The syntax and word-order are still in many important respects Old English'. Nevertheless, '[the] disappearance of the order S. Noun O. V. represents a step towards Modern English' (Mitchell 1964: 124).

3.2   I summarise below, for comparison, the word-order types presented by Traugott (1972: 106–9) for ninth-century OE. This summary illustrates the patterns with respect to only subject (S), object (O) and verb (V), according to clause type. The syntactic units of clauses are here presented without discussion, but are taken as containing one finite verb (I do not know what 'unit' is referred to in Mitchell's (1985: §1881) quotation of Bately's claim that in some OE prose 'the unit is not the phrase or the sentence but the paragraph or even larger sections': but since this is related by Mitchell to problems of punctuating edited versions of OE texts it need not concern us here). On the significance of distinguishing main from subordinate clauses, and, within main clauses, those which open with conjunctions or adverbials, see further Mitchell (1964: 118; 1985: §3889). For a *caveat* on 'relying on element order to decide whether a particular clause is principal or subordinate', see Mitchell (1985: §3889): but see further Mitchell (1985: §3922): 'despite the difficulties, editors of prose texts should not disregard too easily the rule of thumb that after *þær, þanon, þider, þa* and *þonne*, clauses with SV or S ... V are likely to be subordinate'.

3.2.1 A main clause with simple verb has (S)VO, as in (33):

(33) he   underfeng   martydom
      'he' 'receive' 3 sg pret 'martyrdom' acc
      (Bacquet 1962: 71)

except where the object is a pronoun, in which case (S)OV is regular, as in (34) and (35):

(34) hio   hit   gewundað
      'she' 'it' acc 'wound' 3 sg pres
      (Bacquet 1962: 68)

(35) Davið   se witga   ðæt   cyðde
      'David' 'the' 'wise' 'that' acc 'make known' 3 sg pret
      (Bacquet 1962: 68).

Mitchell (1985: §3889) considers among 'unnecessarily sweeping assertions' Traugott's (1972: 107) 'obligatory shift of pronoun objects to preverbal position'; nevertheless, on 'the intervention of a pronoun object or of pronoun objects, direct and/or indirect, between S and V', Mitchell (1985: §3907) remarks: 'this is regular, but not compulsory', and points out 'the vital importance of distinguishing noun and pronoun objects'. (I remain unconvinced by Mitchell's argument (1985: §3907) for S pro O V as a variant of SV, not S ... V: the cited patterns of S pro O V acc could as well be variants of S ... V, not SV.)

3.2.2 A main clause with compound verb, viz. main verb plus dependent verb: infinitive or participle, has (S)VO non-finite V, as in (36):

(36) he   hæfde   folc   gegaderad
      'he' 'have' 3 sg pret 'people' acc 'gather' pa part
      (Bacquet 1962: 112)

except where the object is a pronoun, in which case SOV non-finite V occurs, as in (37):

(37) Ic hi   wille   læran
      'I' 'them' acc 'intend' 1 sg pres 'teach' infin
      (Bacquet 1962: 114).

Given lack of motivation for positing the category *auxiliary* for OE (Lightfoot 1979: §2.2.1; and see Anderson 1976: 43), the finite verb form is here treated as the main verb, with the non-finite form dependent; cf. Traugott's (1972: 106–9) analysis of the finite form as aux, with the non-finite form as the main verb; and

Mitchell's (1985: ch.IX) use of 'V' for non-finite forms, 'v' for finite (where the two co-occur in a clause), implying aux status for the latter. On adjectival inflection of participles see §2.3.3. above.

3.2.3   A main clause initiated by an interrogative, negative or adverb (X) has XVS(O), as in (38), (39) and (41) to (43) (note the interrogative construction without X in (40)):

(38)   hwær   bist   ðu
       'where' 'be' 2 sg pres 'you' nom sg
       (Bacquet 1962: 205)

(39)   hwi   acsast   þu   ma   æfter   ðam
       'why' 'ask' 2 sg pres 'you' nom 'more' 'about' 'that' dat
       (Bacquet 1962: 189)

(40)   eart   þu
       'be' 2 sg pres 'you' nom sg
       (Bacquet 1962: 204)

(41)   ne   cweðe   ic
       'not' 'say' 1 sg pres 'I'
       (Bacquet 1962: 630)

(42)   þa ofslog   Poros   Alexandres
       'then' 'slay' 3 sg pret 'Poros' nom 'Alexander' gen
       hors
       'horse' acc
       (Bacquet 1962: 602)

(43)   ðonne   gefeng   David   his   hearpan
       'then' 'take' 3 sg pret 'David' nom 'his' 'harp' acc
       (Bacquet 1962: 602)

3.2.4   The basic order for all subordinate constructions in ninth-century prose is SOV, as in (44) to (47):

(44)   ðonne ða   lareowas   mid wordum
       'when' 'the' 'teacher' nom pl 'with' 'word'   dat pl
       oðre menn   lærat
       'other' 'man' acc pl 'teach' pl pres
       (Bacquet 1962: 383)

(45)   þeh   hie   sige   hæfden
       'although' 'they' 'victory' acc 'have' pl pret subj
       (Bacquet 1962: 390)

(46)   gif   mon   wif   mid   bearne ofslea
       'if' 'one' nom 'woman' acc 'with' 'child' 'slay' 3 sg pres subj
       (Bacquet 1962: 390)

(47) ðæt ic   mine mægcild   oððe yldran,
      'that' 'I' 'my' 'kin-child' acc 'whether' 'older' acc
      oððe gingran,   mid   wo   fordemde
      'or' 'younger' acc 'with' 'sorrow'   'condemn' 1 sg pret
      (Bacquet 1962: 406)

3.2.5 A main clause introduced by a coordinating conjunction, i.e. one which is not the first in a series of main clauses, has the order of a subordinate clause, viz. (S)OV, as in (48) and (49):

(48) 7   þæt folc   mid   gefeohte sohte
      'and' 'that' 'people' acc 'with' 'battle' dat 'seek' 3 sg pret
      (Bacquet 1962: 148)

(49) 7   monege oþera þeoda   to
      'and' 'many' acc 'other' 'people' gen pl 'to'
      ðæm ilcan gewinne   getugon
      'that' 'same' 'fight' dat 'draw' pl pret
      (Bacquet 1962: 146)

Note also (S)XV (where X is not a direct object) in (50):

(50) 7   mid ealle ofslog
      'and'   'entirely' 'slay' 3 sg pret
      (Bacquet 1962: 140)

The focus in our discussion is on subordinate, and main plus coordinator clauses, and the change in these clause-types from (S)XV to (S)VX (on the change from V second order in main plus 'X' clauses, see §2.3.2 above).

3.3 The situation is not as (simply) clear-cut as implied by Traugott (1972): ninth-century English is already showing signs of patterns commonly attested for eleventh-century OE, suggesting that the move towards SVX was under way by then (but note that the pronoun object is much more consistently pre-verbal in the ninth century). The following data exemplify subordinate and main plus coordinator clauses where the main verb is not final in ninth-century OE.
3.2.1 Subordinate

(51) ðonne he ðurh   dæt woo weorc   forliest
      'when' 'he' 'through' 'that' 'dire' 'deed' acc 'give up' 3 sg pret
      ðone wlite   oðerra godra weorca
      'the' 'splendour' acc 'other' 'good' 'work' gen pl
      (Bacquet 1962: 380)

(52) þæt ðu   lufast   ðone wisdom
      'that' 'you' sg 'love' 2 sg pres 'the' 'wisdom' acc
      ofer   ealle oððre   ðing
      'above' 'all' 'other'   'thing' acc pl
      (Bacquet 1962: 403)

3.3.2   Main plus coodinator: with simple verb

(53)   7   he   wræc   þone aldorman   Cumbran
        'and' 'he' 'avenge' 3 sg pret 'the' 'aldorman' 'Cumbra' acc
        (Bacquet 1962: 72)

(54)   7   þa Denescan ahton
        'and' 'the' 'Danish' 'control' pl pret
        wælstowe   gewald
        'slaughter-place' gen 'power' acc
        (Bacquet 1962: 72)

3.3.3   Main plus coordinator: with compond verb

(55)   7   he hæfde   Poros   monegum
        'and' 'he' 'have' 3 sg pret 'Poros'   'many'
        wundum   gewundodne
        'wound' dat pl 'wound' pa part
        (Bacquet 1962: 112)

(56)   ac   he wolde   ætiewan   his arfæðnesse
        'but' 'he' 'want' 3 sg pret 'manifest' infin 'his' 'piety' acc
        (Bacquet 1962: 114)

3.3.4   Furthermore, along with centre-embedding, as in (57) and (58) we find
extraposition, as in (59), and HA shift, as in (60), in ninth-century prose:

(57)   for ðon þa   feawan þe   þær   ut   oþflugon
        'because' 'the' 'few'   'who' 'there' 'out'   'flee' pl pret
        hæfdon   eft   þa burg   gebune
        'have' pl pret 'again' 'the' 'dwelling' acc 'settle' pa part pl
        (Bacquet 1962: 285)

(58)   7   Aeþelswiþ   cuen   sio   wæs
        'and' 'Aethelswith' 'queen' nom 'who' 'be' 3 sg pret
        Aelfredes   sweostor cyninges forþferde
        'Aelfred' gen 'sister' nom 'king' gen 'die' 3 sg pret
        (Bacquet 1962: 305)

(59)   ðylæs him   ðæs godan weorces   lean
        'lest' 'him' dat 'the' 'good' 'deed' gen 'reward' nom
        losige   ðe   he mid   ðære
        'be lost' 3 sg pres subj 'which' 'he' 'with' 'the'
        steore   gearnian sceolde
        'discipline' dat 'earn' infin 'shall' 3 sg pret
        (Bacquet 1962: 345)

(60)   ic eow   healsige   ðæt ge
        'I' 'you' dat pl 'beseech' 1 sg pres 'that' 'you' nom pl

feden   Godes   heorde   ðe   under   eow
'feed' infin 'God' gen 'flock' acc 'which' 'under' 'you' dat pl
is
'be' 3 sg pres
(Bacquet 1962: 312)

4 Eleventh-century OE Data

4.1   The data consist of subordinate clauses, and main clauses initiated by a coordinating conjunction. The structure of each clause is analysed in terms of CRs pertaining between the verb and any arguments (see §2 above). The finite (main) verb may have a dependent non-finite verb, e.g. as in (62) below. The appropriate structural properties are represented by dependency trees: the head of a clause is the predicative element, viz. the finite verb, whose modifiers are case phrases (either participants of circumstantials, or both, see §2 above). CRs may be expressed by adposition plus inflection (e.g. the PP *on fultume* in (63) below) or by modification of the noun alone (e.g. the NP *hiora yfeles* in (67) below). A participant argument of a verb is shown as dependent on that verb (e.g. the abs in (62) below; a non-participant (circumstantial) argument is dependent on a V node constituting the head of the whole sentence, on which depends in subjunction (i.e. without linear distinction, see Anderson 1977; Böhm 1982; Anderson 1985) also the lower verb (e.g. the circumstantial *næfre* in (67) below). I have followed the traditional assignment of head-hood to the noun in NPs; but for a preferable assignment of head-hood to the determiner or modifier, where present, see Anderson (1976: ch.4; 1979; to appear). Differing interpretations of the internal structures of NPs do not affect the present concern.

    Subject- and objecthood are assigned (but not in the trees) according to the Anderson hierarchy, and its truncation (see §2 above).

    Selected data from the eleventh-century text (Rositzke 1940) are presented according as they represent SXV order (§4.2 below) and SVX order (§4.3 below), illustrating a move towards PE order. This presentation illustrates formally the perceptual complexities of SXV order, as compared to the patterns for SVX order, with regard to interruption of arguments. Arguments may be interrupted in the following ways.

— heavy participants (see §2 above);

— one or more circumstantials (see §2 above);

— where a CR is expressed by an adposition, this may be separated from its argument, e.g. in (61):

(61)   se   here   him   fleah   beforan
        'the' 'army' 'him' dat 'flee' 3 sg pret 'before'
        (Rositzke 1940: AD 1096)

where the adposition *beforan* is separated from the argument *him* by the verb *fleah*.

    The last type of interruption is not treated in the subsequent analyses. I shall concentrate on the order of verb and arguments in the two types of clauses under discussion, focusing on weight of participant argument(s), and presence of circumstantial ones, or a combination of both. Where participants and circumstantials both occur before the finite verb (see e.g. (67) below), tangling (crossing of dependency and/or association lines) results. Now tangling may not necessarily present a perceptual problem in the syntax of a language, cf. e.g. Present-day German, with verb-final subordinate clauses; but where difficulties arise, these may well be associated with syncretism and loss of expression of inflectional morphology. The effects of tangling in late OE may become more pernicious given the increasing syncretism in the expression of inflectional morphology (already evidenced by then), and the gradual loss in English of all case-markers except that for genitive. So, the effects of tangling in a language which is losing its overt inflectional case-markers may contribute, along with those of HAs, to a shift from SXV to SVX in late OE.

Clauses treated in this section have participants which are heavy by virtue of at least lexical weight, as well as possibly constituent weight (see §2.4 above). In §5 (below) we see instances of argument shift where the participant is lexically light (and therefore also without constituent weight), i.e. pronominal (unexpanded, cf. §2.4.2 above).

The following abbreviations are used in the tree-diagrams and comments on them: V: verb; N: noun; Pro: pronoun; D: determiner; M: modifier (adjective, quantifier etc.); A: adverb. Parentheses enclosing one or more argument-types indicate that although that type may not be present in the example cited, the possibility of its occurrence is to be allowed for: e.g. in 4.2.1.2: 'Argument = (abs O) + non-abs participant'.

4.2   SXV order from *OE Chronicle, C Text* (Rositzke 1940)

4.2.1   Subordinate clauses

4.2.1.1   Argument = abs object (0) = participant = heavy

diagram (62)

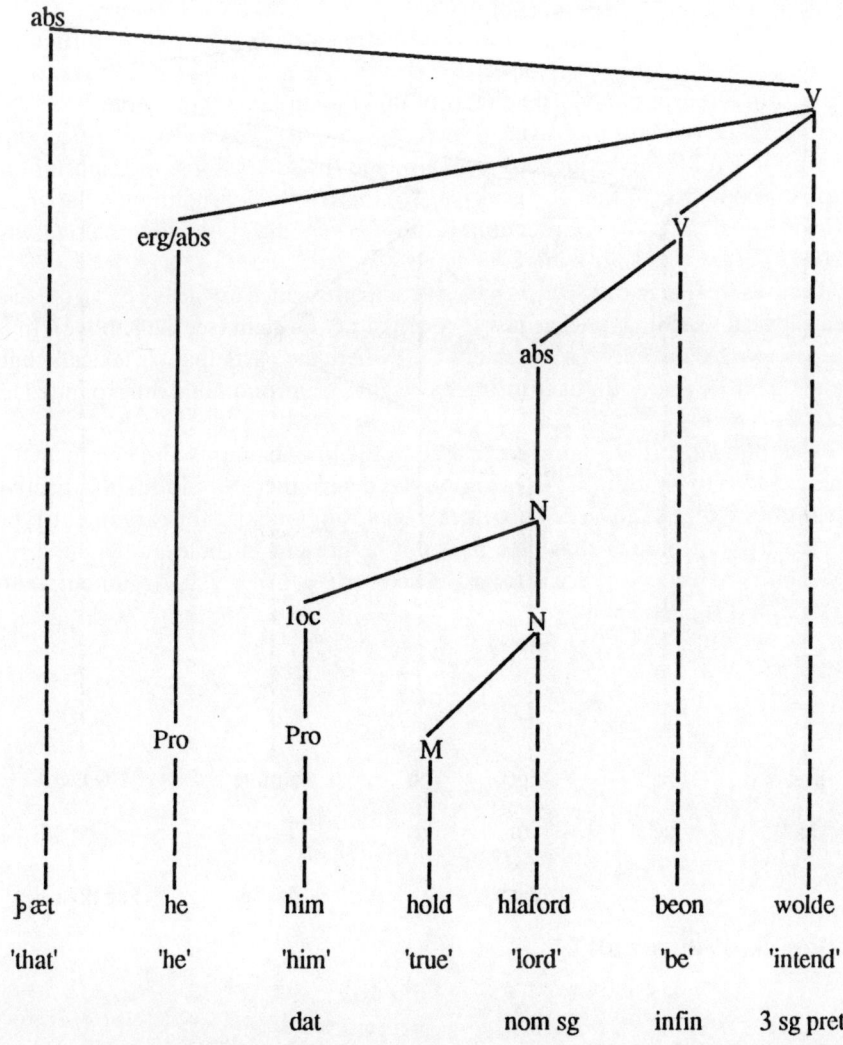

(Rositzke 1940: AD 1014)

Abs is heavy because nominal (*hlaford*) and modified by the dependent loc (*him*) and M (*hold*). Note also the participant dependent V (*beon*), and that the erg/abs subject (S) is dependent on the higher (finite) V, while other arguments depend on the lower V.

4.2.1.2   Argument = (abs S) + non-abs participant

diagram (63)

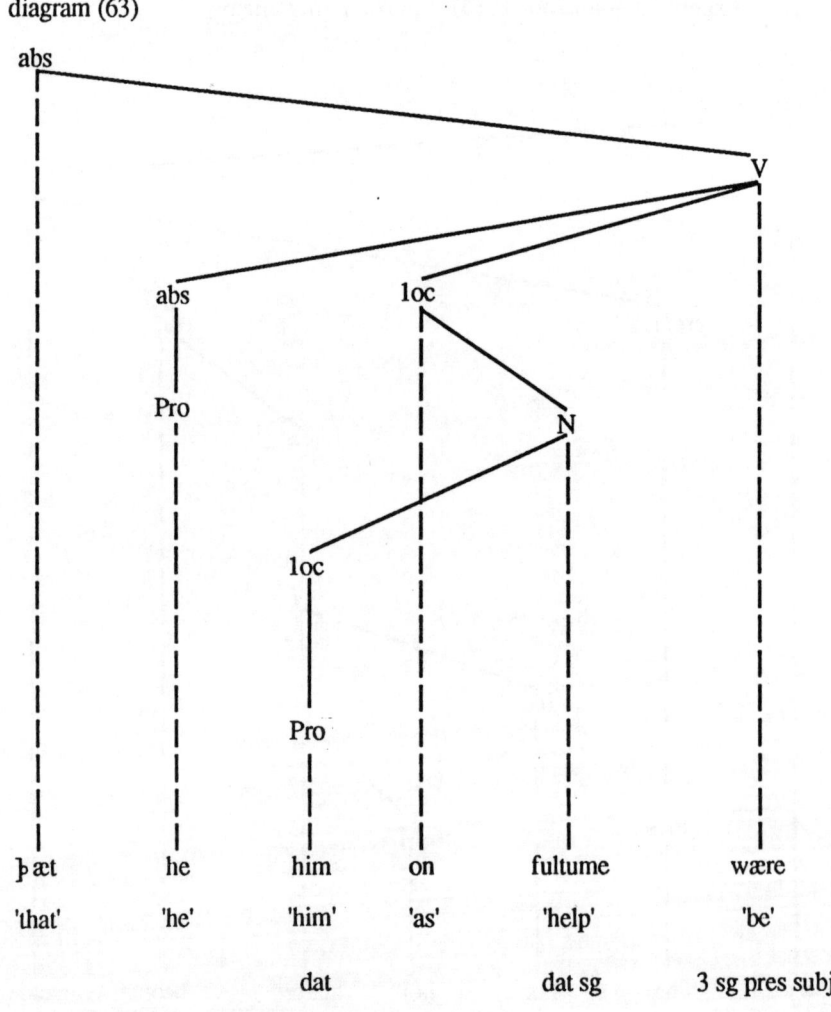

(Rositzke 1940: AD 1049)

S is abs (in the absence of erg); there is no 'direct O', i.e. non-subjective abs. The participant argument is loc, and heavy by virtue of the N (*fultume*) and the dependent loc (*him*). Tangling results from separation by the preposition *on*, of these arguments, which are shown by case-inflection to be related.

diagram (64)

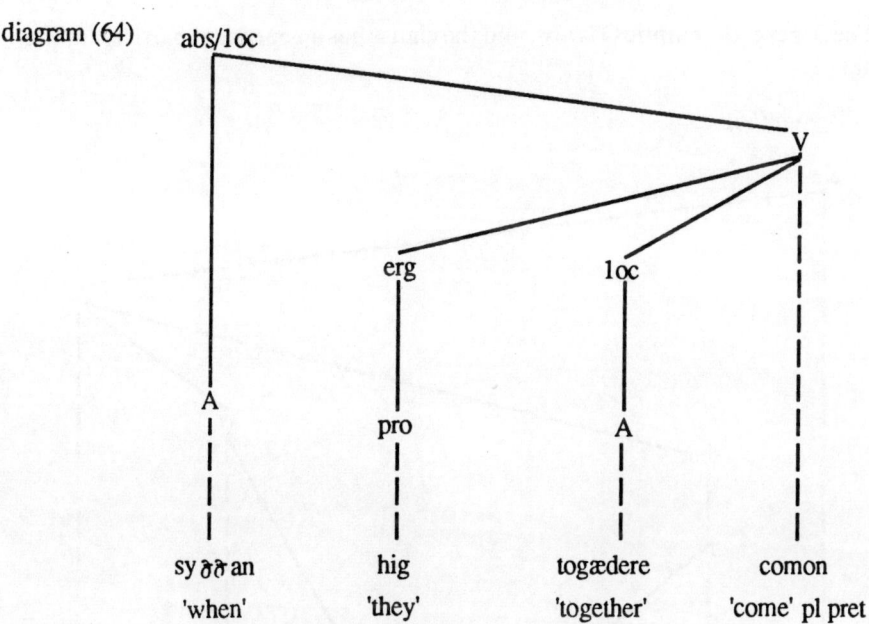

(Rositzke 1940: AD 1052)

There is no abs O; the participant argument is loc.

diagram (65)

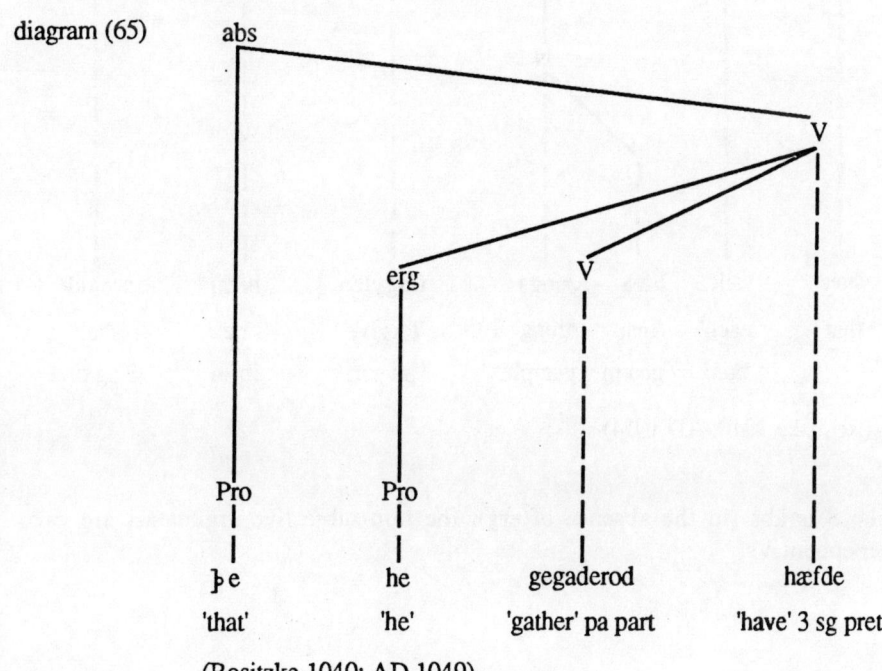

(Rositzke 1040: AD 1049)

c

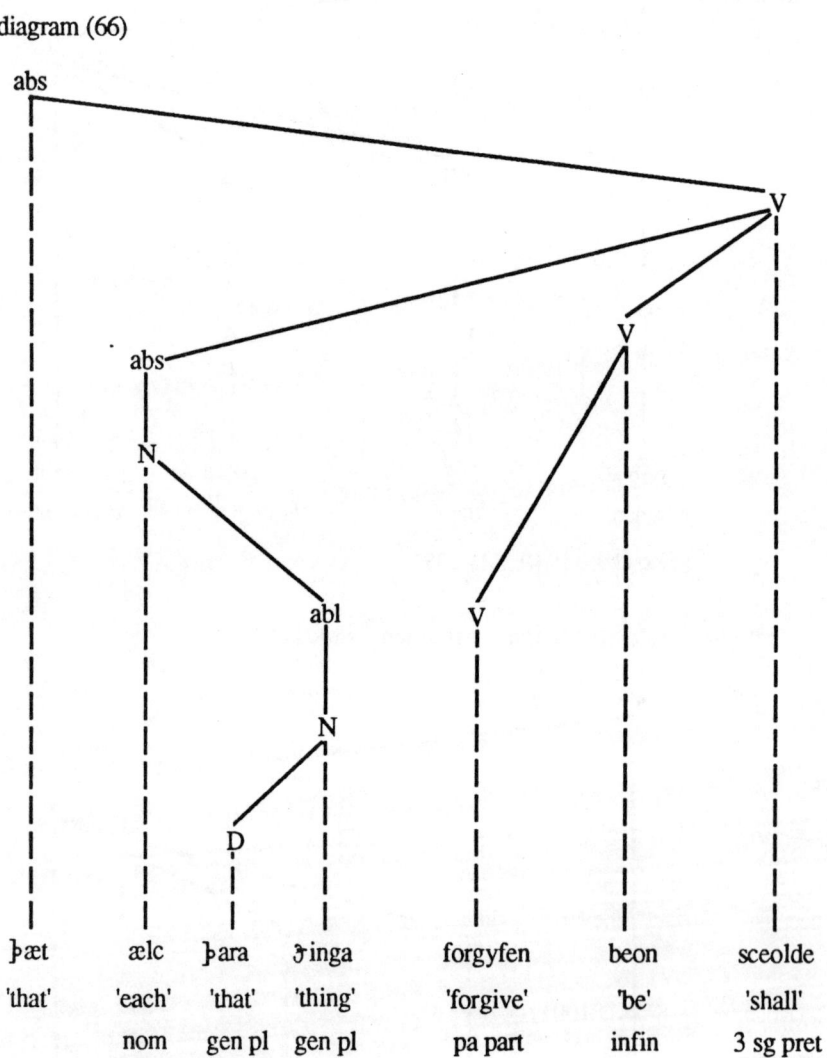

The S is erg, the elliptic O is abs; and the clause has a dependent participant (non abs) V.

diagram (66)

(Rositzke 1940: AD 1014)

The S is abs (in the absence of erg); the non-subjective arguments are two dependent Vs.

4.2.1.3   Argument = (abs O) (+ participant) + circumstantial

diagram (67)

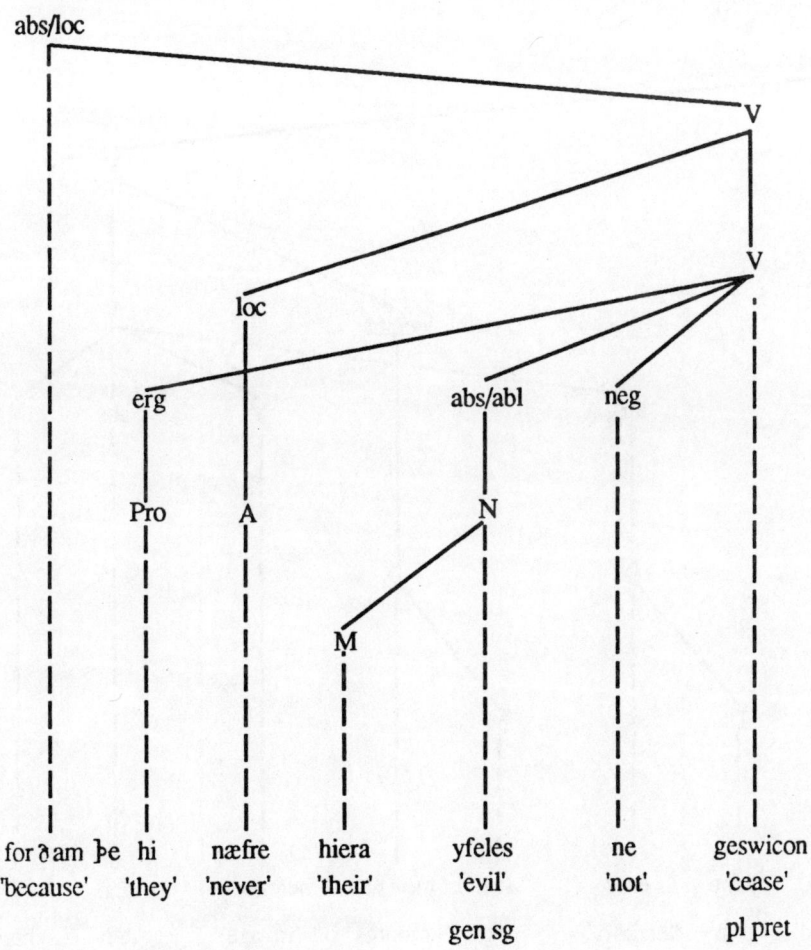

(Rositzke 1940: AD 1001)

The S is erg, and the 'direct O' is abs/abl (see Anderson 1985); the circumstantial is the loc (*næfre*). Note that tangling results from the sequence of circumstantial and abs/abl.

4.2.2　*Main clauses plus coordinators*
4.2.2.1　Argument = abs O = participant = heavy

diagram (68)

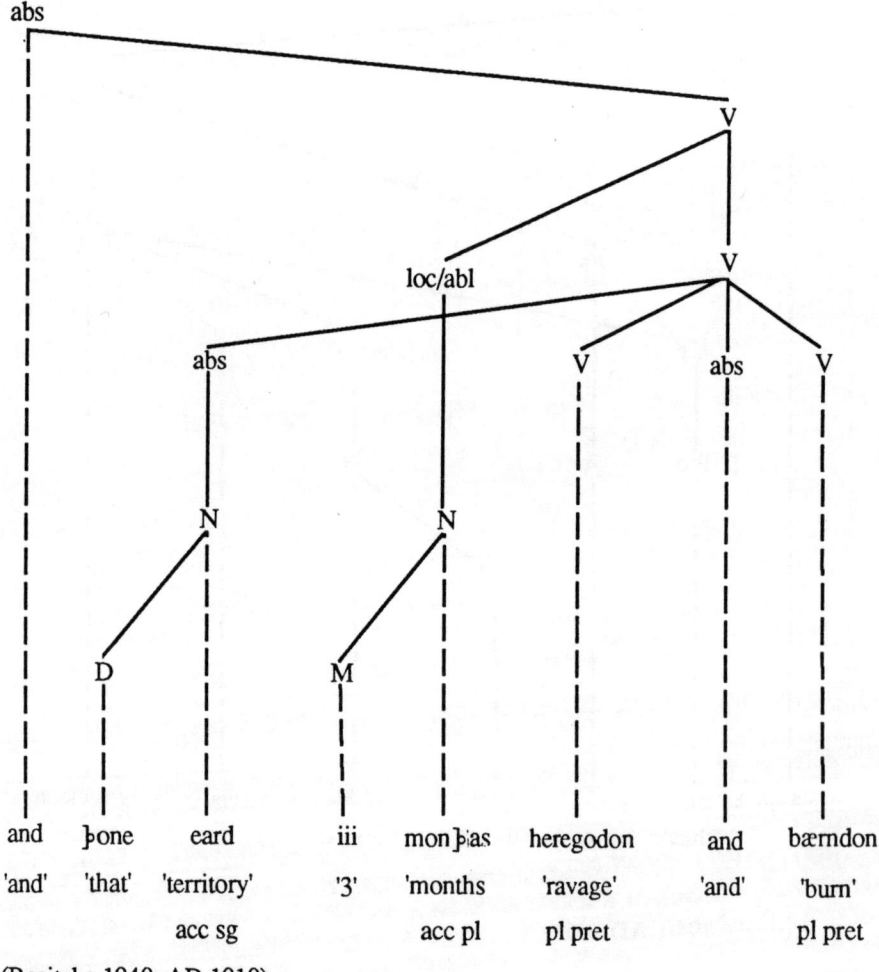

and	þone	eard	iii	mon þas	heregodon	and	bærndon
'and'	'that'	'territory'	'3'	'months	'ravage'	'and'	'burn'
		acc sg		acc pl	pl pret		pl pret

(Rositzke 1940: AD 1010)

The abs (*eard*) is heavy because nominal and modified by the D (*bone*); see also
§4.2.2.3 below: (abs) + circumstantial.

diagram (69)

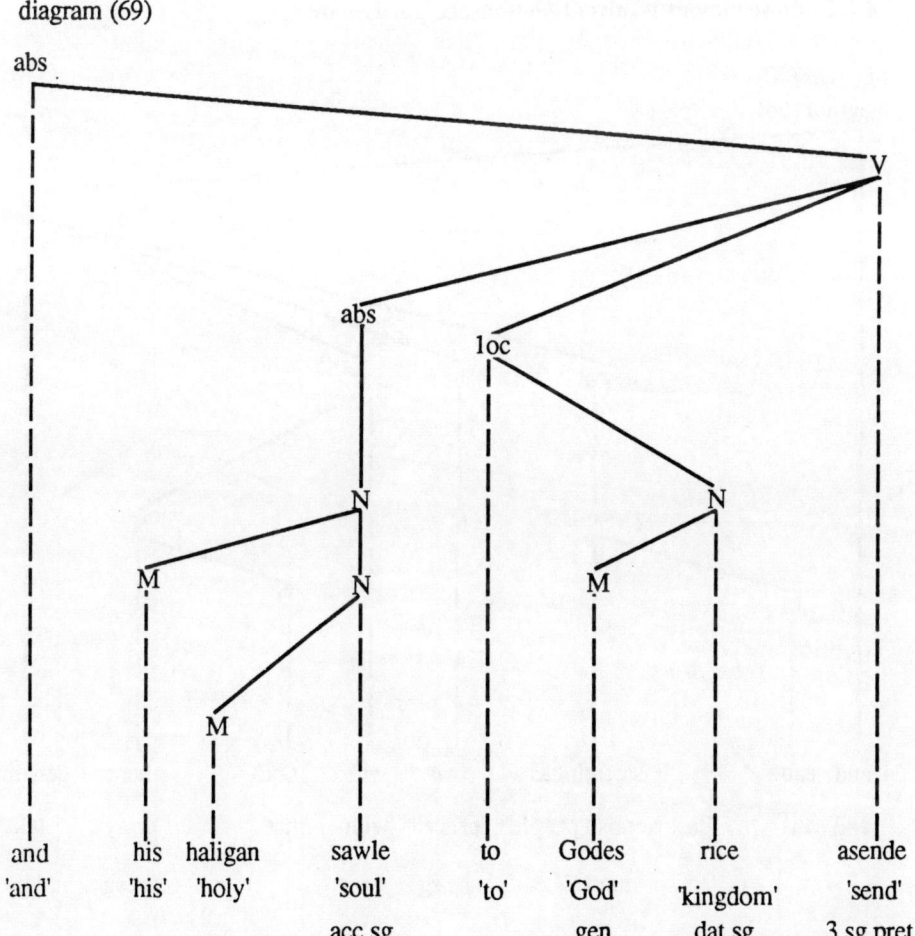

(Rositzke 1040: AD 1012)

The abs is heavy because nominal and twice modified (see also §4.2.2.2 below).

4.2.2.2   Argument = (abs O) + non-abs participant

diagram (70)

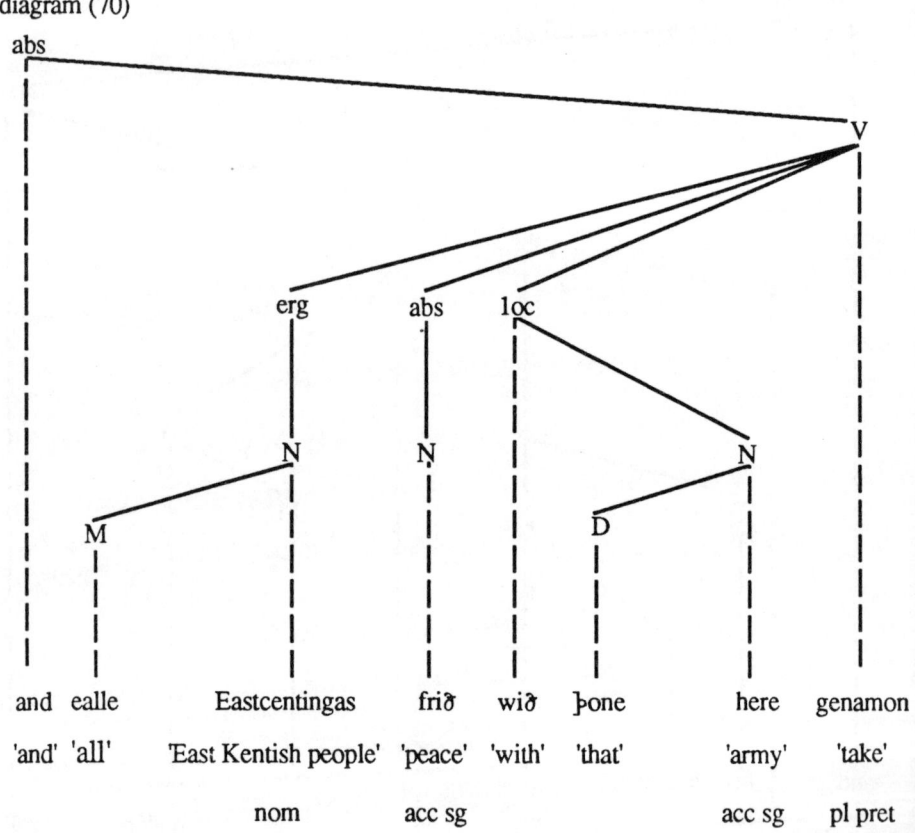

(Rositzke 1940: AD 1009)

The S is erg; the abs is heavy only by virtue of being nominal; but note the heavy non-abs participant: PP with N (*here*) modified by the dependent D (*þone*). See also (69) above, where the abs is heavy by virtue of being nominal, and of modification within the NP; but where there is also a complex non-abs participant, the PP with N (*rice*) modified by the dependent case-marked N (*Godes*).

4.2.2.3   Argument = (abs O) (+ participant) + circumstantial.
See (68) in §4.2.2.1 above, where the circumstantial (loc/abl) argument is heavy by virtue of modification of N (*monþas*) by the M (*iii*). Tangling results from the sequence of abs participant and circumstantial in the V-final clause.

4.2.2.4   The formal representations above illustrate weight of arguments (and combination of arguments) preceding the V, as well as the complexity shown by tangling where both participants and circumstantials precede the V.

Data in §4.3 exemplify changed word-order in subordinate and main plus coordinator clauses (from the same period), where putative perceptual problems are overcome by extraposition or HA shift.

4.3 SVX order from *OE Chronicle, C Text* (Rositzke 1940)

4.3.1 Subordinate clauses

4.3.1.1 Extraposition

(71) below represents the extraposed relative clause that follows the noun clause *and cwæð þæt him hold hlaford beon wolde* (glossed in (62) above):

diagram (71)

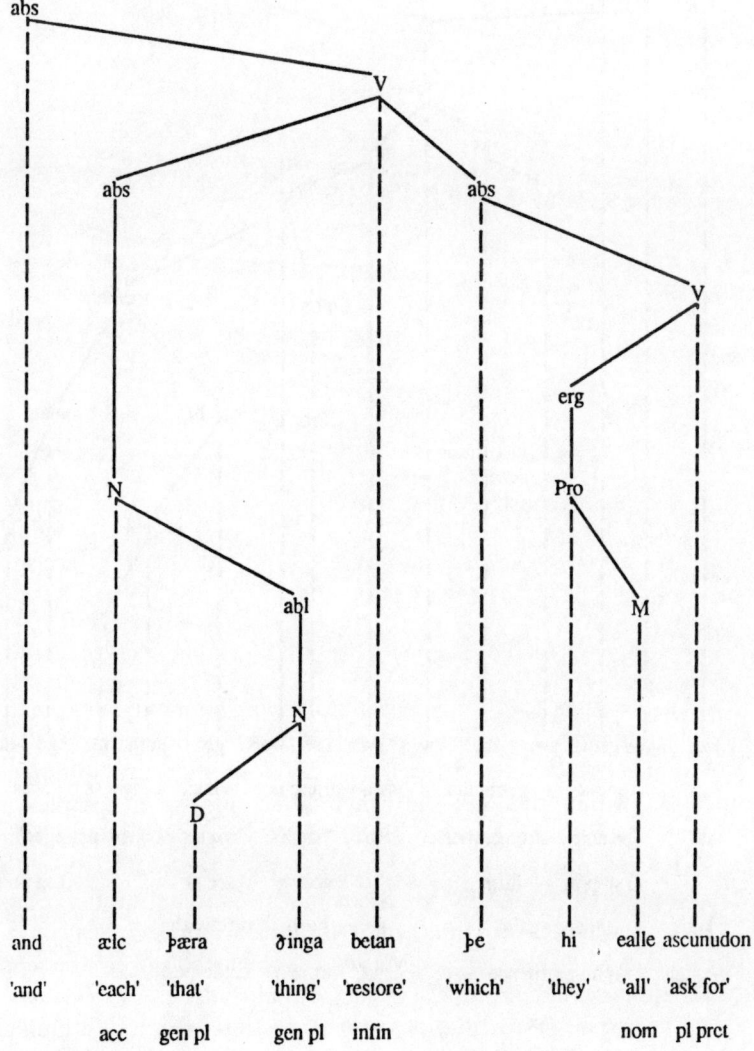

and	ælc	þæra	ðinga	betan	þe	hi	ealle	ascunudon
'and'	'each'	'that'	'thing'	'restore'	'which'	'they'	'all'	'ask for'
	acc	gen pl	gen pl	infin			nom	pl pret

(Rositzke 1940: AD 1014)

Betan is dependent on the main V (*wolde*), and analysed as an infinitive in coordination with the infinitive *beon*, also dependent on *wolde* in the noun clause. The abs participant (*ælc þæra ðinga*) is expanded by the relative clause, extraposed to the right of the V.

4.3.1.2 HA shift: argument = abs O + clause: heavy

diagram (72)

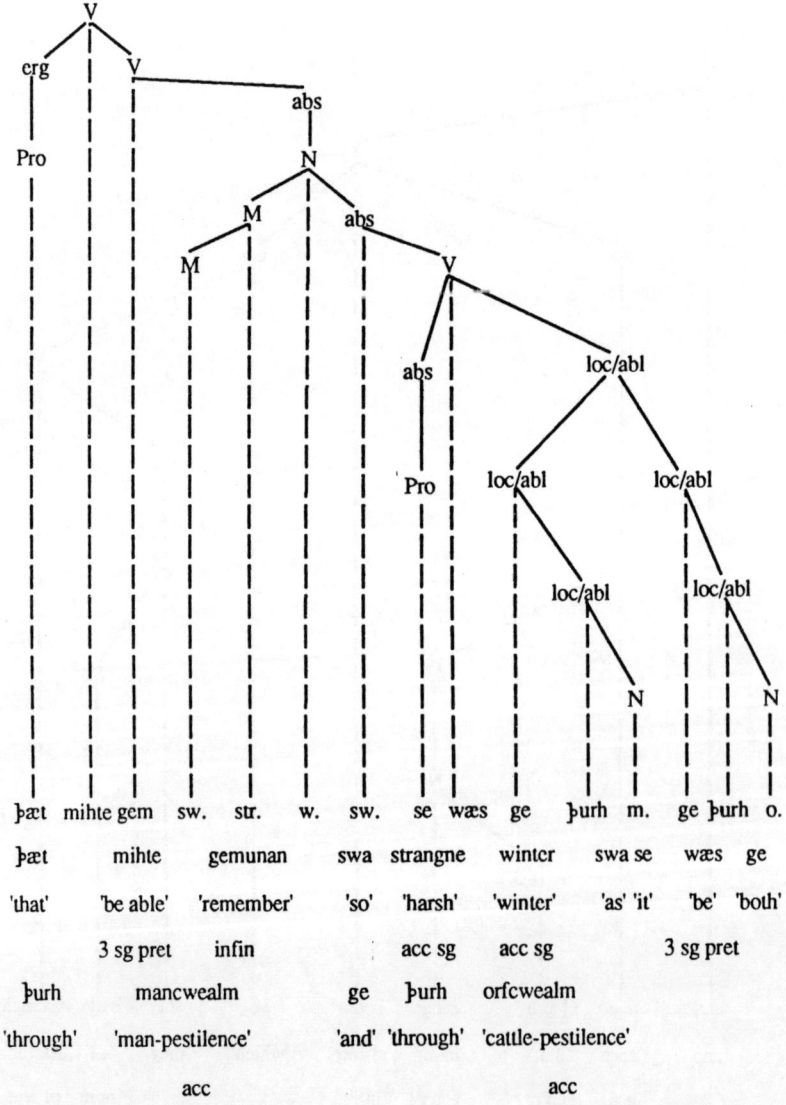

(Rositzke 1940: AD 1043)

diagram (73)

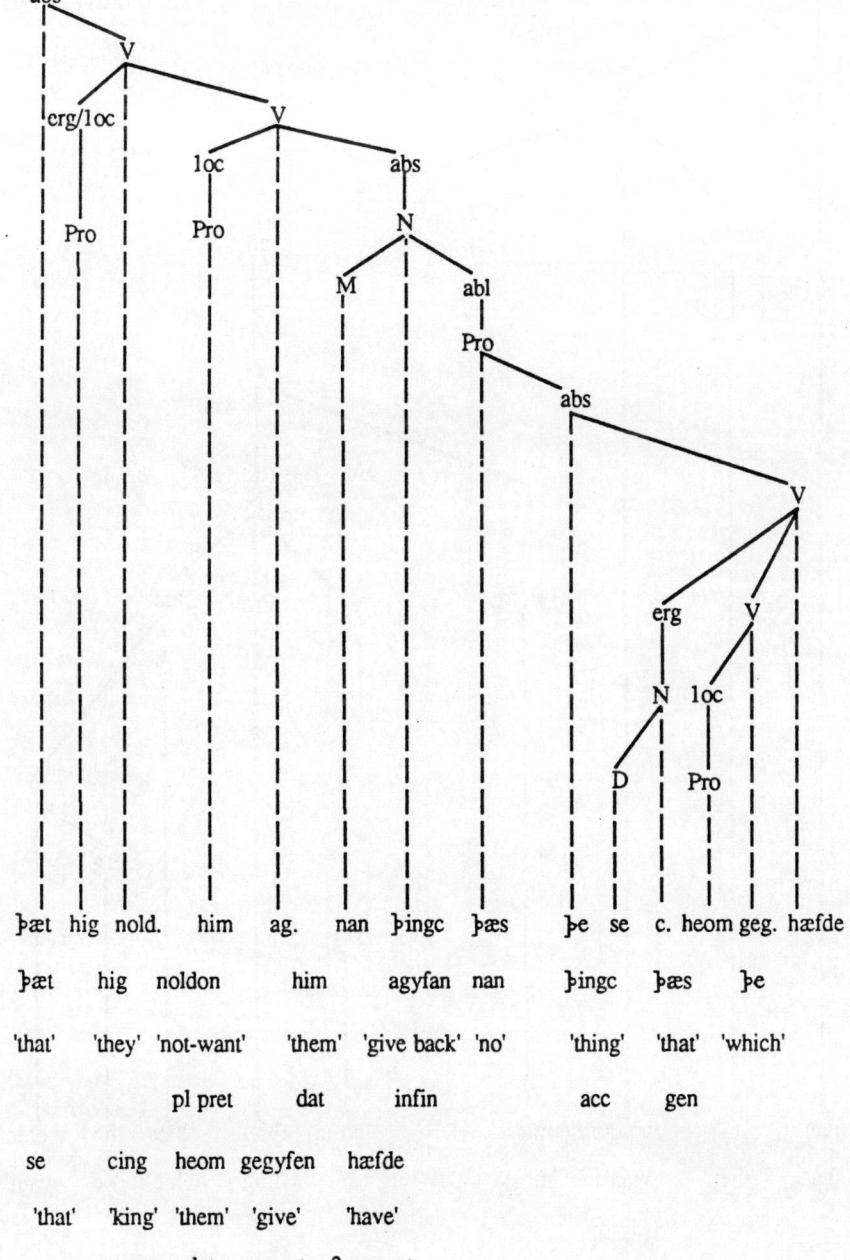

(Rositzke 1940: AD 1049)

diagram (74)

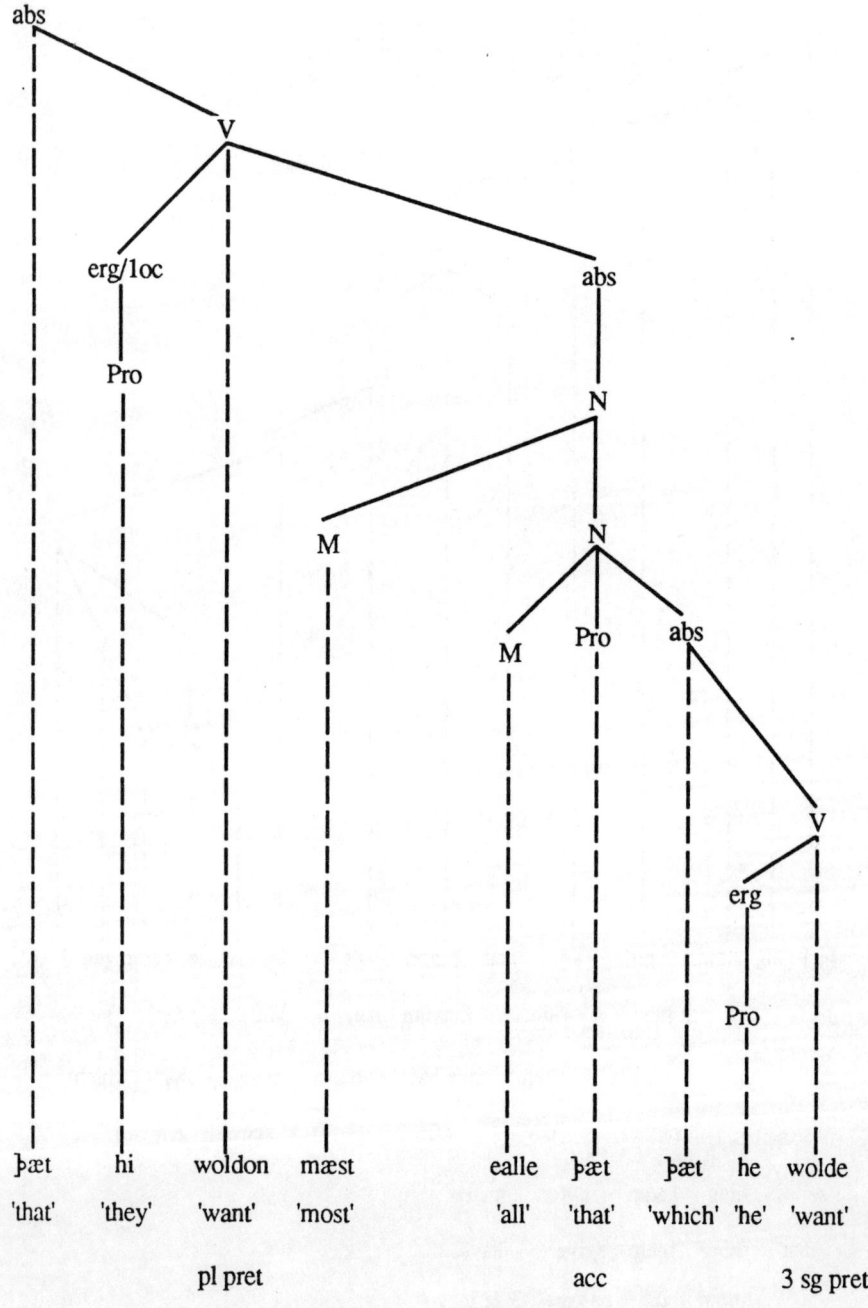

(Rositzke 1940: AD 1052)

4.3.1.3 HA shift: argument = abs O = heavy (non-clausal)

diagram (75)

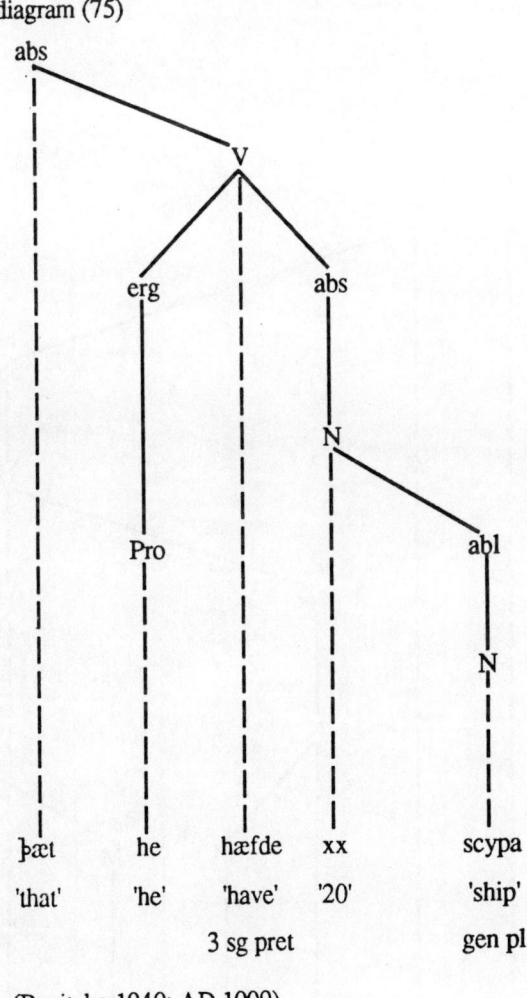

(Rositzke 1940: AD 1009)

The S is erg, and the abs O is heavy by virtue of modification by the dependent abl (partitive: *scypa*).

diagram (76)

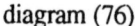

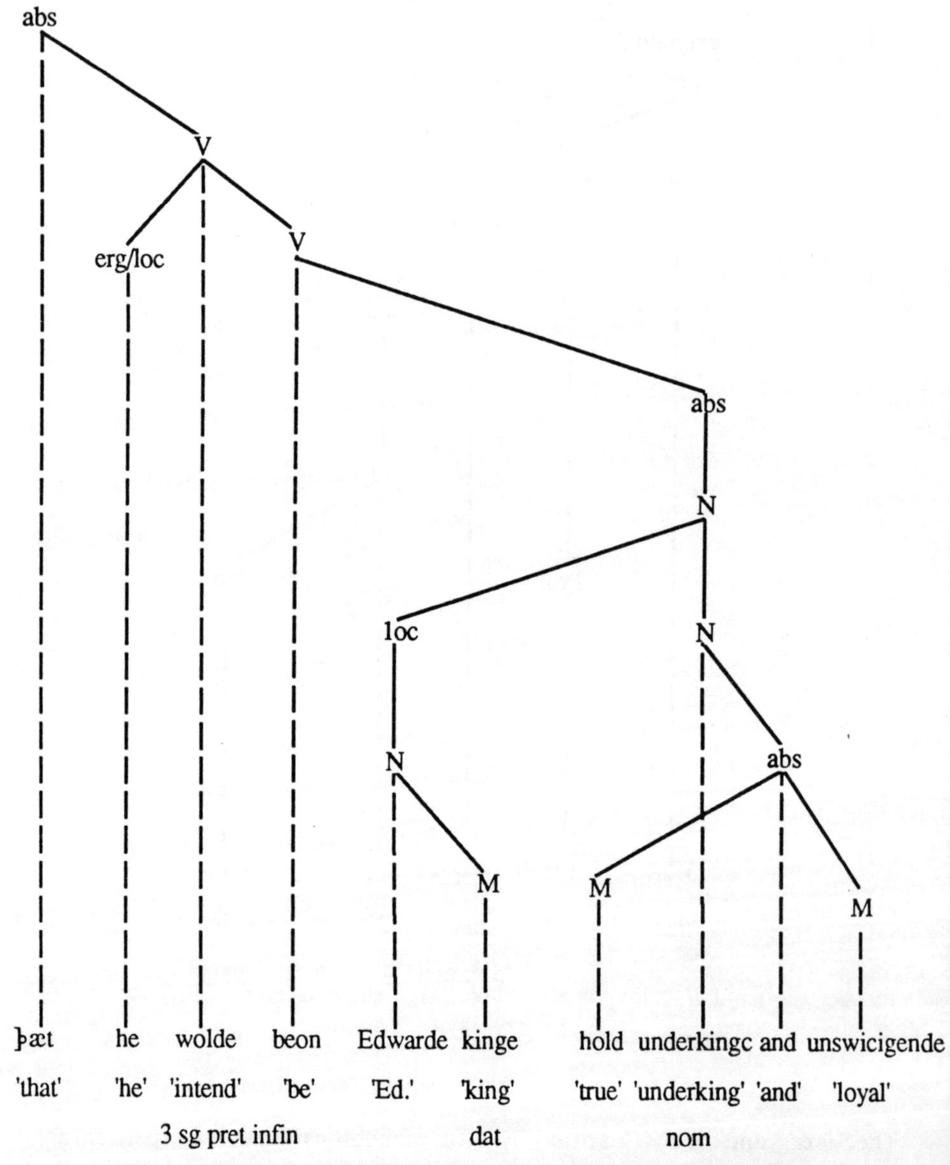

abs

            V

     erg/loc   V

                                abs

                                N

            loc   N

               N   abs

                   M   M   M

þæt	he	wolde	beon	Edwarde	kinge	hold	underkingc	and	unswicigende
'that'	'he'	'intend'	'be'	'Ed.'	'king'	'true'	'underking'	'and'	'loyal'
		3 sg pret infin			dat			nom	

(Rositzke 1940: AD 1056)

Here the abs O is nominal (*underkingc*) and modified to both left and right,
therefore heavy. There is also the dependent V (*beon*) functioning as a non-abs
participant of the main V. Note the tangling effect of the postposed second
modifier of *underkingc (unswicigende)*: cf. e.g. PE (unmarked) 'true and loyal
underking'.

diagram (77)

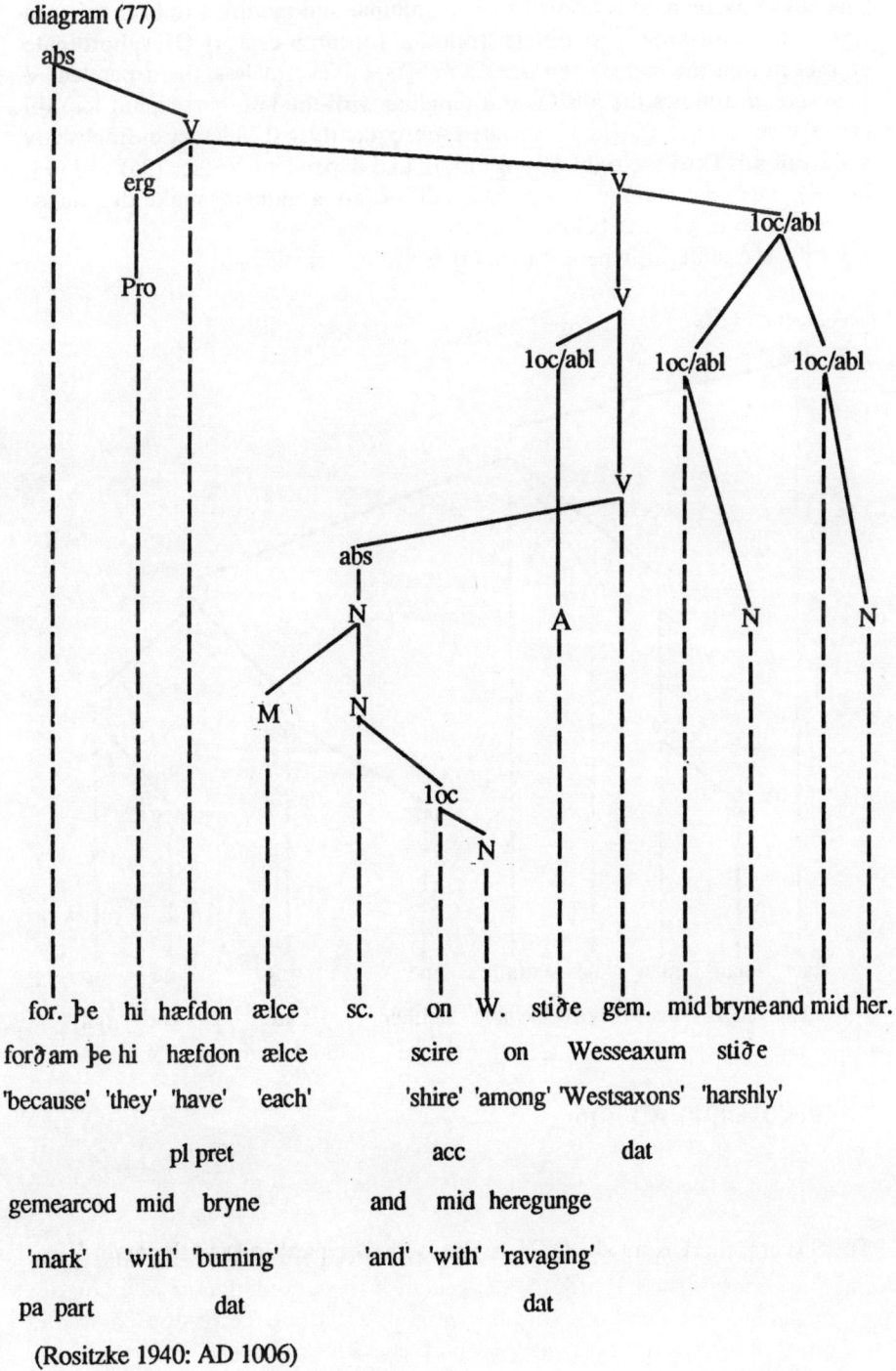

for. þe hi hæfdon ælce   sc.   on W. stiðe gem. mid bryneand mid her.

forðam þe hi hæfdon ælce   scire   on Wesseaxum stiðe

'because' 'they' 'have' 'each'   'shire' 'among' 'Westsaxons' 'harshly'

              pl pret   acc   dat

gemearcod mid bryne   and mid heregunge

'mark' 'with' 'burning'   'and' 'with' 'ravaging'

pa part   dat   dat

(Rositzke 1940: AD 1006)

The abs O participant is heavy because nominal and modified to both left and right. The word-order here differs from that for ninth-century OE subordinate clauses in that the main V (*hæfdon*) is not final. Nevertheless, the dependent V (*gemearcod*) follows the abs O, and tangling with the non-participant loc/abl (*stiðe*) results. Such tangling is avoided subsequently in the history of English by a shift of abs O to the right of both main and dependent Vs (see (85) and (93) below). The post-main V non-participant loc/abl arguments make this clause relevant also to §4.3.1.5 below .

4.3.1.4   HA shift: argument = (abs O) + non-abs participant

diagram (78)

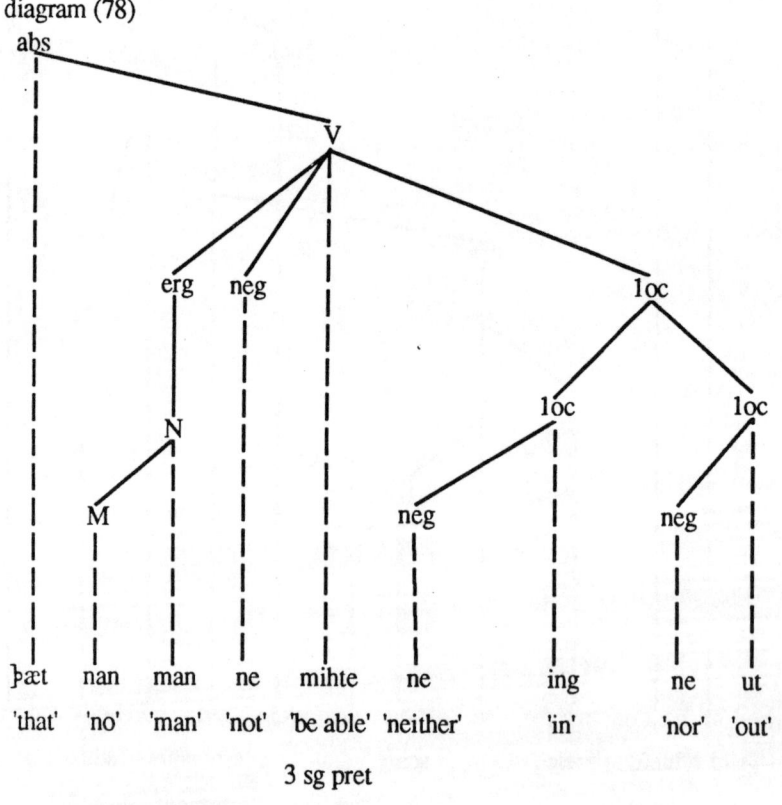

þæt	nan	man	ne	mihte	ne	ing	ne	ut
'that'	'no'	'man'	'not'	'be able'	'neither'	'in'	'nor'	'out'

3 sg pret

(Rositzke 1940: AD 1016)

The S is erg; there is no abs O. Here the loc participant follows the main V.

diagram (79)

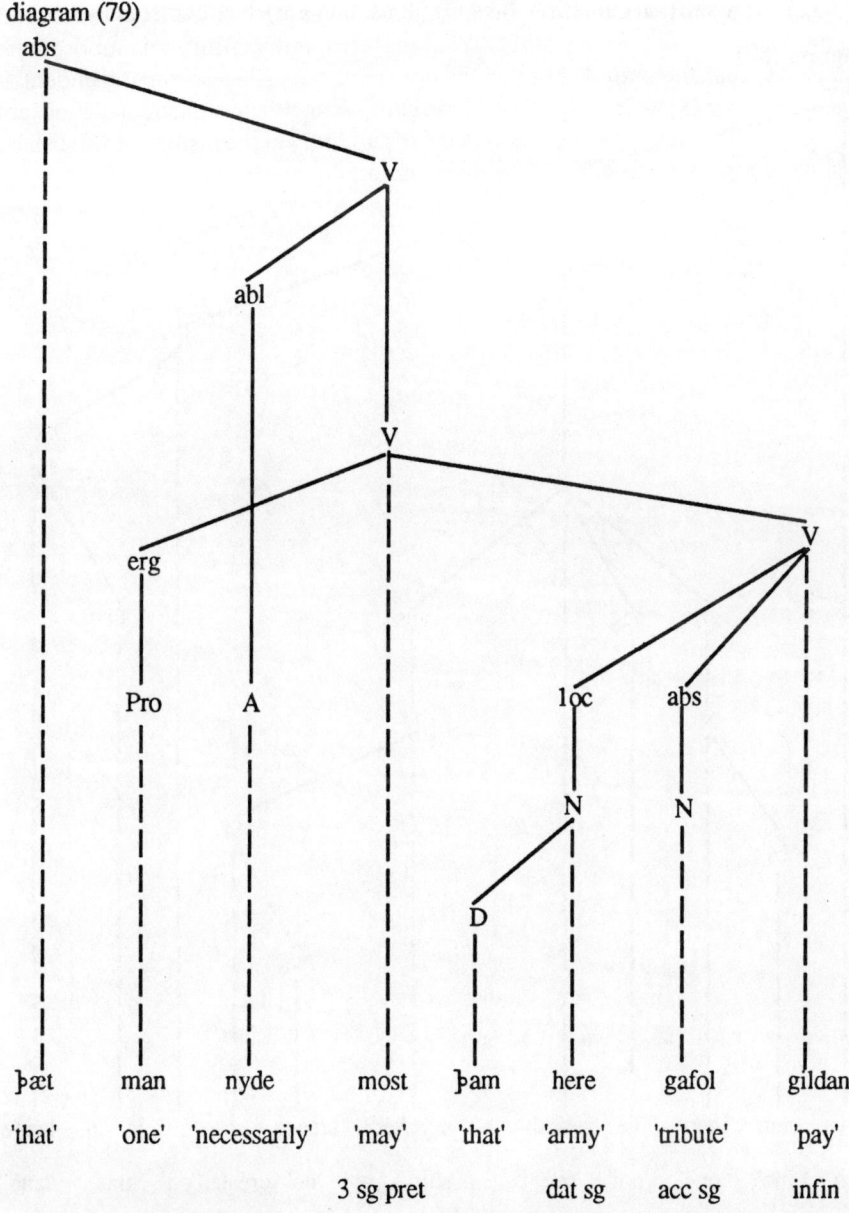

(Rositzke 1940: AD 1006)

The S is erg; the abs O is heavy only by virtue of being nominal: but note the non-abs participant (loc: *þam here*). On the dependent V final, see (77) above.

4.3.1.5   HA shift: argument = (abs O) (+ participant) + circumstantial

diagram (80)

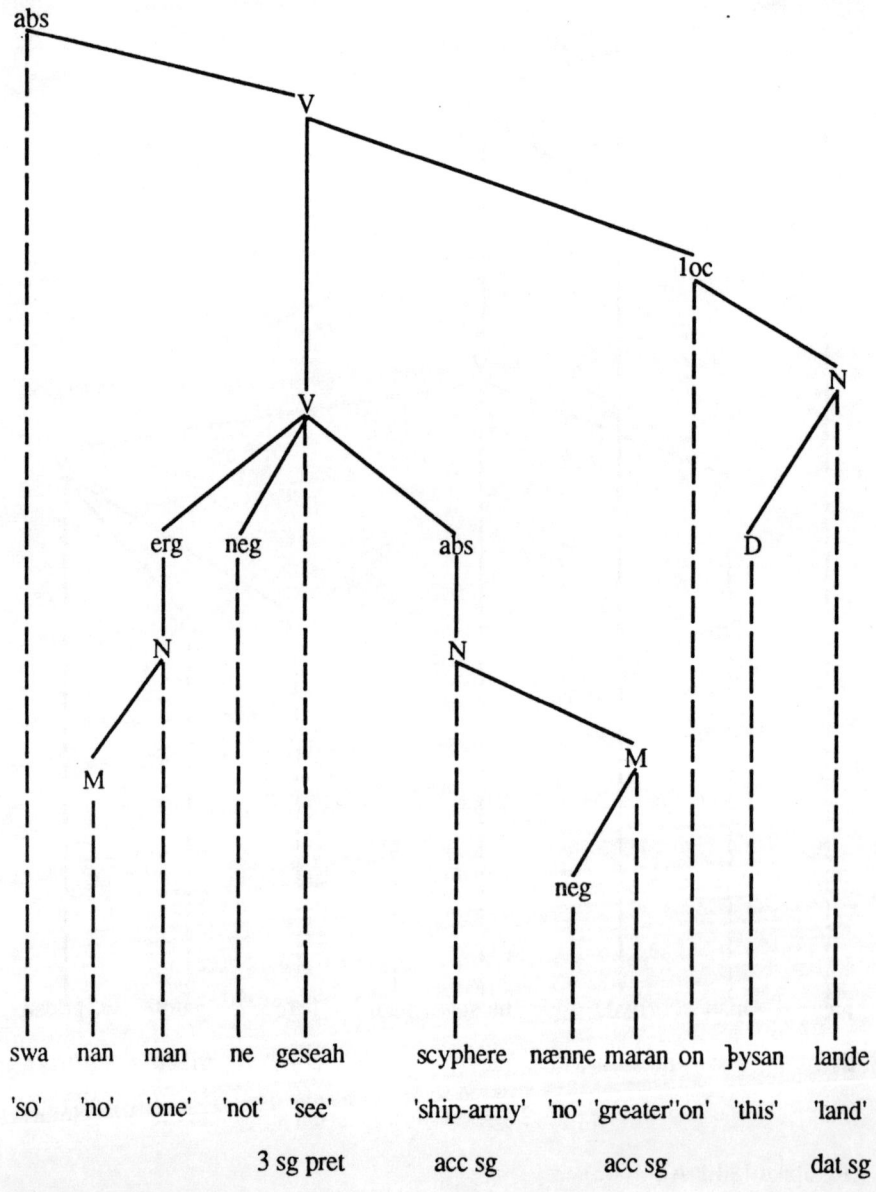

(Rositzke 1940: AD 1045)

The S is erg; the abs O is heavy by virtue of being nominal and modified. Here the non-participant (circumstantial) argument (loc) follows the abs O after the verb (see also (77) above).

We also find examples of argument shift in subordinate clauses with no non-abs participants or circumstantials, where the abs O is heavy only because nominal or adjectival (i.e. with lexical, but not constituent, weight), as in e.g. (81) and (82):

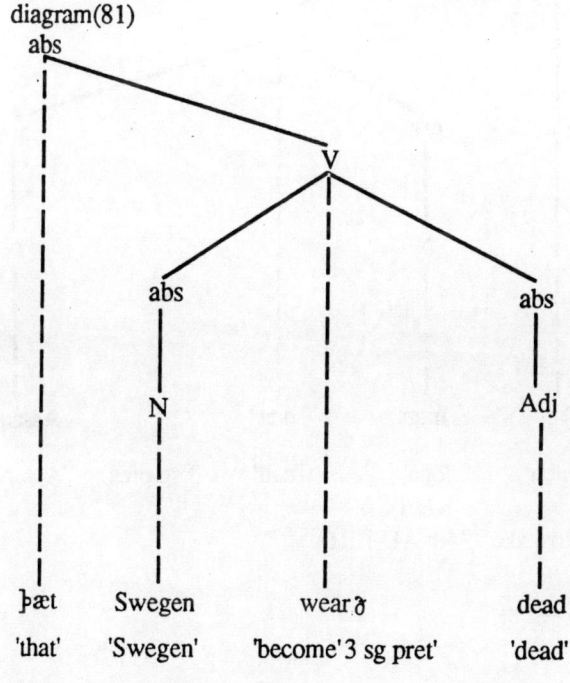

diagram(81)

þæt	Swegen	wearð	dead
'that'	'Swegen'	'become' 3 sg pret'	'dead'

(Rositzke 1940: AD 1013)

where abs is S (in absence of erg);

diagram (82)

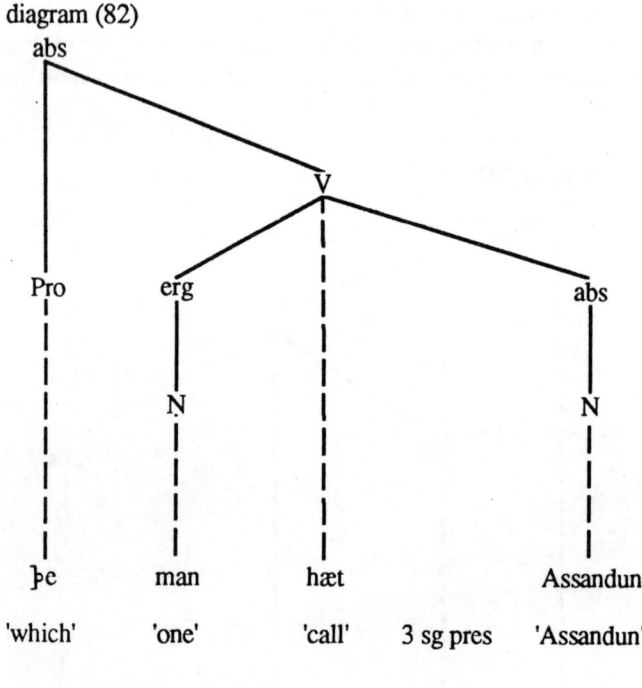

(Rositzke 1940: AD 1016)

Such examples suggest that HA shift is becoming grammaticalised to the extent that the least weighty nominal or adjectival abs O may also follow suit, and hence SVX becomes regular even for subordinate clauses. See further on pronoun Os (lexically light) in §5 below.

4.3.2   *Main clauses plus coordinators*

4.3.2.1   Extraposition

In (83) and (84) the abs participant (*þæt folc mæst eall*, and *þæt god*) is expanded by the relative clause, extraposed to the right of the V.

diagram (83)

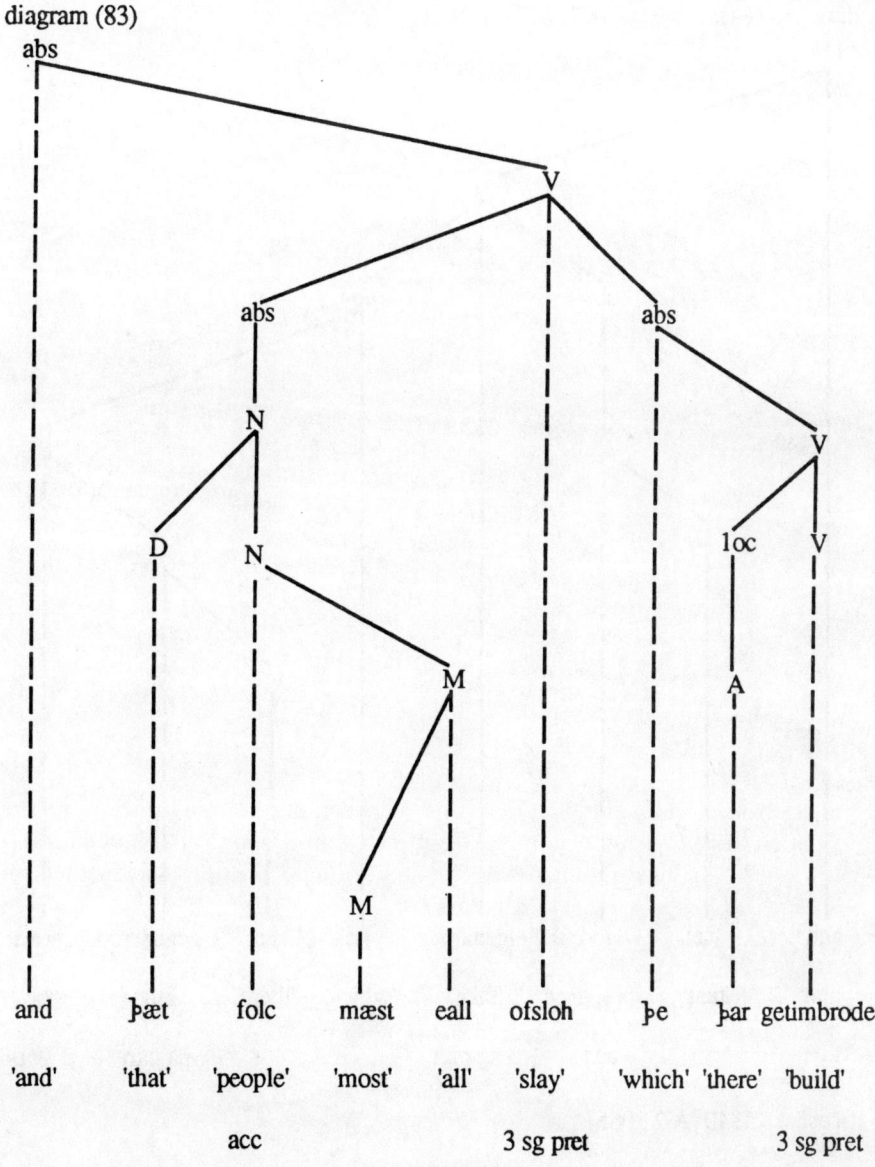

and	þæt	folc	mæst	eall	ofsloh	þe	þar getimbrode
'and'	'that'	'people'	'most'	'all'	'slay'	'which'	'there' 'build'
		acc			3 sg pret		3 sg pret

(Rositzke 1940: AD 1065)

diagram (84).

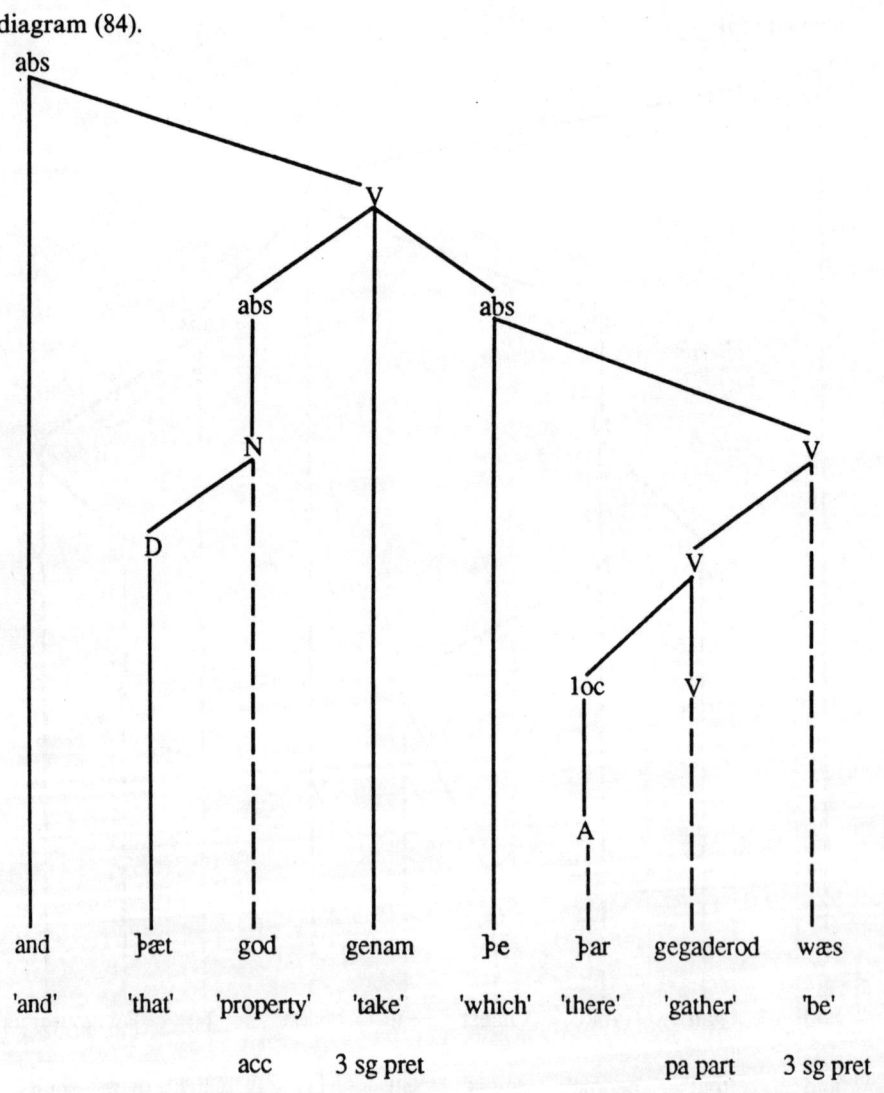

(Rositzke 1940: AD 1065)

4.3.2.2 HA shift: argument = abs O + clause: heavy

diagram (85)

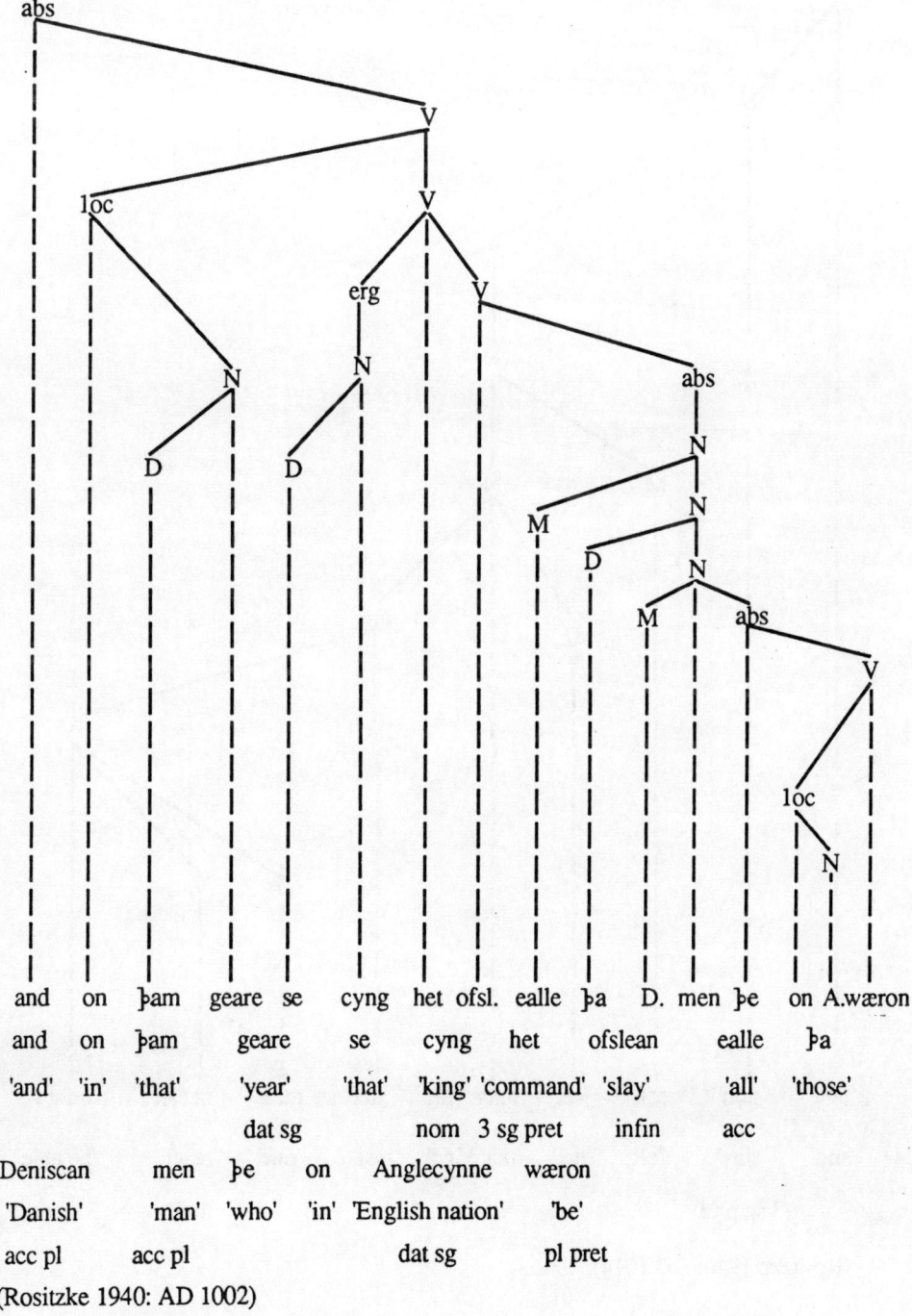

and	on	þam	geare	se	cyng	het	ofsl.	ealle	þa	D.	men	þe	on A.wæron
and	on	þam	geare		se	cyng	het	ofslean	ealle	þa			
'and'	'in'	'that'	'year'	'that'	'king'	'command'	'slay'		'all'	'those'			
			dat sg		nom	3 sg pret		infin		acc			

Deniscan men þe on Anglecynne wæron

'Danish' 'man' 'who' 'in' 'English nation' 'be'

acc pl acc pl dat sg pl pret

(Rositzke 1940: AD 1002)

diagram (86)

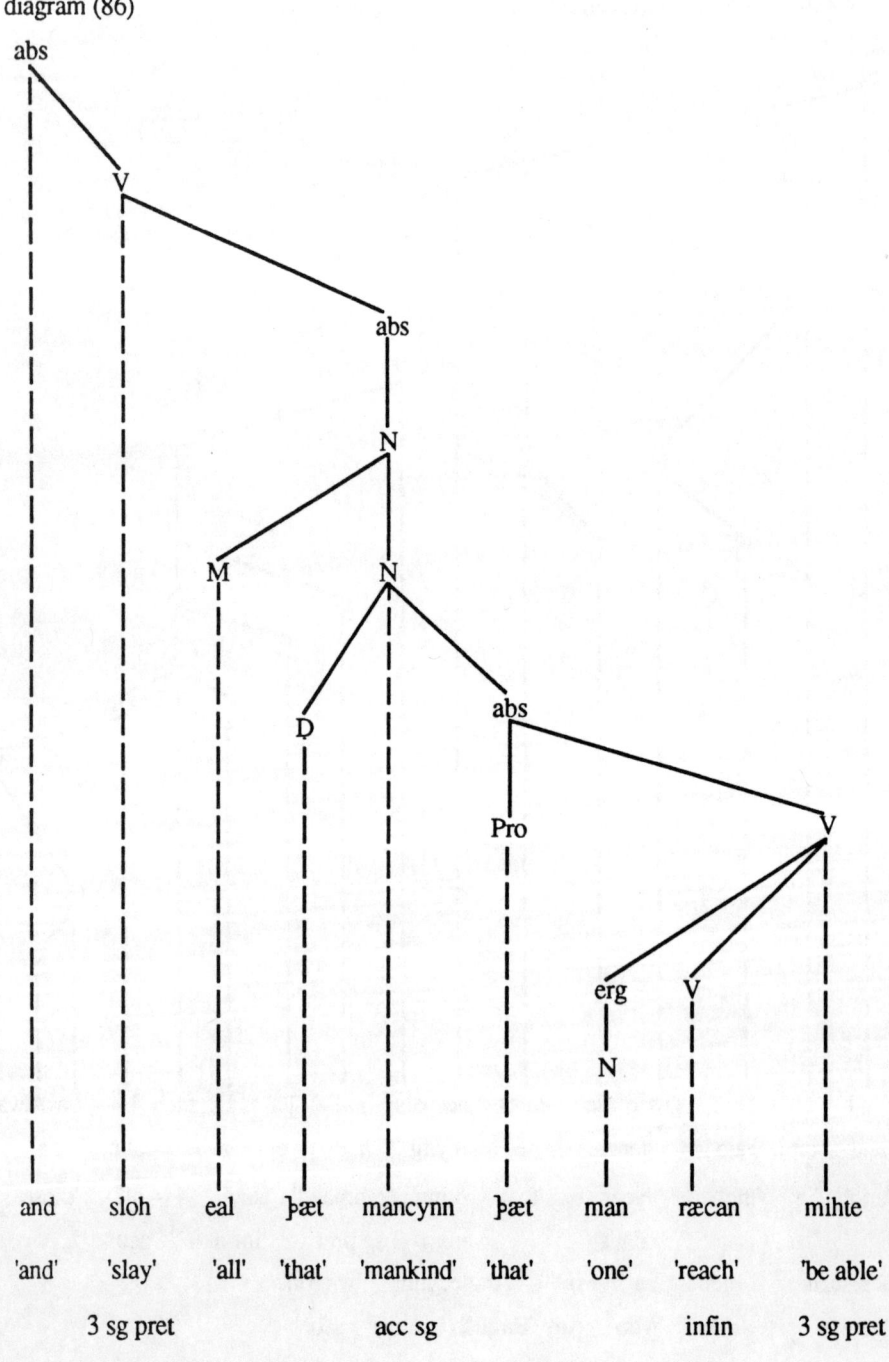

(Rositzke 1940: AD 1014)

diagram (87)

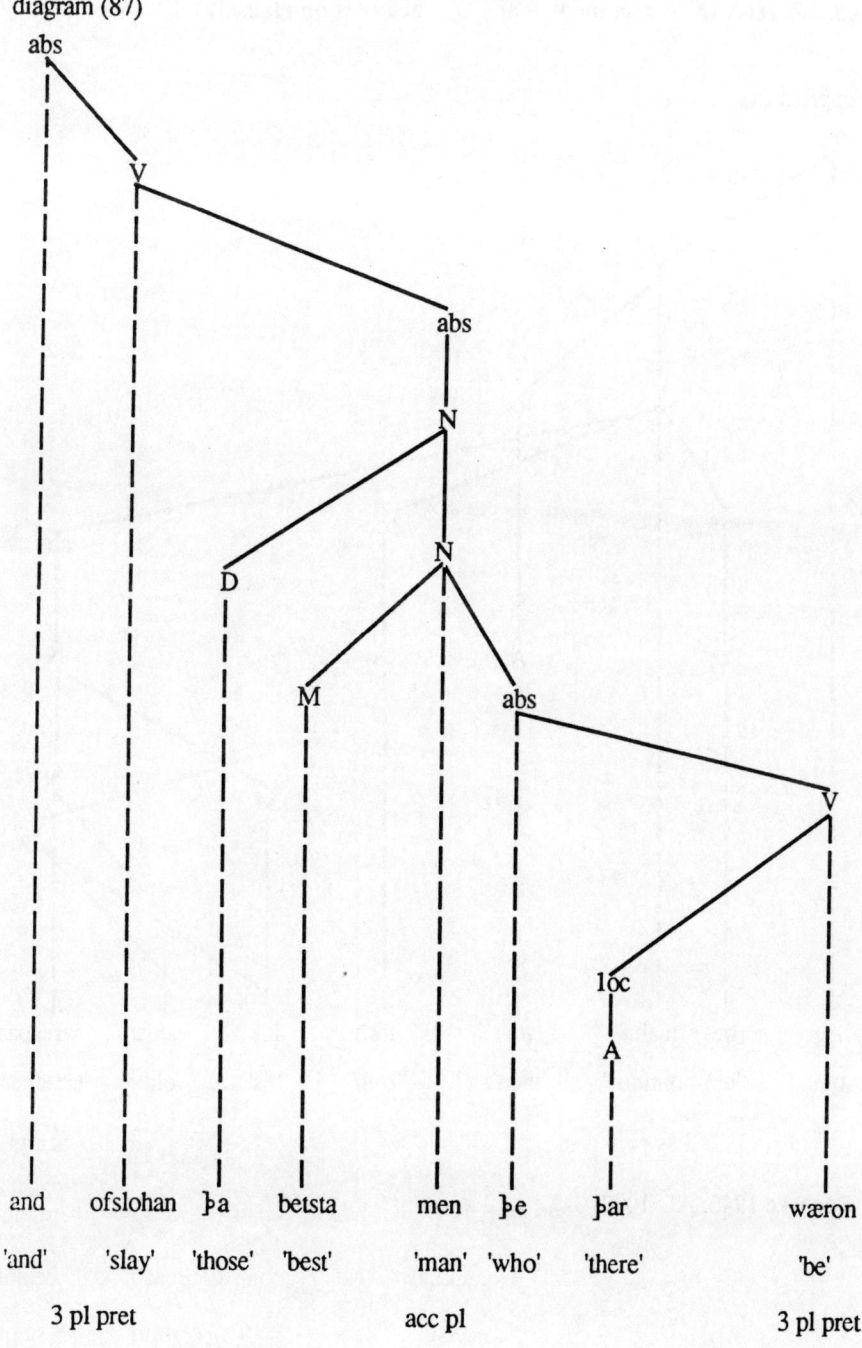

and	ofslohan	þa	betsta	men	þe	þar	wæron
'and'	'slay'	'those'	'best'	'man'	'who'	'there'	'be'

3 pl pret · acc pl · 3 pl pret

(Rositzke 1940: AD 1048)

4.3.2.2   HA shift: argument = abs O = heavy (non-clausal)

diagram (88)

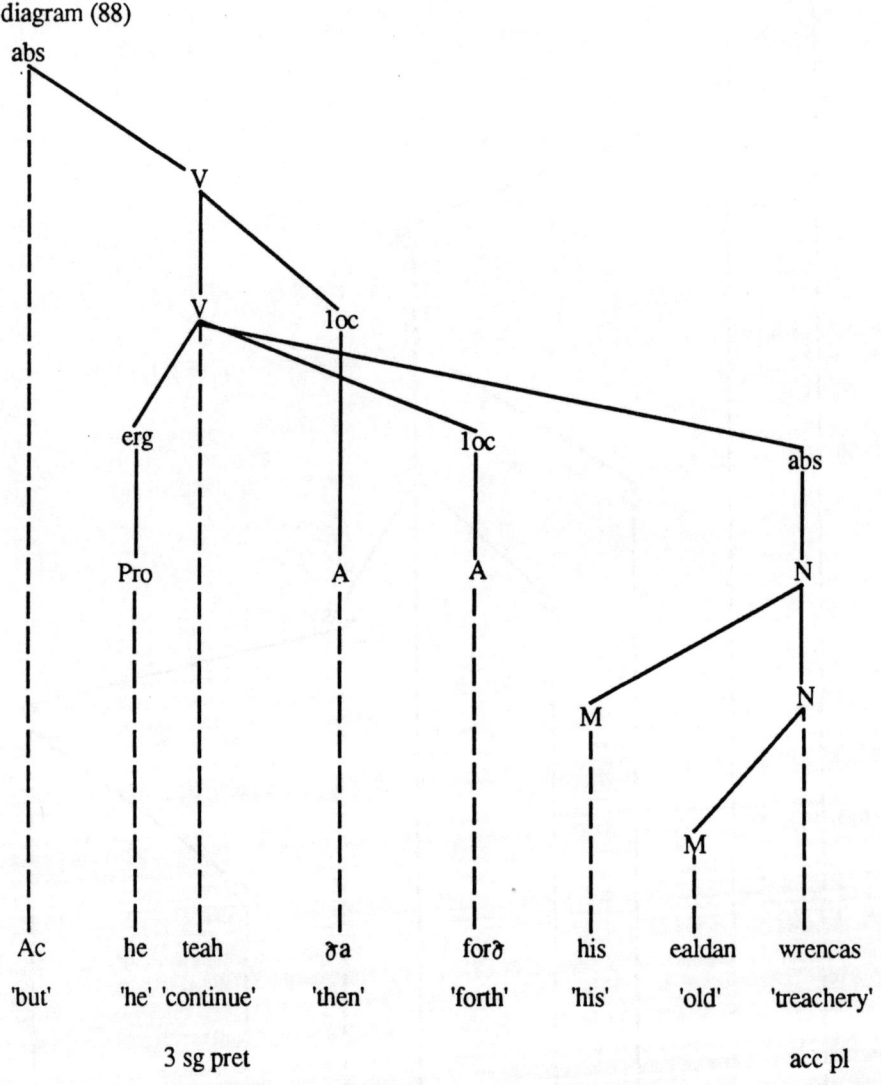

(Rositzke 1940: AD 1003)

diagram (89)

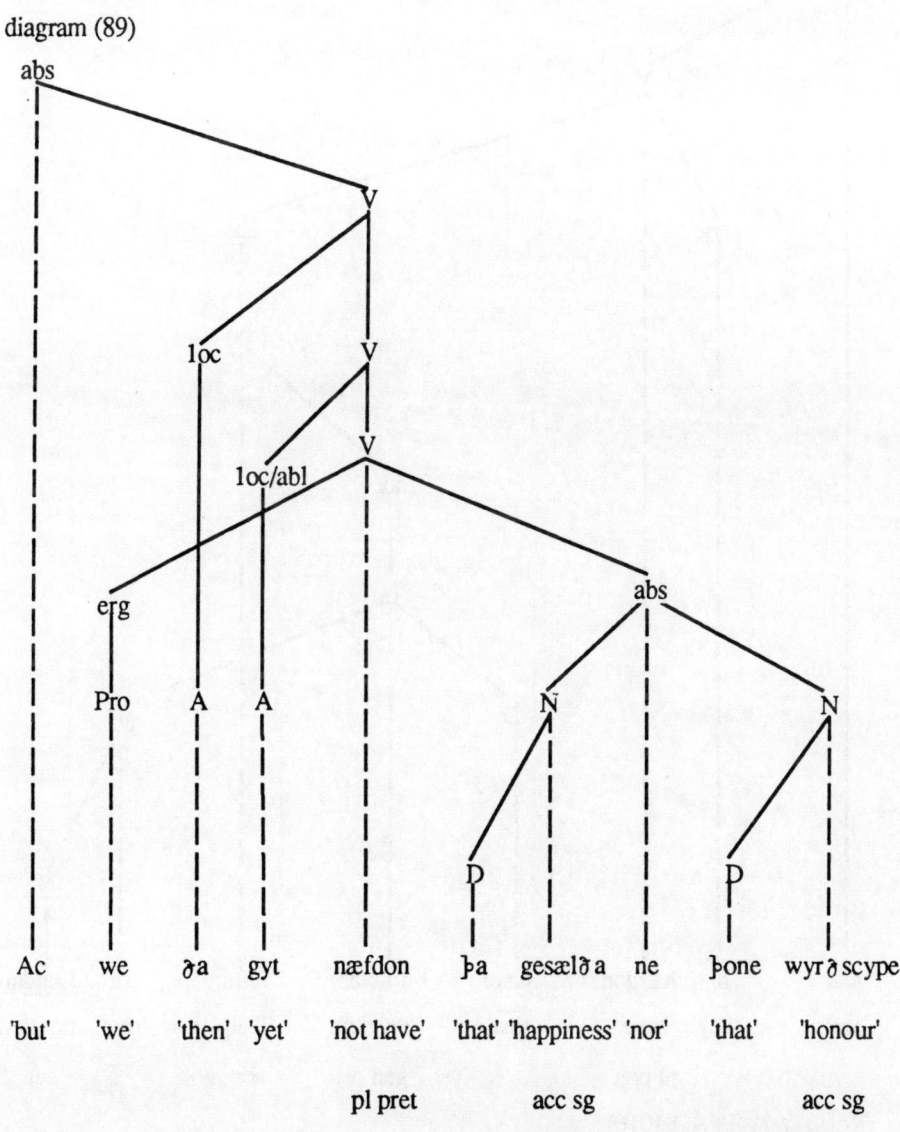

(Rositzke 1940: AD 1009)

diagram (90)

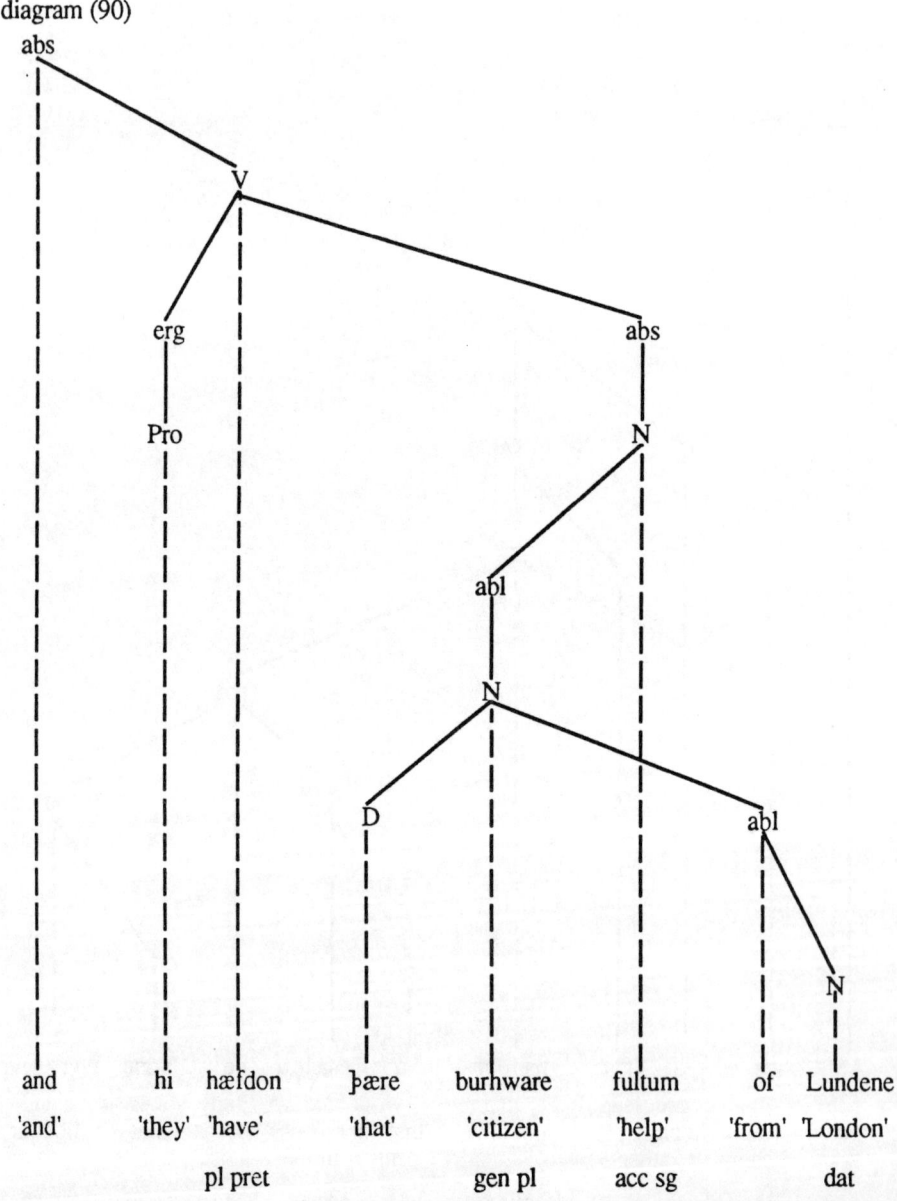

(Rositzke 1940: AD 1016)

In (88), the abs O is heavy because nominal and twice modified to the left; that in (89) is heavy because it contains a coordination of two nominals, each modified by a D; that in (90) is heavy because nominal and left modified by another case-marked noun (*burhware*), itself modified to the left by the D (*þære*) and to the right by abl (PP *of Lundene*).

4.3.2.4 HA shift: argument = (abs O) + non-abs participant

diagram (91)

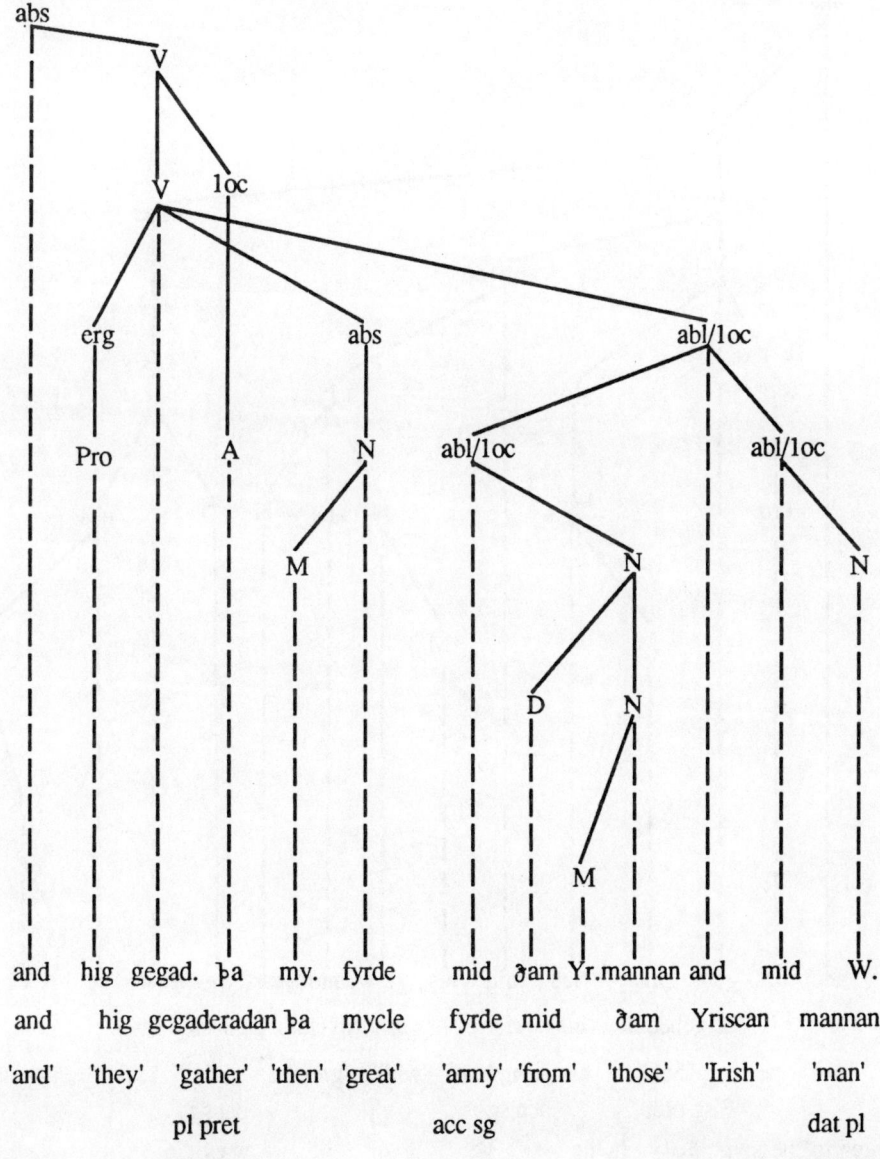

(Rositzke 1940: AD 1055)

4.3.2.5   HA shift: argument = (abs O) (+ participant) + circumstantial diagram (92)

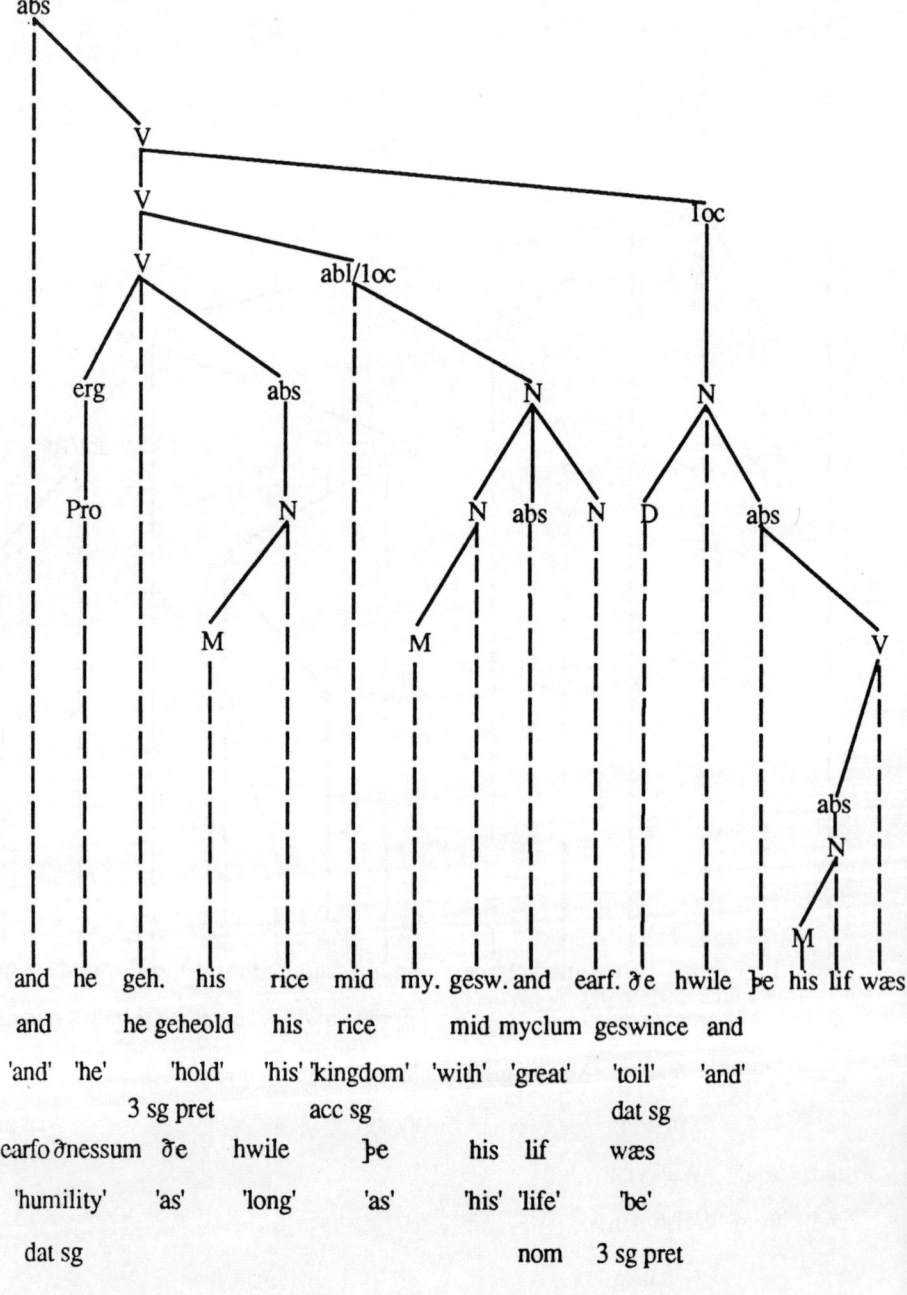

(Rositzke 1940: AD 1016)

diagram (93)

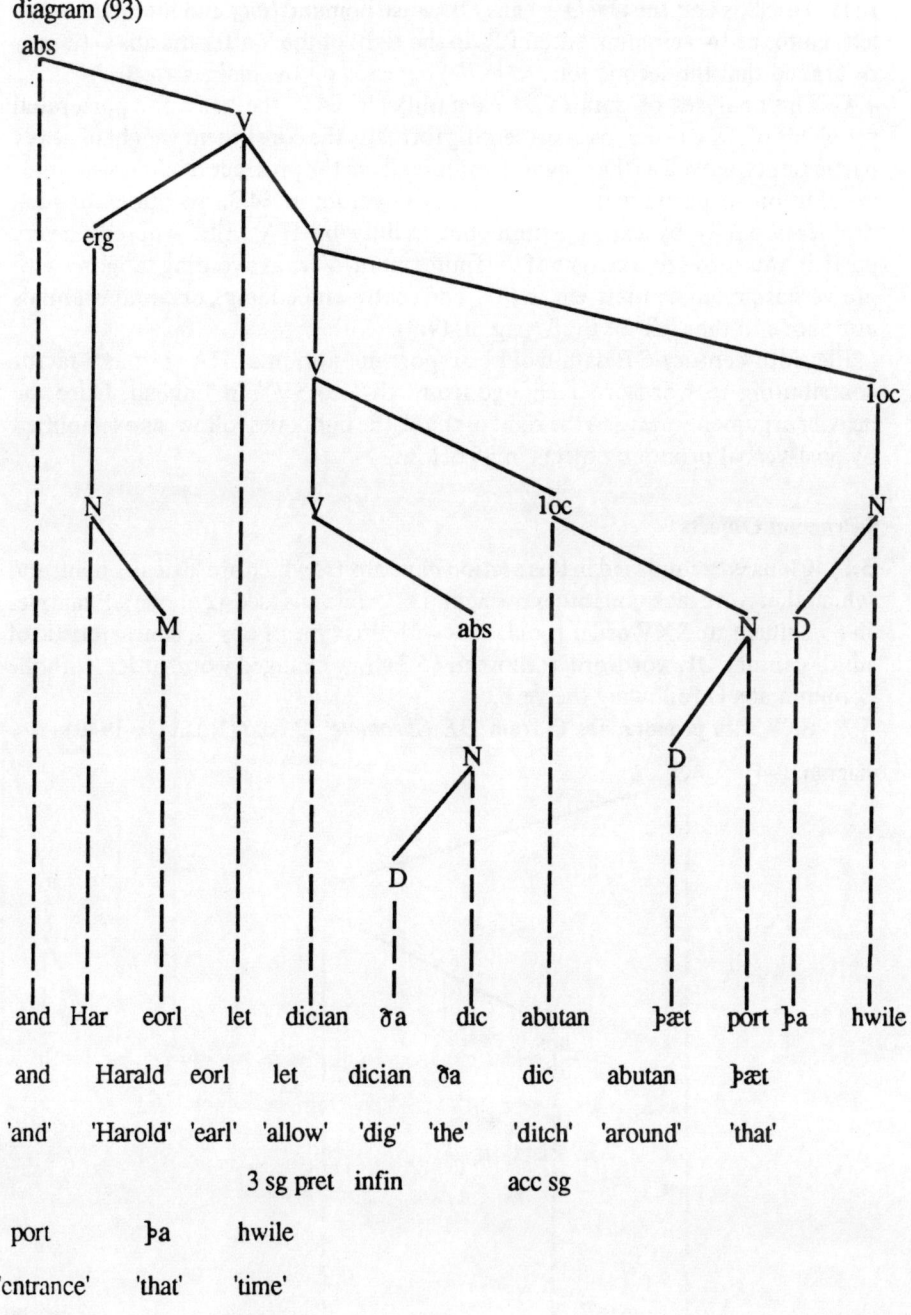

(Rositzke 1940: AD 1055)

In (93) the S is erg; the abs O is heavy because nominal (*dic*) and modified to the left. Note the two circumstantial PPs to the right of the V after the abs O (it may be argued that the second loc (*þa hwile*) depends on the main V (*let*)).

4.4   The analyses of data in §4 exemplify: in §4.2, the basis for perceptual problems of SXV order, by representing formally the constituent weight of heavy participants, as well as the tangling resulting from the presence of circumstantials in addition to participants in pre-verbal position; in §4.3., solutions to such problems partly by extraposition, but mainly by HA shift, whereby heavy participants move to the right of the finite (main) V (thus avoiding tangling with pre-verbal circumstantials, e.g. in (89), and centre-embedding), or circumstantials also move to the right of the V (e.g. in (92)).

Eleventh-century OE data would support the notion of HA shift as a factor contributing to word-order change from SXV to SVX in English. Once the heavier arguments move to the right of the V, the light ones follow, as exemplified by post-verbal pronoun objects in §5 below.

5 Pronoun Objects

5.1   Clauses exemplified in this section have abs Os which are lexically light, and which therefore lack constituent weight, i.e. pronouns (see §2 above). Examples in §5.2 illustrate SXV order for clauses with this type of abs O, characteristic of ninth-century OE word-order; those in §5.3 show changed word-order, with the pronoun abs O following the verb.

5.2   SXV with pronoun abs O from *OE Chronicle, C Text* (Rositzke 1940)

diagram (94)

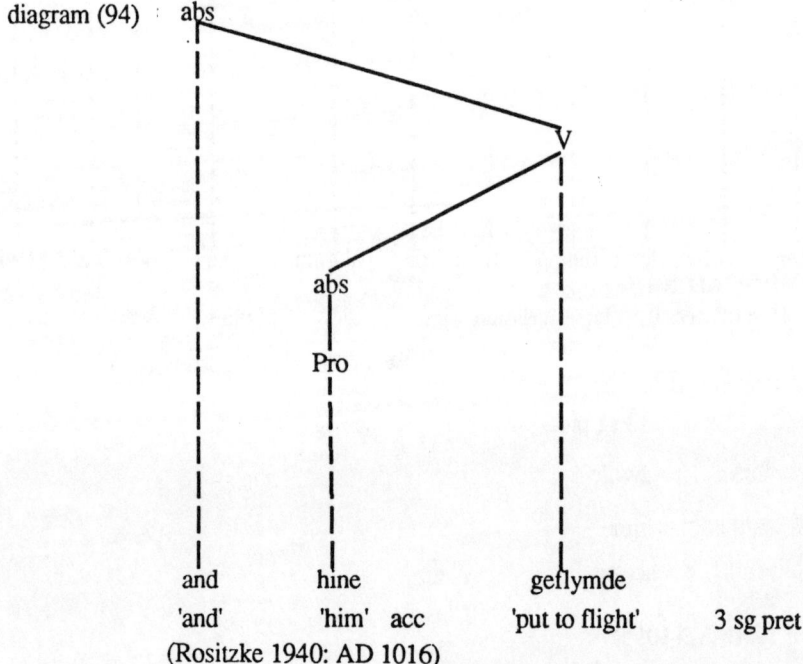

(Rositzke 1940: AD 1016)

diagram (95)

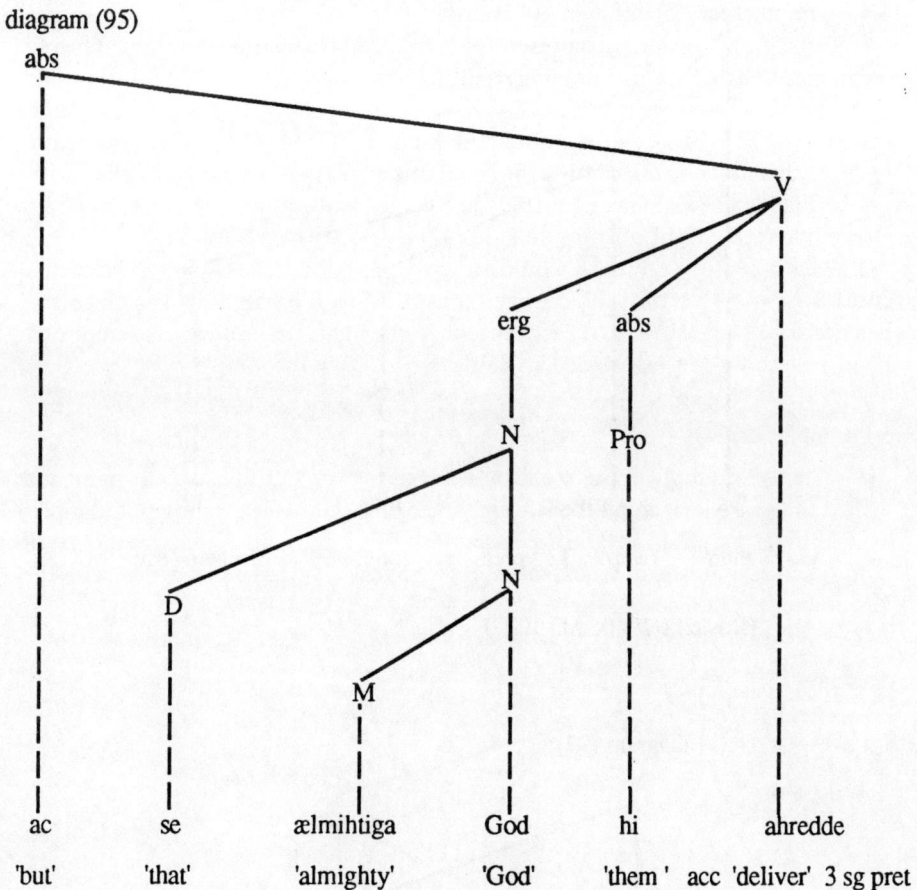

(Rositzke 1940: AD 1016)

5.3   SVX with pronoun abs O from *OE Chronicle, C Text* (Rositzke 1940)

diagram (96)

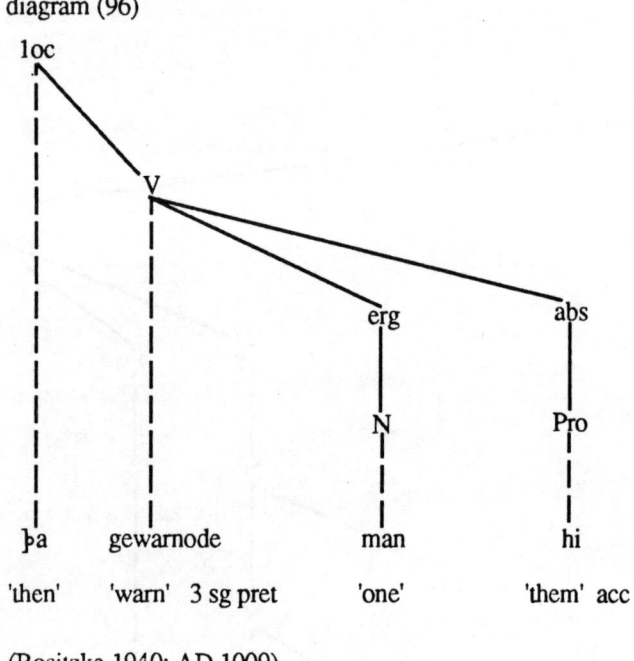

(Rositzke 1940: AD 1009)

diagram (97)

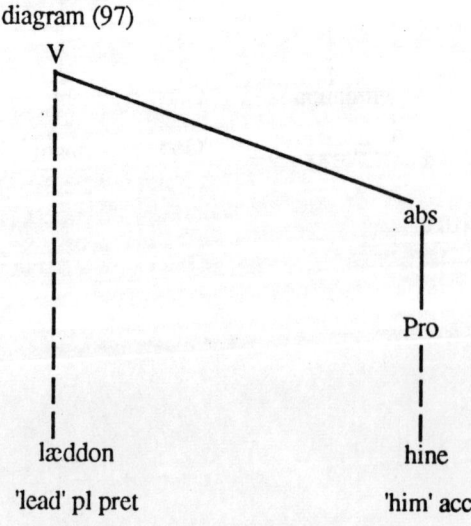

(Rositzke 1940: AD 1012)

diagram (98)

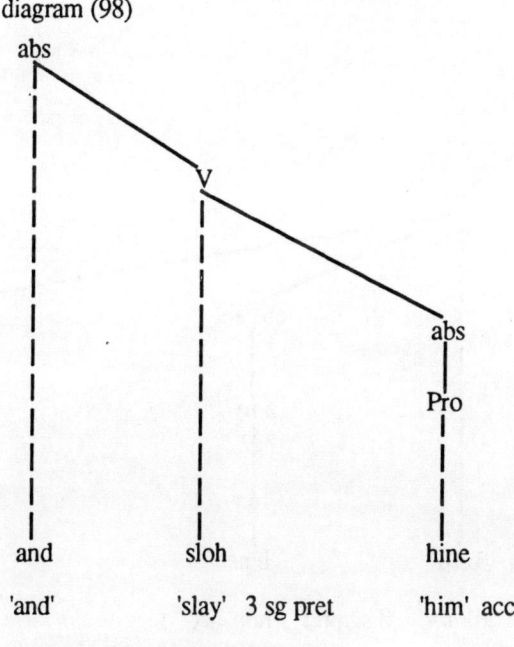

(Rositzke 1940: AD 1012)

diagram (99)

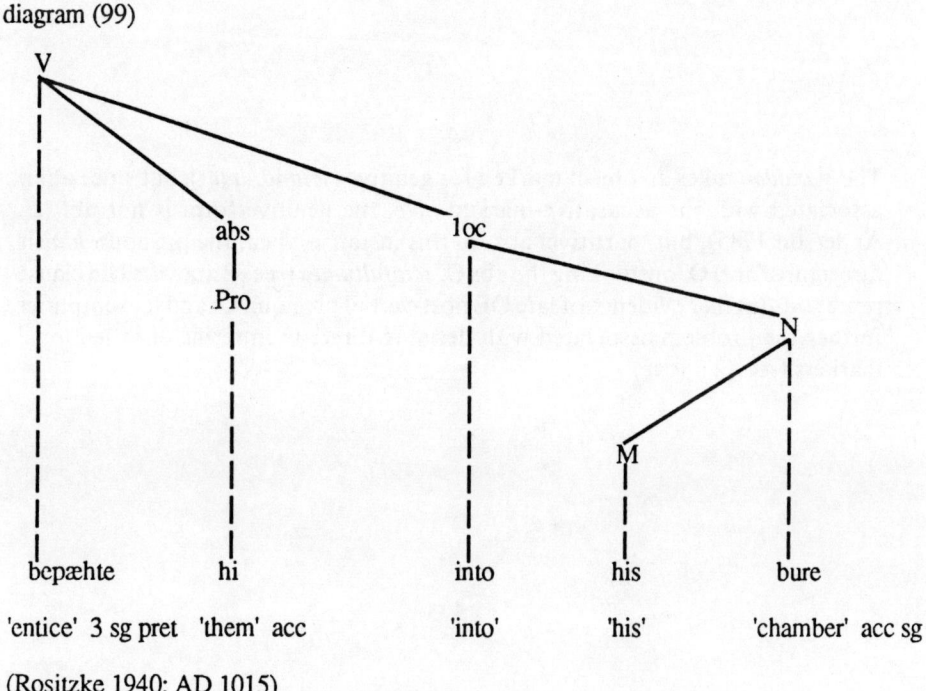

(Rositzke 1940: AD 1015)

D

diagram (100)

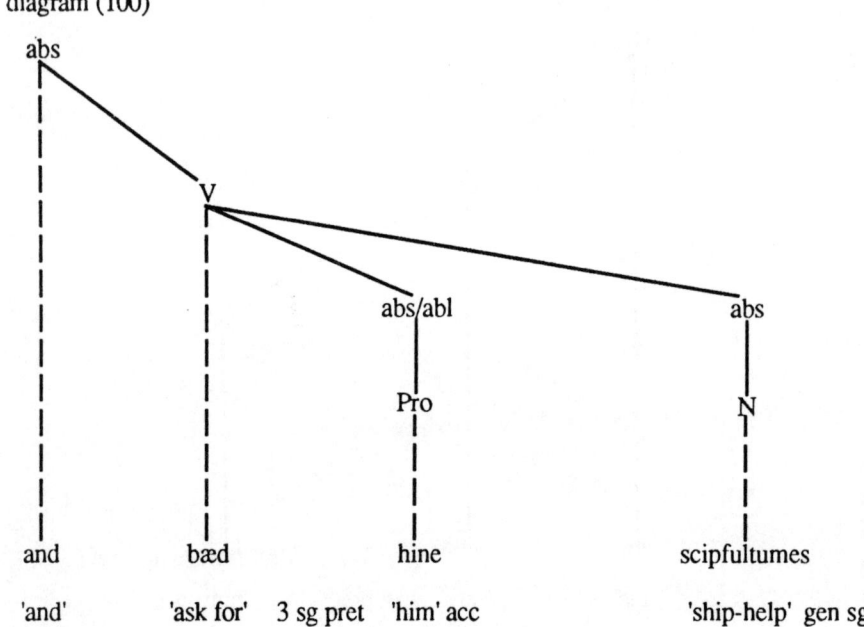

and   bæd   hine   scipfultumes

'and'   'ask for'   3 sg pret   'him' acc   'ship-help' gen sg

(Rositzke 1940: AD 1049)

The V *biddan* takes an object marked for genitive (*scipfultumes*); but since abl is associated with the accusative-marked *hine*, the genitive form is not abl (cf. Anderson 1985), but 'partitive' abs. In this instance, then, the pronoun *hine* is direct (abs/abl) O, outranking the abs O, *scipfultumes* (see §2 above). The clause represents further evidence of late OE post-verbal pronoun O; and it exemplifies further the problem associated with defining direct O in terms of inflectional markers (see §2 above).

diagram (101)

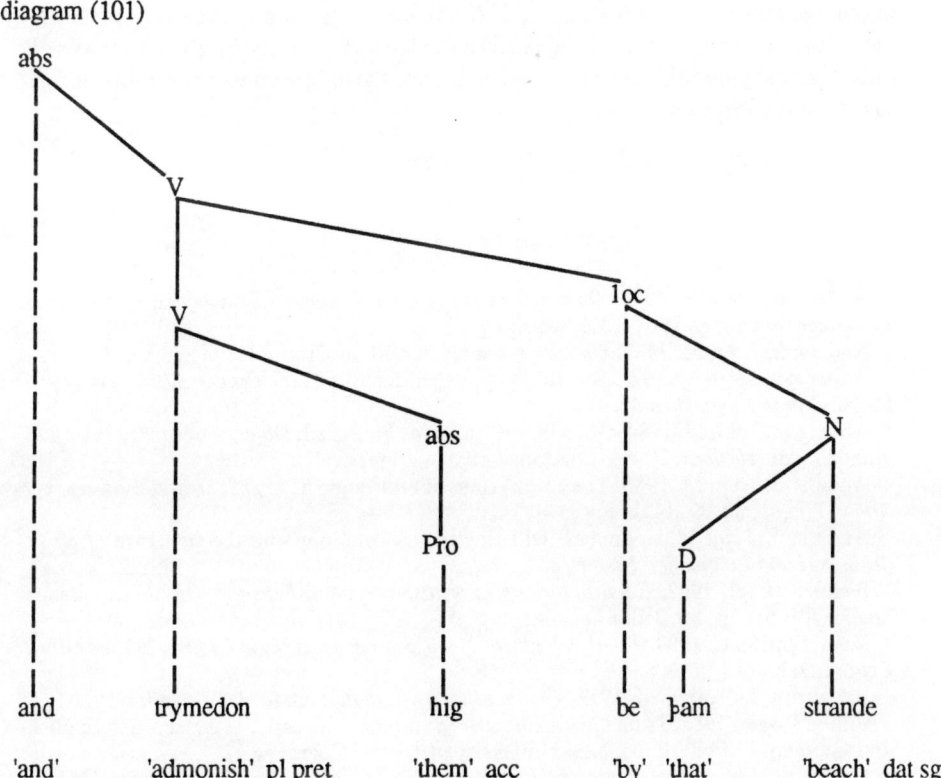

(Rositzke 1940: AD 1052)

Here a non-participant loc follows the abs O (*hig*), thus suggesting HA of the type with abs O + circumstantial. But the lexically empty pronoun, as the lightest abs O type, precedes the verb in ninth-century OE, no matter what other arguments occur in the clause. The post-verbal position of *hig* represents a change in word-order for the pronoun O.

6 The Heavy Argument

Data from eleventh-century OE prose show a mixture of word-order patterns for subordinate and main plus coordinator clauses. This mixture of patterns may be seen as evidence of the change from SXV to SVX in English.

A contributing factor in this change (along with e.g. loss of expression of inflectional morphology and resulting problems associated with effects of tangling) is seen to be the tendency for HA shift (illustrated in §4.3.1.4 above) as a solution to the perceptual problems imposed by SXV order. The data in §5.3

above represent the final stage of HA shift, viz. its grammaticalisation: SVX order has become the prevailing pattern in eleventh-century English, so that not only heavy arguments occur post-verbally, but the lightest ones are established in the same position.

REFERENCES

Anderson, John M. 1976. *On serialisation in English Syntax.* Ludwigsburg Studies in Language and Linguistics 1. Ludwigsburg.

Anderson, John M. 1977. *On case grammar.* London: Croom Helm.

Anderson, John M. 1979. Serialisation, dependency and the syntax of possessives in Moru. *Studia Linguistica* 33. 1–25.

Anderson, John M. 1984. Objecthood. In Frans Plank, ed. *Objects: towards a theory of grammatical relations*, 29–54. London: Academic Press.

Anderson, John M. 1985. The case system of Old English: a case for non-modularity. *Studia Linguistica* 39. 1–22.

Anderson, John M. to appear. Old English morphology and the structure of noun phrases. *Folia Linguistica Historica.*

Bacquet, Paul. 1962. *La structure de la phrase verbale à l'époque Alfredienne.* Paris: Société d'Éditions: les Belles Lettres.

Bean, Marian C. 1983. *The development of word-order patterns in Old English.* London: Croom Helm.

Bethurum, Dorothy, ed. 1957. *The homilies of Wulfstan.* Oxford: Clarendon Press.

Böhm, Roger. 1982. Topics in localist case grammar, with especial reference to English and German. D.Phil. thesis, New University of Ulster, Coleraine.

Bosworth, Joseph and T. Northcote Toller. 1898. *An Anglo-Saxon dictionary.* Oxford: Oxford University Press. Supplement by T. Northcote Toller. 1921. Addenda and corrigenda by A. Campbell. 1972. Oxford: Oxford University Press.

Campbell, A. 1959. *Old English grammar.* Oxford: Oxford University Press.

Campbell, A. 1970. Verse influences in Old English prose. In J. L. Rosier (ed) *Philological essays in Old and Middle English language and literature in honour of Herbert Dean Meritt.* 93–8. The Hague.

Clark, C., ed. 1970. *The Peterborough Chronicle, 1070–1154*, 2nd edn. Oxford: Oxford University Press.

Colman, Fran. to appear. On some morphological formatives in Old English. *Folia Linguistica Historica* 6.

De Armond, Richard C. 1984. On the development of the verb phrase node in English syntax. In N. F. Blake and Charles Jones, eds. *English historical linguistics: studies in development.* CECTAL Conference Papers Series, 3, 205–226. Sheffield: Department of English Language, University of Sheffield.

Derbyshire, Desmond C. 1981. A diachronic explanation for the origin of OVS in some Carib languages. *Journal of Linguistics* 17. 209–220.

Dik, Simon C. 1978. *Functional grammar.* Amsterdam: North Holland.

Fries, Charles C. 1940. On the development of the structural use of word-order in modern English. *Language* 16. 199–208. Reprinted in Roger Lass, ed. *Approaches to English historical linguistics*, 303–310. New York, 1969: Holt, Rinehart and Winston.

Gardner, F. F. 1971. *An analysis of the syntactic patterns of Old English.* The Hague: Mouton.

Hopper, P. J. 1975. *The syntax of the simple sentence in Proto-Germanic.* The Hague: Mouton.

Hyman, L. M. 1975. On the change from SOV to SVO: evidence from Niger-Congo. In C. N. Li, ed. *Word-order and word-order change*, 113–148. Austin: University of Texas Press.

Lehmann, W. P. 1974. *Proto-Indo European syntax*. Austin: University of Texas Press.

Lightfoot, David W. 1979. *Principles of diachronic syntax*. Cambridge: Cambridge University Press.

Matthews, P. H. 1981. *Syntax*. Cambridge: Cambridge University Press.

Mitchell, Bruce. 1964. Syntax and word-order in the Peterborough Chronicle 1122–1154. *Neuphilologisches Mitteilungen* **65**. 113–44.

Mitchell, Bruce. 1985. *Old English syntax*. Oxford: Oxford University Press.

Mitchell, Bruce and Fred C. Robinson. 1982. *A guide to Old English: revised with texts and glossary*. Oxford: Basil Blackwell.

Postal, Paul M. 1974. *On raising: one rule of English Grammar and its theoretical implications*. Cambridge, Mass. and London, England: The M.I.T. Press.

Quirk, Randolph and Sidney Greenbaum. 1977. *A university grammar of English*. London: Longmans.

Quirk, Randolph and C. L. Wrenn. 1957. *An Old English grammar*, 2nd edn. London: Methuen.

Rositzke, Harry August. 1940. *The C-text of the Old English Chronicles*. Beiträge zur englischen Philologie, **xxxiv**. Bochum-Langendreer: Verlag Heinrich Pöppinghaus.

Ross, John R. 1967. Constraints on variables in syntax. Ph.D. dissertation, M.I.T.

Shannon, A. 1964. *A descriptive syntax of the Parker manuscript of the Anglo-Saxon Chronicle from 734–891*. The Hague: Mouton.

Swinney, David A. 1981. Lexical processing during sentence comprehension: effects of higher order constraints and implications for representation. In Terry Myers, John Laver and John Anderson, eds. *The cognitive representation of speech*, 201–209. Amsterdam: North Holland.

Traugott, Elizabeth Closs. 1972. *A history of English syntax*. New York: Holt, Rinehart and Winston.

Vennemann, T. 1974. Topics, subjects and word order: from SXV to SVX via TVX. In J. M. Anderson and C. Jones, eds. *Historical linguistics I*, 339–376. Amsterdam: North Holland.

Vennemann, T. 1975. An explanation of drift. In C. N. Li, ed. *Word-order and word-order change*, 113–148. Austin: University of Texas Press.

Vincent, Nigel. 1976. Perceptual factors and word order change in Latin. In Martin B. Harris, ed. *Romance syntax: synchronic and diachronic perspectives*, 54–68. University of Salford.

Wagner, Karl Heinz. 1969. *Generative grammatical studies in the Old English language*. Heidelberg: Julius Groos Verlag.

3

THE STATUS OF VOICED FRICATIVES IN OLD ENGLISH

John Anderson

There is a general consensus that Old English (OE) possessed a series of voiced fricatives: cf. e.g. Sweet 1882:§3, Campbell 1959: §50, Pilch 1970:58, Kuhn 1970, Lass and Anderson 1975:ch.V. This consensus is perhaps all the more remarkable given that, with the possible, temporary exception of the velar, voiced fricatives are not contrastive in OE. Nor (no doubt as a consequence of this) are they consistently and simultaneously distinguished in spelling from both voiceless fricatives and voiced plosives: throughout most of the OE period, most occurrences of the alleged voiced fricatives are spelled in the same way as their voiceless congeners; exceptional again is the voiced velar, which, it is usually considered, shares its orthographic representation with its plosive congener, with which it is not in contrast, and with the (voiced) palatal continuant.

It is not my concern here to dispute the hypothesis that such a sound-type be attributed to OE. Reconciliation of both subsequent and reconstructed previous developments with the spellings attested in OE depends on the appropriateness of just such an assumption.

For example, the graph <f> in OE is usually interpreted (with refinements we shall return to) as representing a voiced fricative only word-internally when it occurs between graphs which themselves represent (for the most part, rather uncontroversially) voiced sounds. Thus, <f> in the forms in (1):

(1)   a. *fot* 'foot'
        b. *hlaf* 'bread'
        c. *eft* 'afterwards'

represents a voiceless fricative [f], in that only one voiced segment is immediately adjacent; whereas in (2):

(2)   a. *ġiefan* 'give', *seofon* 'seven'
        b. *wulfas* 'wolves', *drifan* 'drive'

<f> is interpretable as representing [v]. This is consistent with the later history of these segments, including the phonemicisation of /v/: cf. e.g. Kurath 1956 — but also Sledd's (1958: §1.2) qualification of that account. Moreover, [v], or [β] (see further note 11 below), is a plausible mutual 'target' for the two major developments that collapse in it: viz. the fricativisation of Indo-European (IE) /bʰ/, or the voicing of Germanic /f/ as a consequence of Verner's Law (2.a); and the pre-OE voicing of /f/ between voiced segments (2.b). And the spelling <f> in OE seems to be quite appropriate for a segment [v] which differs minimally from [f], also so represented, and which is not in contrast with [f].

90

What is not in question here, then, is the plausibility of associating a series of voiced fricatives with the phonology of OE. Rather, what I am going to suggest is that the synchronic status of the (non-velar) voiced fricatives is rather less uniform than has been supposed (Pilch 1970:§6) or implied (Campbell 1959:§50), and that, on the other hand, the velar is less distinctive than e.g. Vachek (1964) suggests. §1 below looks at the apparent distribution of voiced fricatives, particularly as compared with other obstruents; §2 offers a phonological interpretation of this distribution, and looks more closely at the significance of the orthography in this regard; §3 proposes a characterisation (in terms of dependency phonology — cf. e.g. Anderson and Jones 1974, 1977, Anderson and Ewen 1980b; Durand 1986) of the proposed phonological interpretation.

1 Distribution of the Voiced Fricatives, and of their Voiceless and Plosive Congeners

Given the kind of distribution alluded to above, ascription of homorganic voiceless and voiced fricatives to a single contrastive unit, or phoneme, might suggest itself as appropriate. And this does indeed seem to be borne out by an inspection of the distribution of the non-grave pairs, the dentals [θ]/[ð] and the sibilants [s]/[z].

1.1 [s] and [θ] (the latter spelled either <þ> or <ð> occur only initially and finally, and medially in gemination[1] and juxtaposed to a voiceless segment, as in (3):

(3)   a. *seofon* 'seven', *sittan* 'sit'
        b. *hus* 'house', *ċeas* 'chose'
        c. *cyssan* 'kiss'
        d. *læst* 'least'

and (4):

(4)   a. *þeġn* 'thane', *þolian* 'suffer'
        b. *pæþ* 'path', *cwæþ* 'said'
        c. *scaþþan* 'injure'
        d. *sniþst* 'you (sg.) cut'[2]

We might take 'finally' to mean, as a first approximation, 'word-finally', as in (3/4.b), or, possibly, 'morpheme-finally' when followed by a voiceless segment (or cluster), as in, say, (5):

(5)   *ċiest* 'you (sg.) choose', *sniþst* 'you (sg.) cut'

However, reference to morpheme is unnecessary, given that (5) are simply instances of type (d) of (3/4). This seems appropriate in view of the fact that a morpheme boundary in itself does not inhibit voicing of a morpheme-final fricative (as in the infinitives *ċeosan* 'choose' or *sniþan* 'cut'). On the other hand, the behaviour of the prefixes in (6):

(6)   a. *mis-lædan* 'mislead', *mis-don* 'act wrongly'
       b. *wiþ-lædan* 'lead away', *wiþ-drifan* 'repel'

where the prefix-final fricatives are, despite the following (and preceding) voiced segments, apparently voiceless (given e.g. subsequent developments) might suggest that the morphological boundary is relevant. However, what may rather be relevant is the placement of the boundary of the foot, which is initiated by a stressed syllable (e.g. Abercrombie 1965): 'primary stress' is borne by the second syllables in (6), and thus we can say that foot-finally the fricatives are voiceless.[3]

'Initially' in the above formulation must apparently be glossed as '(either word- or) morpheme-initially': (3/4.a) are word-initial, and so morpheme-initial; (7) are morpheme- but not word-initial, and voiceless despite the preceding (and following) voiced segments:

(7)   a. *beseon* 'look about', *onsettan* 'bear down'
       b. *aþencan* 'devise', *underþiedan* 'subjugate'

The [s]/[θ] in the examples in (7) are both foot- and morpheme-initial. That the morpheme boundary is the crucial one is suggested by the forms in (8), which show initial [s] in a suffix, despite a preceding (and following) voiced segment:

(8)   *wynsum* 'pleasant', *fremsum* 'benign', *wilsum* 'desirable'

The pairs of identical graphs in (3/4.c) represent geminate (or long) [s] and [θ]; there are no (contrastive) voiced fricative geminates. Nor can voiced fricatives be adjacent to a voiceless segment: (3/4.d) and (5); in general, non-geminate obstruent clusters are voiceless in OE.

[z] and [ð] (the latter again spelled either <þ> or <ð>) occur only medially in words between voiced segments and provided a foot boundary does not immediately follow (cf. (8)) and a morpheme boundary does not immediately precede (cf. (8)); i.e. as in (9):

(9)   a. *dysiġ* 'foolish', *husl* 'eucharist'
       b. *æþele* 'noble', *baþian* 'bathe'

Perhaps, then, we can formulate the distribution of these voiced and voiceless congeners as in (10):

(10)   a. [z]/[ð] in the environment: [+ voice] X____Y [+ voice], within
                                             the word,[4] and where X and Y are
                                             non-segmental and X ≠ morpheme
                                             boundary and Y ≠ foot (or root-
                                             initial — see note 3 above)
                                             boundary

       b. [s]/[θ] elsewhere

That is, [s] and [z] and [θ] and [ð] are respectively in complementary distribution, provided that phonological and morphological boundaries are distributionally relevant.

Moreover, in these various positions one of the voiceless/voiced pair of fricatives is in contrast with their plosive congeners. Compare with the examples in (3)–(8) those in (11):

(11)   a. *turf* 'turf', *set* 'seat', *sittan* 'sit', *æt-reċċan* 'deprive of', *be-tæċan* 'teach', *winter-tid* 'winter'.

         b. *dæġ* 'day', *slæd* 'valley', *biddan* 'ask', *mid-help* 'assistance', *be-dælan* 'deprive of' *þeow-dom* 'servitude', *swicdom* 'fraud'

and consider the (near-)minimal pairs in (12):[5]

(12)   a. *seon* 'see', *teon* 'construct'; *þyrstiġ* 'thirsty', *dyrstiġ* 'bold'; *sinc* 'treasure', *þing* 'thing', *tind* 'prong', *ding* 'dungeon'

         b. *wraþ* 'twisted', *wrat* 'wrote', *rad* 'rode', *ras* 'rose'; *liþ* 'joint', *lid* 'ship'

         c. *wriþon, writon, ridon, rison*, preterite plurals

It therefore seems appropriate to assign [s] and [z] and [θ] and [ð], respectively, to a single phonological unit,[6] a unit whose allophony is formulable as in (10) above.

However, it is not at all clear that the same status should be accorded to the voiced labial fricative.

1.2 Lass (1969b:4–5) offers a formulation of the status of [v] 'from a structural viewpoint' which suggests a parallelism with the [ð] situation we have just described: 'OE had a phoneme /f/, with probable allophones [f] initially, finally and medially when double, and [v] between voiced elements. That is, [f] and [v] are manifestations of *one* unit in the *langue* (opposed to /s/, /þ/ and so forth), as shown by the fact that they are in *complementary distribution* ...' I do not wish to deny that for most of the OE period [f] and [v] are in complementary distribution; and their respective occurrences correspond to the pattern for voiced and voiceless fricatives formulated in (10). This distribution is illustrated in (1) (for [f]) and (2) (for [v]) above, and in (13):

(13)   a. *pyffan* 'puff', *offrian* 'offer'

         b. *drifst* 'you (sg.) drive'

         c. *of-sittan* 'sit on'

         d. *be-fæstan* 'fasten'

         e. *þrym-ful* 'glorious'

in which <f> represents [f]; with, it should be conceded, [ff] being rather marginal (Hogg 1982). And again we find a contrastive voiceless plosive in all these positions. Compare e.g. (14):

(14)   a. *fell* 'ruin', *pell* 'pall'

         b. *scof* 'shaved', *scop* 'shaped'

         c. *hoffing* 'circle', *hoppere* 'dancer'

         d. *scafen* 'shaved', *scapen* 'shaped', past participles; *stafum* 'staves', *stapum* 'grass-hoppers', dative plurals

in which [f] contrasts with [p] initially and finally and in gemination (a–c), and there is a medial contrast between [v] and [p].

However, a labial fricative contrasts only initially and in gemination with whatever is represented by <b>, presumably through most of OE a bilabial plosive, given (in particular) subsequent history:

(15)   a. *fæc* 'space', *bæc* 'back'
        b. *pyffan* 'puff', *hebban* 'raise'

Notice this means, among other things, that [v] is in complementary distribution with [b] as well as with [f]. And, though it shares friction with [f] (and not [b]), it is voiced like [b] (and not [f]). Thus, [v] shows complementarity of distribution and phonetic affinity with respect to two alternative partners. Such a pattern suggests neutralisation rather than allophony: [v] realises the neutralisation of the /f/ ≠ /b/ opposition in certain positions. Assignment of [v] to a /f/ phoneme involves an arbitrary decision which in turn requires that /b/ be represented as showing a defective distribution.

1.3   Vachek (1964) proposes an alignment for the OE voiced velar fricative that involves neither neutralisation nor co-allophony with its voiceless congener. Partly, this can be associated with the fact that [ɣ] apparently occurs outside the environment specified by (10.a). Specifically, it seems to be in contrast, at least in early West Saxon and perhaps elsewhere (Campbell 1959: §§446–7), with [x] word-finally, as illustrated in (16):

(16)   *mearh* 'horse', *mearg* 'marrow'; *fleah* 'flew', *flog* 'flayed'

<h> represents [x] and <g>[ɣ], it would appear, given subsequent developments. <g> also represents a voiced velar initially and medially, as illustrated by the examples in (17):

(17)   a. *god* 'good', *ges* 'geese'
        b. *dagas* 'days', *lagu* 'law'

And <h> also occurs initially, and, beside (graphs representing) voiceless segments, medially, and in gemination:

(18)   a. *habban* 'have'
        b. *aht* 'something'
        c. *hliehhan* 'laugh'

On the basis of such distributions, Vachek proposes two distinct phonemes (and cf. here Campbell 1959: §50, Stockwell and Barritt 1961, Kuhn 1970: §5.3): the first includes final and geminate [x] and whatever initial <h> represents, [x], or on the basis of subsequent developments in particular, perhaps already [h]; and it is in contrast with a voiced velar phoneme, represented <g>. Both of these are in contrast initially and finally with a voiceless velar plosive, spelled <c>:

(19)   a. *guþ* 'war', *cuþ* 'known'; *hal* 'whole', *cal* 'cole-wort'; *har* 'hoary', *gar* 'spear'
        b. *fleah* 'flew', *breac* 'used'; *mearh* 'horse', *mearg* 'marrow', *mearc* 'limit'

In view of the later development of what is represented by final <g> (devoicing to [x] or [f]) and medial <g> ('vocalisation'),[7] its characterisation as a voiced velar fricative in these positions in OE is plausible. However, the initial velar appears subsequently as a plosive [g], as it does after a nasal and when geminate, as in (20):

(20)   *singan* 'sing', *cyning* 'king'; *frogga* 'frog', *sceacga* 'hair'

Given Vachek's analysis, then, are we dealing here with a plosive or a fricative phoneme? In any case there is no voiced velar plosive vs. fricative contrast: compare the medial contrast between [ð]≠[z]≠[d]. But the continuant vs. non-continuant character of the phoneme is less determinate than in the case of /b/.

Let us consider more carefully the probable distribution of [g] and [γ] and their status in various positions. The distribution of [γ] is not suggestive of a phonemic voiced fricative. Notice firstly that, as with the labials, there is no medial voiced/voiceless fricative contrast: [x,h] are excluded from environment (10.a). Again, medially we find only voiceless stop vs. voiced fricative in voiced environments:

(21)   *bocian* 'give a charter', *bogian* 'inhabit'

Thus, medial [γ] again (cf. [v]) manifests a neutralisation, rather than an allophone of the velar phoneme represented elsewhere by <g>. Secondly, the final contrast between final [γ] and [x] appears to be eliminated in the course of the OE period (cf. again Campbell 1959: §447, where e.g. back spellings such as *mearg*, for *mearh*, are noted). These are the two environments in which the evidence for a fricative value for what is represented by <g> is strongest; and in them [γ] is either non-contrastive (with [x]) or only transiently so.

Initially, in gemination and post-nasally, the velar segment represented by <g> is subsequently a plosive. Moreover, there is apparently (with an exception we shall return to) no reason to suppose — and it is thus simpler not to suppose —that in such positions IE /gʰ/, /dʰ/ and /bʰ/ ever developed into fricatives in Germanic. The earliest evidence and subsequent development of the Germanic languages suggests a plosive value (Moulton 1954, 1972); evidence for an intermediate voiced fricative stage is lacking. That is, rather than supposing that IE /bʰ/ passed uniformly into a voiced fricative in Germanic (as is commonly assumed — Moulton 1972: 164), thus /bʰ/ → /β/ → [b ~ β], we can base on the available evidence only a development of the character of /bʰ/ → [b ~β]. However, initial /gʰ/ is possibly exceptional here. The evidence of Dutch initial [γ,χ] is not crucial, in that this could represent an innovation. Rather more striking is the evidence from palatalisation in pre-OE to which we return below, which strongly suggests that at that period the descendant of IE /gʰ/ was fricative in initial position.[8]

In OE fricatives do not occur after a tautosyllabic nasal (cf. §2.1 below). Does, then, post-nasal [g] also represent the neutralisation of /x/ and the phoneme elsewhere spelled <g>? Presumably not, since the absence of tautosyllabic nasal + fricative clusters in all positions represents a basic law of OE syllable structure rather than involving the neutralisation of particular oppositions in specific environments (cf. Anderson and Ewen 1981). We have, then, at best a weak preference for reconstructing the velar phoneme represented by <g> as a plosive, /g/.[9]

If we assume a voiced velar plosive (or obstruent) phoneme /g/, which shares with /x/ a neutralisation [ɣ] in the (10.a) environment, then the velar obstruent subsystem is after all much less idiosyncratic than might be supposed in comparison with the subsystems at other places of articulation. This is not to deny the distinctive history of medial [ɣ] in not deriving in any instance from voicing of pre-OE /x/, which was rather lost in this picture. But in OE the parallel with the distribution of [v] is rather close, particularly latterly.

These observations, on the other hand, do not support Pilch's proposal (which he opposes to the view expressed by Vachek which is described above) that [ɣ] is the medial allophone of a phoneme /x/ which is distinct from both /h/ and /g/. Such a proposal, apart from implying a rather eccentric orthography, as diagrammed in (22):

(22)   GRAPH represents   PHONE realises   PHONEME

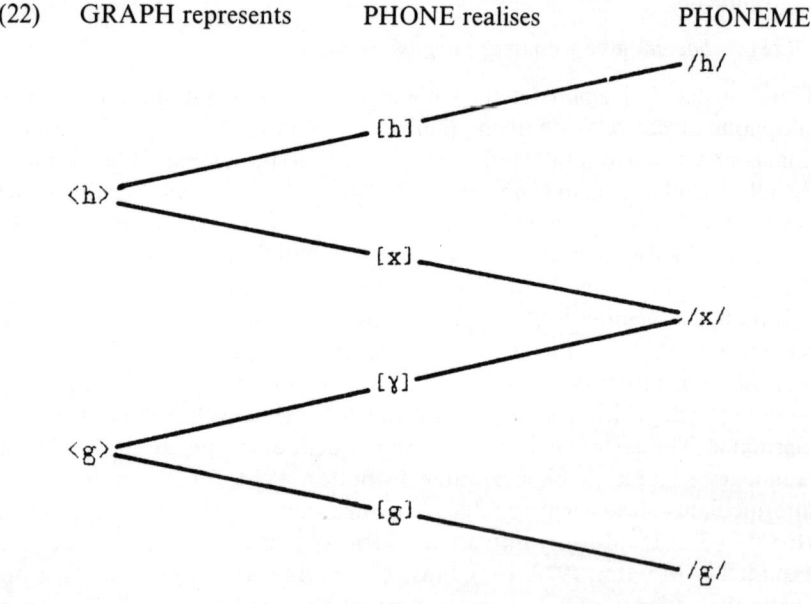

involves several defective distributions, and a phonemic distinction, between /h/ and /x/, based on Biblical loanwords spelled with initial <ch> (e.g. *Chana*), which Pilch interprets as representing /x/. — This despite the fact that he neglects the admittedly transient but much better supported final contrast between [x] and [ɣ].[10] Whatever the status of the /x/≠/h/ contrast, the assignment of non-final [ɣ] to /x/ is no more warranted than it is to /g/: either assignment is arbitrary.

1.4   On the assumption of a /g/ phoneme, this final contrast between [x] and [ɣ] is all that distinguishes the distribution of the velar obstruents from that of the labial. Its existence depends on the delayed implementation in the case of velars of the process of final fricative devoicing that has already operated with the labials. Its early non-operation with respect to even the latter is perhaps evidenced by spellings with final <b>, as in (23), from the Epinal gloss:

(23) *salb* 'ointment', *theb-* 'thief', *halb-* 'half'

(cf. Campbell 1959: §444). That these represent a voiced fricative is suggested by the subsequent development to a voiceless fricative represented <f> and by a source in both medial and final position in fricativisation of IE /bʰ/ and Verner's Law voicing of /f/.[11]

Thus, throughout most of OE with the labials, and latterly with the velars, not only is the fricative/voiced plosive opposition neutralised medially (in environment (10.a)), but there is also neutralisation finally, realised as [f] and [x] in this case. We also find only [f] and [x] in the environment of voiceless segments (cf. (1.c), (18.b)).

We must now, in §2, consider rather more carefully the nature of these neutralisations. All I have been trying to show in this section is that attribution of allophonic status to [v] and [ɣ] disguises their lack of congruence with [ð]; as a consequence, defective distribution must be accorded to /b/, and /g/ or /x/. The controversy over the phonemic assignment of [ɣ] (cf. Pilch and Vachek) underlines the arbitrariness of the decision. But this is also true of [v]: complementary distribution with both [f] and [b] and phonetic affinity with both argues, as we have seen, for neutralisation rather than allophony. And the natural basis for the neutralisations suggested in §§2–3 below also throws into question an interpretation involving defective distribution. My assumptions are that arbitrary phonemic assignments are to be avoided and attribution of defective distribution minimised. This is made possible in a principled way by the recognition of neutralisation.

1.5   Before proceeding further with a consideration of the proposed neutral-isations, however, we must also take into account one further aspect of the system that involves both representation by <g> and more neutralisation. For OE orthography also represents a (voiced) palatal by <g>. I shall symbolise the major realisation of this as [j]; it was, perhaps, given that one of its sources is the Germanic approximant /j/, and in the light of subsequent developments ('vocalisation'), already frictionless in OE, though its other source is in the palatalisation of [ɣ]: cf. here e.g. Campbell 1959: ch.IX.B, Lass and Anderson 1975: ch.IV, Kuhn 1970: §9.2, Hogg 1979. [g] (or [ɣ]) and [j] contrast initially in the foot/word, as suggested by (24):

(24)   *guma* 'man', *ġung/ġeong* 'young'; *gylden* 'golden', *ġift* 'gift'

(where as elsewhere *ġ*, by editorial tradition, represents the palatal). But finally only the palatal appears after a front vowel (including one that is separated from it by a liquid) and only [ɣ] after a back:

(25)   a. *sweġ* 'sound', *byrġ* 'cities'
        b. *plog* 'plough', *burg* 'city'

Medially there is at best a rather restricted contrast: only the palatal is found between front vowels (including one that is separated from it by a liquid) and only [γ] after back:[12]

(26)   a. *siġe* 'victory', *belġe* 'I get angry'
        b. *plogum* 'ploughs', dative, *burgum* 'cities', dative, *burge* 'city's'

but where there is a preceding front vowel and a following back we find such contrasts as (27):

(27)   *feġan* 'join', *wegas* 'ways'; *dryġe* 'dry', *nigon* 'nine'

The palatals here reflect a [γ] palatalised before an original [j/i] (which also mutates the preceding vowel) lost in such instances before the period of extant OE texts. We have, then, a surface contrast here in OE, provided that palatalisation cannot be motivated as an allophonic rather than a morpho-phonemic regularity. (On subsequent 'reversion' of such palatals to [γ] see Luick 1914–40: §373.a.5, Campbell 1959: §439.)

Thus, finally and for the most part medially, the (voiced) palatal and velar are non-contrastive. Again, there is a neutralisation; but here the representative of the neutralisation is determined simply by the quality of the adjacent vowels: we have alternative assimilatory neutralisations (see further §2).

Notice finally here the difference between the palatals developed medially after a nasal and in gemination and those developed elsewhere. Post-nasally, we find an affricate, [dʒ], as in *sengan* 'singe'; or *fenġ* 'grasp'; so too in gemination, as in *seċġan* 'say'. Elsewhere, as we have noted, we probably have a palatal approximant. Now, in gemination and after a nasal is where we can reconstruct a plosive [g] as representative of the velar. Finally, we have [γ]. So, under palatalisation, the plosive develops to an affricate, the fricative to an approximant. But the palatalisation of initial /g/ produces an approximant which falls together with Germanic /j/. This at least suggests that, after all, at some point initial /g/ was a fricative and may have remained so through most of OE: see further Luick 1914–40: §633, Hogg 1979: 93–6.

2 Interpretation of the Status of the Voiced Fricatives, and of their Orthography

2.1 I have suggested that [v] and [γ] in environment (10.a) represent the neutralisations of the /f/≠/b/ and /x/≠/g/(≠/j/) contrasts, respectively, which involve a distinction in both voice and continuancy. As such, [v] and [γ] are the products of an assimilatory neutralisation, in terms of the typology of neutralisation agency proposed by Anderson and Ewen 1981.[13] Crucial are the adjoining voiced segments rather than structural considerations; (phonological and morphological) boundaries merely delimit the domain within which the neutralisation occurs. The nature of the assimilatory process is rather clear in the case of /f/ and /x/, which merely 'assimilate to' the voicing of the environment. But with /b/ and /g/, a stop articulation 'becomes' continuant. We cannot formulate this as assimilation to the (voiced) continuancy of the adjacent segments, since the adjacent voiced segments need not be continuant, as in (28):

(28)   *hæfde* 'had', *hogde* 'thought'

where [v] or [γ] is followed by a voiced plosive. We return in §3 to a formulation of the property shared by continuancy and voicing that is the basis for the assimilation.

We should, however, note at this point that the product of the neutralisation is a segment to whose characterisation are crucial properties which are 'marked' with respect to other suspensions of oppositions. Thus, voicing can be said to be marked, given that the realisation of the word-final suspension of the voiced and voiceless fricative opposition is voiceless. And continuancy of obstruents is marked, since e.g. only plosives occur after tautosyllabic nasals; in Ingvaeonic languages all nasals are lost before fricatives: cf. e.g. OE *þuhte* 'seemed' with its infinitive *þyncan*, OE *fif* 'five' with Old High German *fimf*, OE *fus* 'eager' with Old High German *funs*, OE *liþe* 'mild' with Old High German *linde* (Campbell 1969: §§119,121). As confirmation, note that root-final obstruents assimilate to the voicelessness of an inflexional consonant, whereas such consonants assimilate to the non-continuancy of the root-final segment: so, *bint* 'he binds', a degemination of /bintt/ from root /bind/ plus inflexional /θ/.

These language-particular reflexions of markedness coincide with the status that can be accorded to the properties on universalist grounds; voicing of obstruents and frication are 'inherently marked': see further §3 below. The markedness of [v] and [γ] supports the view that the neutralisation in their case is indeed assimilatory rather than simply suspension of an opposition in some structurally specified position.

We can designate [v] and [γ] realisations of the archiphonemes, here represented //v// and //γ// associated with medial neutralisation of the /f/≠/b/ and /x/≠/g/ oppositions, respectively. They embody a constraint on the representations that can be accorded to words in the lexicon: only the archiphonemes (and thus neither phoneme) can appear in environment (10.a).

In the case of the labials (and latterly the velars) neutralisation can also be associated with final position: there is no final contrast either between /b/ and /f/; here we find only [f]. This is usually regarded as a realisation of the phoneme /f/. But, given the absence of contrast with /b/, it is surely more appropriate to regard final [f] as realising //v// in final position: //v// shows final devoicing. The product of the neutralisation is in this instance determined by structural considerations, viz. final position.

However, presumably then <f> in *eft*, etc. also represents //v// Thus, the distribution of voicing with fricative archiphonemes, as well as phonemes, is dictated by (10). And, in that case, <h> in *aht* (18.b) represents the variant of //γ//associated with an adjoining voiceless segment. On the other hand, it is arguable that the absence of a voiced obstruent here follows from a requirement that obstruent clusters necessarily agree in voice: we have here not neutralisation but cluster concord with respect to voice. Further, obstruent clusters which agree in continuancy are also excluded. Thus, the present instances of [f] and [x] are not appropriately characterised as realising a segmental archiphoneme; but their occurrence follows from laws of basic syllable structure (cf. again Anderson and Ewen 1981).

We can thus characterise the status of the various obstruents in OE as in (29):

(29)

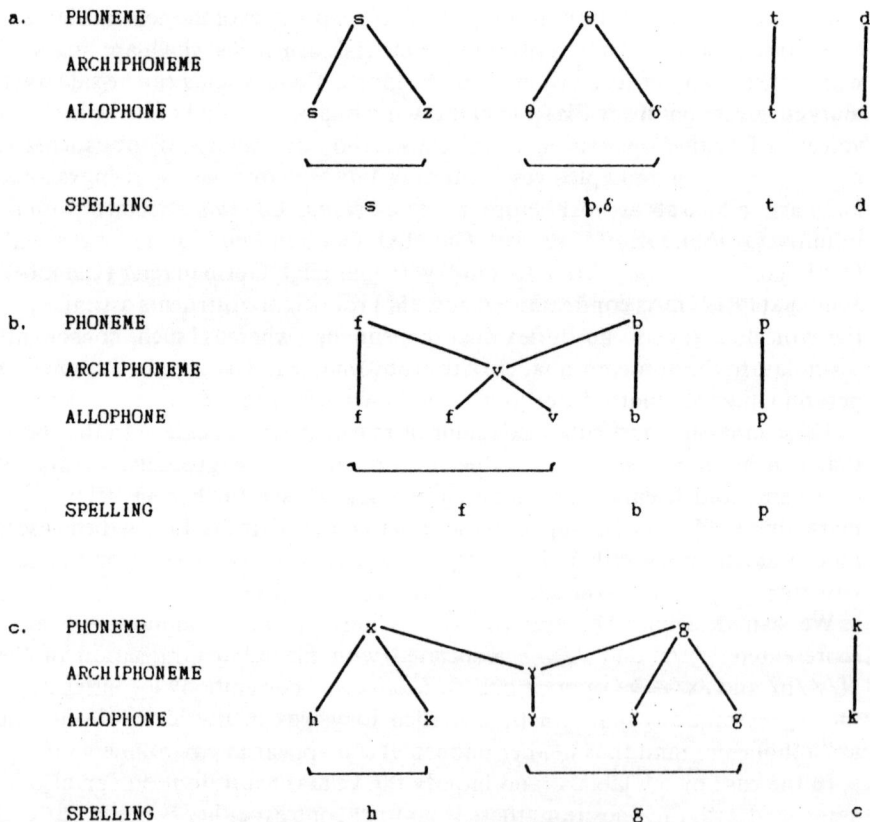

in which is displayed the range of neutralisations and reconstructible allophonies we have been looking at.

2.2   The orthographic system of OE might be taken to support the view that [v] is an allophone of /f/, which phoneme is uniformly spelled <f>; whereas [γ] belongs to a different phoneme from its voiceless congener [x]: /x/ is spelled <h>, but [γ], as in all circumstances a member of the /g/ phoneme, is spelled <g>. (Cf. again Vachek 1964.) But, as we have seen, such a formulation of the status of these voiced fricatives simply obscures the characterisation of their distribution by assimilating the situation with the labials to that appropriate for the dental-alveolars and by rendering the velars more idiosyncratic than is warranted. Moreover, a purely phonemic interpretation of the orthography fails to account for the use of <g> for /j/: see further §2.3 below.

I have argued that an interpretation involving neutralisation more adequately characterises the relevant distributions. And, I shall now suggest, it is quite compatible with the orthographic evidence. For what (29) reveals is that the orthographic representation accords a distinct symbol to each phoneme (with variation in the case of <þ> and <ð>) and that archiphonemes share their representation with the phoneme with which they also share an allophone. Thus we have the phoneme-graph correspondences: <s>=/s/, <þ,ð>= /θ/, <t>= /t/, <d>=/d/, <f>=/f/, <b>=/b/, <h>=/x/ and <g>=/g/. And the archiphoneme //v// is spelled <f>, given that it shares an allophone [f] with /f/; whereas //γ// which shares an allophone [γ] with /g/, is accordingly spelled <g>: see (29).

2.3 Such an interpretation is supported by spelling practice in relation to the neutralisation noted in §1.5, one we have so far not considered in this section. In §1.5 we observed that the [γ]/[j] opposition is neutralised in certain contexts (recall examples (25)/(26)). Thus, [g]/[γ], [h] and [j] are in contrast initially. Finally [γ] and [j] do not contrast; which occurs depends on the quality of the preceding vowel. So we can posit a final archiphoneme //G// in contrast with final /x/. //G// is a non-anterior obstruent neutral between /g/ and /j/, which has two segmentally determined (and again assimilatory) realisations, [γ] and [j]. Medially, there is a firm contrast only after a front vowel and before a back (cf. (27) — but recall note 12). Where [γ] contrasts with [j] it represents the archiphoneme //γ// which neutralises /g/ and /x/. Where (and if — note 12) there is so such medial contrast between [γ] and [j] (as, say, in (25)/(26)), they realise the neutralisation of all of /x/, /g/ and /j/: i.e. we have a hyper-archiphoneme ///Γ/// which is the neutralisation of two archiphonemes and is realised as [γ] or [j].

Thus, we should substitute for (29.c) the pattern of neutralisation shown in (30):[14]

(30)

/g/ and /j/ are both spelled <g>; this infringes the requirement that each phoneme be given a distinct graph. This is presumably permitted as a consequence of the fact that //G// and ///Γ///share allophones with both /j/ and /g/ (on the assumption that /g/ has a (initial) [γ] allophone): in order for these archiphonemes to be associated with a single graph and also to be spelled in the same way as the phonemes they share allophones with, the phonemes themselves must be spelled in the same way. (Similarly, all of /k/, /tʃ/ and their final neutralisation //K// realised [k] or [tʃ], are spelled <c>.) What emerges overall is that the realisations of this complex of neutralisations are spelled in accordance with their voice, <h> if voiceless, <g> if voiced.

That this grouping implied by the spelling is systematic is confirmed by the testimony of alliterative practice in early OE (provided we make the reasonable assumption that the alliteration is not 'eye-alliteration'). Lass and Anderson (1975: ch.IV, §7) note with regard to this set of consonants that 'the principle behind alliterative choice . . . seems to be neither phonetic likeness nor identity of lexical origin'. For instance, (31):

(31)   ġeong in ġeardagum, þone God sende

(Beowulf, 1.13; Klaeber 1950)

alliterates /j/, [j] with /g/, [γ]. Lass and Anderson devise principles governing alliterative and spelling practice which depend on a rather abstract analysis of the segments concerned. We can alternatively refer these principles to the neutralisation pattern prescribed by (30): initial [γ] and [j] may alliterate because, although they are in contrast in initial position, they are also allophones of the archiphoneme //G//. An analysis of the surface oppositions of OE which does not recognise archiphonemes throws no light on this whatsoever. Both spelling and alliterative practice reflect some such neutralisation pattern as is given in (30).

2.4 Subsequently, as we have seen, the final contrast between /x/ and //G// manifested as [x] vs. [γ], also disappears, in some varieties of OE, at least, as a consequence of the extension of final devoicing of fricatives to the velars. And we find spellings such as *ploh* rather than *plog*, as well as back spellings like *mearg* for *mearh*. If at the same time initial /g/ is developing to a plosive, then the pattern for the velars given in (29.c) (if we once again ignore for the moment the palatals) comes to be replaced by one that is isomorphic to that associated in (29.b) with the labials; a pattern to which the orthography is no longer so appropriate.

If, as in (30), we relate this later velar system to the palatal one, we get (32): That is, the archiphoneme //γ// has now extended to final position, realised as [x] and in contrast with /j/; and //G// is now virtual, it has no realisation. //γ//shares an allophone with /x/ and no other phoneme; and this allophone of /x/ is now limited to in gemination. ///Γ/// shares an allophone with /j/. And /g/ is quite isolated. These developments prepare the way for the breakdown of this complex and defective system of neutralisation, which is not obviously preferable conceptually to defective distribution; and for the adoption of a different basis for the spelling.

(32)

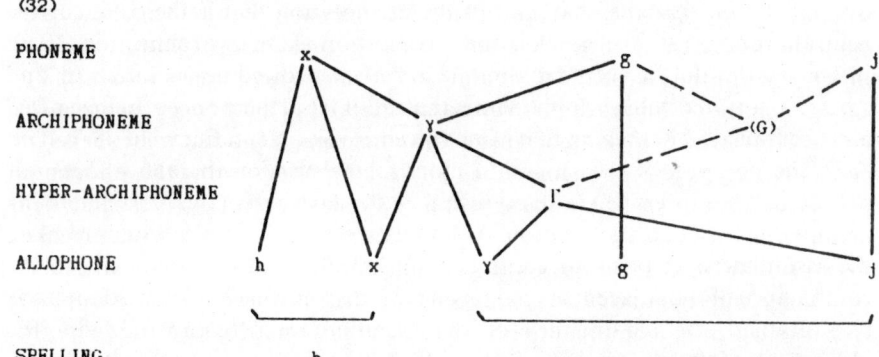

With degemination of /xx/ and /gg/ and the loss of /– ə/ there develops a medial and final contrast between /x/ and /g/; while medial and then final (with loss of /– ə/) [γ] weakens and falls together with /w/, and eventually 'vocalises', as does non-initial [j] (cf. again Colman 1983). The OE pattern of allophony and neutralisation is replaced by one involving a contrast between /x/ and /g/ which is not neutralised in environment (10.a), and lacking both [γ] and non-initial [j] (and [w]).

Of course, this account is a gross over-simplification; and diverse patterns of development present themselves in the course of the Middle English period. So, in the mid-thirteenth century *Ancren Riwle*, /x/, spelled <(c)h>, contrasts initially and medially (at least) with /g/, <g>, and (initially) with /j/, <3>. Whereas in (slightly earlier) *The Owl and the Nightingale* <3> represents [j] initially but otherwise [x] and unvocalised [γ]; and <g> represents /g/ *passim*: [j], [x] and [γ] are in complementary distribution.

Either by such a realignment as is implied by this last system of representation or, eventually, via loss of (non-initial) [x] in most dialects, and the disappearance of the original clusters represented by <hl>, <hr> and <hn>, initial [h] is left isolated as an alternative (word- or foot-initial) syllable initiator to ϕ.[15]

The other voiced fricatives phonemicise as a consequence of degemination and the loss of /–ə/. With loss of /–ə/ and the introduction of loanwords with initial voiced fricatives (*vertu, zele*, etc.), they achieve contrastive status even in positions where they formerly did not occur at all; though the phonemic status of [ð], in particular, remains rather marginal, given the morpho-syntactic limitations on its distribution.[16] And only with /v/ is the phonemic status given anything approaching a consistent representation by subsequent English orthography.

3 Characterisation of the Voiced Fricatives, and of their Phonological Status

I have suggested that in OE the voiced fricatives [v] and [γ] implement the neutralisation of the /f/≠/b/ and /x/≠/g/ contrasts, respectively. Now, in the case of /f/ and /x/ the character of the assimilation that is the basis for the neutralisation is rather clear from the specification of the environment in (10.a); just as /θ/ develops a voiced allophone in between voiced segments, so /f/ and /x/ are associated with archiphonemes that differ from them only in being voiced and occur instead of them in that same voiced environment. But what of /b/ and /g/? The notation of (10.a) — or a more formal version thereof — does not permit us to express their relationship with their respective corresponding archiphonemes as an assimilation. As I pointed out in §2.1, we cannot formulate the assimilation as being to continuancy; that /b/ and /g/ assimilate to the continuancy of the adjacent voiced segments is disconfirmed by such examples as (24). Rather, the continuancy of the archiphonemes (compared with the plosiveness of the phonemes) reflects assimilation to voicing. I suggest that this failure of the notation is a reflexion of an inadequacy in phonological representations based on binary distinctive features.

In the theory of phonological representation which has come to be known as 'dependency phonology', segments are characterised in terms of the presence or absence of basic elements, or atoms, designated components. These are, further, grouped into sub-segments, or gestures, which constitute a systematic partitioning of the set of components into subsets which can function as units: i.e. there are recurrent phonological regularities whose optimal expression requires reference to just such groupings (see e.g. Lass 1976: ch.6, Anderson 1980, Ewen 1980: §5.2, Anderson and Ewen 1987: particularly part II. Finally, and perhaps most relevantly to our present concerns, of a pair of co-present components one may dominate or preponderate over the other: the dominated component is said to be dependent on the other.

Thus, within the categorial gesture, which specifies the 'major class' (including voicedness) to which the segment belongs, various segment types are distinguished in terms of the presence and combinatorial (dependency) status of the two components |V| (roughly, maximisation of periodicity) and |C| (roughly, energy reduction), where the verticals enclose components. A segment whose categorial gesture contains only |V|, i.e. a vowel, is represented as {|V|}. A segment whose categorial gesture contains |C| (possibly together with |V|), i.e. a consonant, is represented as {C}, where the absence of verticals indicates that |C| may not be the only component present. If both |V| and |C| are present, then they may be combined in various ways: |V| may preponderate, here represented {V⇄}; |C| may, represented {C⇄}; or they may be equipollent (mutual dependency), represented {V:C}. In the categorial gesture up to two instances of each of |V| and |C| may co-occur; but if, say, two |V|'s are present, one must depend (asymmetrically) on the other if |C| is also present.

Various segment types are thus characterised in (33):

(33)   a.   {|V|} = vowels
       b.   {|V|⇄ C} = sonorant non-vowels
       c.   {|V:C|} = voiceless fricatives
       d.   {|C⇄V|} = voiced plosives
       e.   {|C|} = voiceless plosives

where (33.b) requires that with (non-vowel) sonorants a |V|, uncombined with anything else, has a dependent |C|, which may be combined;[17] (33.c) indicates that voiceless fricatives are segments whose categorial gesture contains only an equipollent |V| and |C|; voiced plosives contain only a |V| dependent on a |C|, as in (33.d); and (33.e) specifies voiceless plosives as characterised by the sole presence of |C| — they are the 'optimal consonants'.

The various types are ranged hierarchically in (33) in terms of decreasing preponderance of |V|: uniqueness, through preponderance, equipollence and dependence, to absence. This defines the sonority hierarchy which underlies a wide spread of phonological phenomena, such as syllable structure, lenition and fortition, etc.[18] Their inherent representations also hierarchise these segment types, in terms of relative complexity, with respect to 'markedness', which again underlies a spread of phenomena, from staging of acquisition and loss to simple likelihood of occurrence and the implicational relations based on such — such that, e.g., presence of voiceless fricatives or voiced plosives in a system implies the presence of voiceless plosives.[19] This is not the place, however, to attempt to demonstrate the general appropriateness of such a notation.

What is our concern here is the characterisation of voiced fricatives. Voice in obstruents is indicated by the presence of a dependent |V|, as in (33.d); friction by equipollent co-presence of |V| and |C|.[20] Voiced fricatives are thus most appropriately characterised as in (34):

(34) $\{|V:C \rightleftarrows V|\}$ = voiced fricatives

This correctly represents their relative markedness: systems which contain voiced fricatives will also typically contain voiceless fricatives and voiced plosives. So too is their place on the sonority hierarchy appropriately represented. They contain an extra |V| in comparison with both voiceless fricatives and voiced plosives, and are thus immediate targets for lenition of either, as in the present case.

The archiphonemes //v// and //γ// in OE can be characterised as assimilatory neutralisations of /f/ and /b/ and /x/ and /g/, respectively, by virtue of their displaying, in a highly |V|-full environment (voiced segments — i.e. segments with non-equipollent §V| on both sides), an additional |V| component over both voiceless fricatives and voiced plosives. We can represent the situation as in (35):

(35)

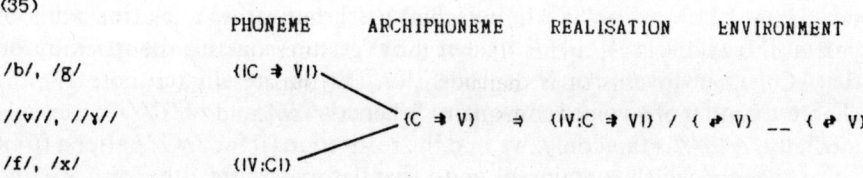

	PHONEME	ARCHIPHONEME	REALISATION	ENVIRONMENT
/b/, /g/	{lC → Vl)			
//v//, //γ//		{C → V) → {lV:C → Vl) / (∂ V) __ (∂ V)		
/f/, /x/	{lV:Cl)			

where |⇄C| and |⇄V| indicate a |C| or |V| that is not dependent; and the specification for the archiphoneme indicates that other components may be present besides the |C| and dependent |V|: the element is an obstruent, with dependent |V|, without further specification. It is thus neutral between voiced plosive ({|C ⇄ V|}) and fricative, in which the |C| and |V| are mutually preponderant. In the |V|-full environment represented in (35), where, as noted, |⇄V|, the presence of a non-equipollent |V|, specifies 'voiced', the archiphoneme is realised via addition of a second |V|: {|V:C⇄V|} is the only possible categorial representation consisting of a non-dependent |C| and two |V| components.

The final variant of //v// and latterly of //γ// differs in showing structurally determined suppression of the governing |V|: the realisation of the archiphoneme, as with any fricative, in this position is {|C:V|}, a voiceless fricative. Thus, finally, {C⇄V} is interpreted as {|C:V|}.

//v// and //γ//themselves, like /f/ and /x/ or /b/ and /g/, differ in the specification for the articulatory gesture (roughly, indicating place of articulation). Whereas //v// (and /f/ and /b/) is {|u|} (grave, labial), //γ// (and /x/ and /g/) is {|l,u|} (lingual and grave, i.e. velar). (See again Anderson and Ewen 1980b.) Though the neutralisation is concerned only with the categorial gesture, we can nevertheless limit it to obstruents that are in articulatory terms {u}, thus excluding dental/alveolars. The target for the neutralisation is thus segments which are {{C⇄V} {u}}, i.e. grave obstruents which are either voiced or fricative (where the inner parentheses enclose the individual gestures).

//G// on the other hand, represents a neutralisation in the articulatory gesture as well as the categorial: it is a voiced consonant which is neutral between palatal and velar, and obstruent and sonorant, as shown in (36):

(36)

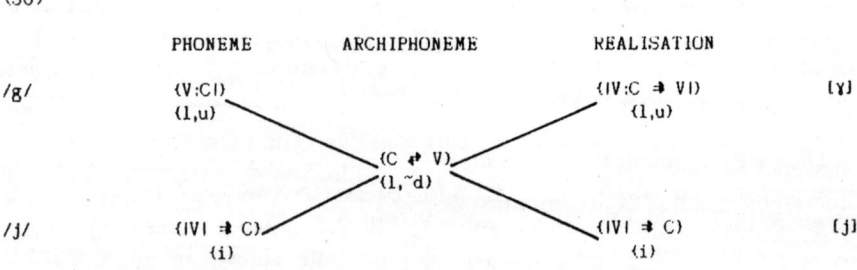

The archiphoneme is specified as having an articulatory gesture which contains |l| combined with some other component with is not |d| (dental). Hence //G// is not dental {|l,d|}, alveolar {|l|} or labial {|u|}, but rather a neutralisation of palatal {l,i} and velar {|l,u|}.[21] Its categorial gesture contains the specification that |C| either governs or is dependent on |V| unilaterally (cf. note 19), the characterisation of a voiced consonant. Whereas //γ//and ///Γ/// occur only medially, //G// is final only: we find the realisation [j] for //G// after a front vowel, i.e. one which contains |i| in its articulatory gesture; otherwise, we find [γ].

///Γ///is the medial neutralisation of /x/, /g/ and /j/, or of //γ// and //G// and can thus be characterised as in (37):

(37)

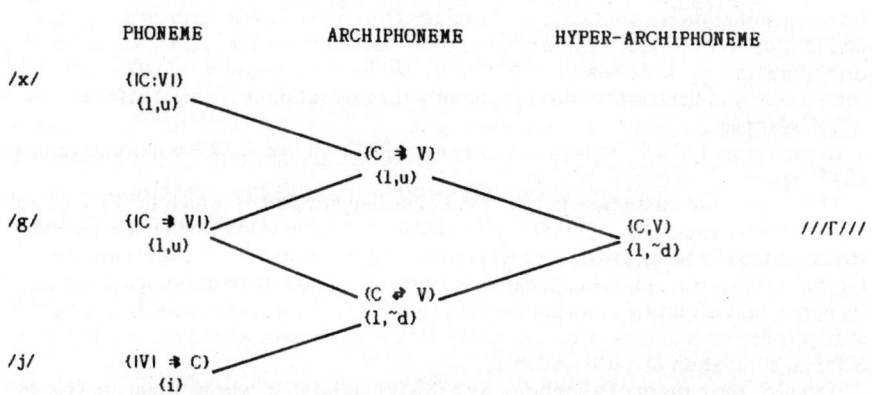

///Γ/// is thus characterised as a non-labial, non-dental, non-alveolar {l,~d})
consonant {C} whose categorial gesture contains a |V|, the absence of a
specification for the relationship between |C| and |V| indicating that it involves a
neutralisation of whether the consonant is simply fricative {|C:V|}, voiced
plosive {|C⇄V|} or approximant {|V⇄C|}. Its realisations are as for //G// (cf.
(36)). However, the environments are medial, but again assimilatory, as
suggested in §1.5.[22]

The hierarchy of archiphonemes in (37) shows progressive and orderly
neutralisation of the oppositions evident in the position of maximum
differentiation, the initial one. Such a characterisation is not available to a
notation based on binary features, as the neutralisations involve being able to
represent what is in common between different features, such as e.g. voice,
continuancy, sonorancy, which share the component |V|, crucial to the
expression of ///Γ/// The archiphonemes involve progressive weakening of
constraints on how |V| and |C| can combine. The theory of representation
adopted in this section thus allows an appropriate characterisation of the
hierarchical status of archiphonemes.

NOTES

*I am grateful to Fran Colman and other 'members' of the class of '83 for their (mostly)
patient comments on my presentation of the material which forms the basis for this study.
The present version also benefited from a perusal by the afore-named and by Richard
Hogg and Roger Lass. All remaining errors are mine alone.
1. Kurath (1956) argues that it is appropriate to suggest a contrastive status for gemination
(or length) of consonants only in word-, or more specifically, foot-medial position
between (short) vowels. Word-final doubling of consonant graphs in forms like *bed(d)*
'bed' is inconsistent, and such doubling may represent, Kurath suggests, orthographic
analogy with members of the same paradigm, like the genitive singular *beddes*, in which
there is consistent doubling in medial position to indicate a contrastive geminate.
However, such consonants are historically long and continue to be in morphophonological

alternation with long consonants, as in the instance just cited. Given that the dating of final degemination is uncertain, I have excluded forms like *cryb(b)* 'crib' in discussing the distribution of /b/ in §1.2 below and in formulating the principles governing orthographic representation in §2.3. Consonant length between a (short) vowel and a sonorant is non-contrastive, but presumably the realisation is a long consonant, as in *ap(p)las* 'apples'.

2. Examples are typically morphologically complex, such that $<$þ,ð$>$ is morpheme-final: cf. (5) below.

3. This formulation assumes that even in nouns like *mis-dæd*, in which the first syllable bears 'primary stress', the segment represented by $<$s$>$ is foot-final, in that the 'secondary stress' on the following syllable initiates a new, subordinate foot (cf. Anderson 1986). If this seems unwarranted, then appeal must be made here too to morphological structure. As noted, that a following morphological boundary is not as such crucial is suggested by examples like *stafas* 'staffs', with medial [v]. However, perhaps what is relevant is position before the initiation of a root syllable.

4. Actually, the pattern of allophony with [θ]/[ð], at least, in words which are typically unstressed, such as forms of the personal and demonstrative pronouns, modifiers and adverbs, is uncertain. Certainly, *this, that, there, then, thou*, etc. emerge later with voiced initial fricatives; and it would appear that the date of voicing is not to be precisely determined.

5. The opposition of voice with plosives is suspended in certain circumstances, as e.g. after syllable-initial [s]. And in general voicing is homogenous in obstruent clusters; indeed, monomorphemic obstruent clusters are voiceless (cf. e.g. Pilch 1970: §§10–1). Also, as we note in §2 below, with obstruents the opposition of continuancy is suspended after nasals.

6. Lass and Anderson (1975: ch.VI, §2.2.3) argue that this unit is itself an 'archi-segment', neutral for voice, rather than a voiceless fricative phoneme. This distinction is, however, rather unimportant in the context of the present discussion, though their suggestion does seem to me to be rather more faithful to the pattern of contrast — and see further note 9 and §3 below. Adoption henceforth of the notation /s/ is not intended to pre-empt a decision on this issue.

7. Final [γ] apparently devoices, as we have already noted, falling together with /x/, which itself disappears in most dialects (*plough*) or is substituted for by /f/ (*enough*); medially it weakens to [v] and, on loss of final /ə/, 'vocalises' — i.e. becomes part of the syllabic nucleus, as part of a diphthong (*law*, which shows subsequent monophthongisa-tion). On these developments, see Colman 1983.

8. See §1.5 below, and cf. Moulton 1972: 173; Hogg 1979, 1982, where in addition the marginality of /gg/ is indicated. Moulton also notes (1972: 173) that Latin *graecus* 'Greek' is borrowed into e.g. OE as *crecas* (plural); and other early Germanic spellings suggest an initial voiceless plosive for this form in Germanic. And he concludes: 'The only likely explanation for this is that ... PGmc. had no initial [gr-] but only [kr-] and [ɡr-]; and that, in borrowing Lat. *graecus*, Gmc. [kr-] was used as the nearest phonetic equivalent of Lat. [gr]'. It seems to me that in the absence of the palatalisation evidence this would be merely suggestive.

9. Perhaps, however, we should think of /g/ (and /b/) as an 'archi-segment', neutral as to continuancy: cf. again on /s/ etc. Lass and Anderson 1975: ch.VI, §2.2.3. In terms of the dependency notation proposed in §3 below, the phoneme will be most appropriately characterised as a plosive (just as /s/ will be voiceless), given relative simplicity of the representations, the absence of a /g/≠/γ/ (and /b/≠/v/) contrast, and the evidence for some realisations as [g] (and [b]). See further Staun 1983.

10. A somewhat similar system is suggested for late OE by Fisiak 1968: §2.54; but the motivation for this is not specified. Moulton (1954:26) suggests 'since [h] was not distinguished by the feature of velar articulation, it was a separate phone [h]'. But I do not find this at all compelling as an argument, given that [h] as a putative allophone of /x/ is still distinguished by absence of labial/dental/ ... articulation from /f/, /ð/, etc., with

which (unlike with [x]) it is in contrast in initial position. (See too Stockwell and Barritt 1961: 79–80, Kuhn 1970: §§5.33–.35.) The existence of early forms like *thohae* (cf. Luick 1914–40: §§656, Campbell 1959: §236(3)) does not provide support for a /h/≠/x/ contrast but rather indicates the reside of a medial contrast between whatever is represented by <h> and whatever by <g>. This does not survive. Only with degemination of /xx/ would a medial contrast between [x] and [γ] arise again. Certainly medial <hh> is not always maintained as a spelling in the OE period: more frequently than with other double graphs we find a simplex <h> rather than <hh> (though the inconsistency is not as great as it is in final position with all double graphs). (Cf. Campbell 1959: §66.) However, this may be merely graphic: given that [γ] is spelled <g> and that [x] does not occur medially, doubling of the graph is redundant.

11. Notice that in the Epinal gloss the product in medial position of fricativisation of /b^h/ and of the Verner's Law-ing of /f/ (exemplified in (2.a) above) is also distinguished orthographically from the pre-OE /f/ which undergoes voicing (cf. (2.b)) as <b> vs. <f>: *aelbitu* 'swan', *gaebuli* 'tribute', instrumental; *giroefa* 'reeve', *uulfes* 'wolf's'. (See again Campbell 1950: §444.) Presumably, this either indicates the continued absence of voice in the latter case (*pace* Pheifer 1974: §69) or represents the maintenance of some other distinction between the old and the new sources of [v]. This might involve bilabial vs. labiodental place of articulation or plosive vs. fricative manner. — But if the latter were the case this would require the positing of a development for non-initial IE /f/ through [v] by Verner's Law and then [b] (parallel to IE /θ/ — -*cweden*, past participle of *cweþan* 'say', etc.) back to [v]. In early texts we also find <d> used not just for medial [ð] but also for final [θ], with <th> limited to initial position (Campbell 1959: 23, note 3). Given all this, the final <b> in the forms in (23) might be interpreted as representing bilabial articulation rather than necessarily voice.

12. These formulations may well be too strong in their limitation of the circumstances for contrast. Weak verbs of class II appear to provide instances [j] and [γ] whose occurrence is not in conformity with the generalisations offered above. In contracted verbs in particular, an original [j] can come to follow a back vowel (*contra* what is illustrated by (26.b)), whether a back or a front vowel follows: *sceoġeað* 'shoe', (verb) plural, *goiende* 'lamenting', -*scoġen* 'shoe', subjunctive plural (Campbell 1959: §761(7)). Cf. too the name *Boia/Boġa*, recorded e.g. as a moneyer's name on coins associated with the Taunton mint (Colman 1981: 110–1). Similarly, if the <g> in *swigian* 'be silent' represents a velar and if the <i> represents a vowel rather than a semi-vowel, then it contravenes the generalisation which is illustrated by (26.a). However, a sequence of front vowel + [j] + [i/j] is not to be expected at this date: so maybe merely a reformulation of the complementarity is required in this case, such that what is represented by <i> is grouped with the back vowels in such circumstances. At any rate, it is possible that [j] and [γ] are more generally, if still marginally, contrastive in medial position. Notice too that with respect to the generalisation illustrated by (26.b) 'back' includes whatever the Germanic diphthongs represented by <ea,eo> in OE had developed into.

13. Cf. too, of course, Trubetzkoy 1939; also Martinet 1936, Lass 1984: ch.3. The framework proposed by Anderson and Ewen is rather closer to that advocated by Martinet or Lass in e.g. not restricting neutralisations to bilateral oppositions, which in turn results from a view of the concept as 'neutralisation, not of pairwise oppositions, but of features or feature sets' (Lass 1984: §3.3). For an implementation of such a view see §3 below.

14. If it were the case that [j] and [γ] are fully contrastive medially (cf. note 12), then ///Γ/// need not be posited; and rather medial [γ] should be assigned to //γ// in all instances. This does not affect the argument given below concerning the basis for the spelling and alliterative conventions. Nor, incidentally, does the existence of mainly early spellings with <i> for [j], which convention represents an alternative orthographic solution to the situation described here but one which was not generally adopted in OE.

15. Anderson 1969 suggests, given the association of both [h] and full aspiration with the

beginning of (word- or foot-initial) syllables, that [h] is the equivalent with a zero-consonant syllable initiation to aspiration with plosive initiations. That is, we have a proportion $C^h : C :: \phi^h : \phi$ (e.g. *pit : bit :: hit : it*). Compare: a) *history*, b) *hysterical*, c) *behest*, where [h] begins a syllable that is either word-(a,b) or foot- (a,c) initial; with d) *petal*, e) *potato*, f) *repeat*, wherein strongly aspirated [p^h] shows the same distribution. [h] is also marginally present foot-medially (*mayhem, Meehan*), which position is also characterised by (reduced) aspiration. This structural parallel, despite the difference in phonological status between [h] and aspiration (e.g. /p/, though non-aspirated, does at least occur word-and-foot-medially, whereas [h] does not; word- or foot-initially [h] contrasts with ϕ and [p^h] and with [b]), does at least suggest a reinterpretation of [h] compared with what seems to be appropriate to its patterning in OE. Notice too that in South African English (at least) it is arguable that 'ϕ' is realised word-initially as [ʔ] (Lass 1983).

Already in Middle English [h] is typically spelled differently from [x] (and whatever other variants we can associate with the development of OE [x]). But for the most part (though cf. the system of *The Owl and the Nightingale* alluded to above), this is in itself scarcely evidence for a change in phonemic status at that point, rather than a reflection of a changed scribal practice, or indicating perhaps at most 'the loosening of the allophonic relationship between the two sounds' (Vachek 1964: 12), if that means anything. It certainly gives us no motivation for suggesting for OE a phoneme /h/, distinct from /x/.

16. In Present-day English initial [ð] is limited to a few closed-class words, and so marginally contrastive (*thy* vs. *thigh*), and instances of medial [θ] are not numerous (*Ethel, methyl, ether*, and a few others, mainly scientific loans). Final [ð] is perhaps more evident, but much concentrated in derived verbs (*seethe, bathe*, etc.).

17. The representation in (33.b) allows for the fact that the dependent |C| may either occur alone or in combination, with another |V|. Thus, nasals are differentiated (apart from by presence of a nasal gesture) from liquids as {|V⇉C|} vs. {|V⇉C,V|}, which reflects among other things the higher status of liquids on the sonority hierarchy (see further below; and, for more detailed discussion, Ewen 1977, 1980: §6.1, 1982, Anderson and Ewen to 1987: ch.4). Notice that the representation for liquids introduces a second |V|. As indicated above, this seems to represent an absolute limit: no more than two tokens of the same component may appear in a single gesture, and even then one must be (asymmetrically) dependent on the other, or simply juxtaposed in the absence of the other component: {|V,V|}, for example, is a tense vowel (Anderson to appear). The characterisation for voiced fricatives proposed below utilises the same capacity, within the same limits.

18. See e.g. Anderson and Jones 1977, Anderson and Ewen 1980b: §4.1, 1987: ch.4, Ewen 1977, 1980: §6.3 (and on markedness §6.2), 1982, Davenport and Staun 1980, Ó Dochartaigh 1980, Jones 1976.

19. The presence of a dependent |V| is associated with voice only in the case of obstruents (segments which are {⇄ C}): a voiced obstruent is {C⇉ V}. Voice in sonorants ({C⇄}) is usually non-contrastive; and no such specification is necessary. However, the class of voiced segments can be characterised in terms of the notation {⇄V}, i.e. |V| either unilaterally governs (including nothing) or depends; a voiced consonant is {C⇄ V}. The latter specification excludes voiceless fricatives and plosives, in which either |C| and |V| are equipollent or |C| appears alone. See further Anderson to appear.

20. This specification assumes that /s/ and /θ/ are distinguished (whatever else differentiates sibilants from other fricatives) at least by place of articulation. |d| also distinguishes, where necessary, between bilabials {|u|} and labiodentals {|u,d|}.

21. [dʒ] appears to be a variant of //G// and /j/ occurring after nasals and in gemination. As a variant of /j/ it is in contrast with [g] in these positions after front vowels: cf. *senġan* 'single', *singan* 'sing'; *fenġ* 'grasp', *feng* 'took'; *secġan* 'say', *eggjan* 'excite', *(ear)wicga* 'earwig'. But since the affricate phonemicises in final position on degemination (thus *wecġ* 'wedge' —contrast *weġ* 'way' —and *bryċġ* 'bridge' —Moulton 1954: 25), /j/ elsewhere, realised as [j] or [dʒ], should be regarded as an 'archi-segment'.

REFERENCES

Abercrombie, David 1965. A phonetician's view of verse structure. Ch.3 of *Studies in phonetics and linguistics*. London: Oxford University Press.

Anderson, John M. 1969. Syllabic or non-syllabic phonology? *Journal of Linguistics* 5. 136–42.

Anderson, John M. 1980. On the internal structure of phonological segments: Evidence from English and its history. *Folia Linguistica Historica* 1. 165–91.

Anderson, John M., ed. 1982. *Language form and linguistic variation: Papers dedicated to Angus McIntosh*. Amsterdam: John Benjamins.

Anderson, John M. 1986. Suprasegmental dependencies. In Durand, 55–133.

Anderson, John M. to appear. The essentially concrete character of dependency phonology. In Festschrift for Robert P. Stockwell.

Anderson, John M. and Colin J. Ewen, eds. 1980a. *Studies in dependency phonology*. Ludwigsburg studies in language and linguistics, 4.

Anderson, John M. and Colin J. Ewen 1980b. Introduction to Anderson and Ewen 1980a: A sketch of dependency phonology, 9–40.

Anderson, John M. and Colin J. Ewen 1981. The representation of neutralisation in universal phonology. *Phonologica 1980*, 15–22.

Anderson, John M. and Colin J. Ewen 1987. *Principles of dependency phonology*. Cambridge: Cambridge University Press.

Anderson, John M. and Charles Jones 1974. Three theses concerning phonological representations. *Journal of Linguistics* 10. 1–26.

Anderson, John M. and Charles Jones 1977. *Phonological structure and the history of English*. Amsterdam: North-Holland.

Campbell, A. 1959. *Old English Grammar*. London: Oxford University Press.

Colman, Fran 1981. A philological study of the moneyer's names on coins of Edward the Confessor. D.Phil. thesis, University of Oxford.

Colman, Fran 1983. 'Vocalisation' as nucleation. *Studia Linguistica* 37. 34–51.

Davenport, Mike and Jørgen Staun 1980. A Grimm fairy tale med (måske) en Rask slutning. In Anderson and Ewen 1980a, 205–25.

Durand, Jacques, ed. 1986. *Dependency and non-linear phonology*. London: Croom Helm.

Ewen, Colin J. 1977. Aitken's Law and the phonatory gesture in dependency phonology. *Lingua* 45. 141–73.

Ewen, Colin J. 1980. Aspects of phonological structure with particular reference to English and Dutch. Ph.D. thesis, University of Edinburgh.

Ewen, Colin J. 1982. The phonology of the Welsh mutations. In Anderson, 75–95.

Fisiak, Jacek 1968. *A short grammar of Middle English, I*. Warsaw: Państwowe Wydawnictwo Naukowe.

Hogg, Richard M. 1979. Old English palatalization. *Transactions of the Philological Society*, 89–113.

Hogg, Richard M. 1982. Two geminate consonants in Old English? In Anderson, 187–202.

Jones, Charles 1976. Some constraints on medial consonant clusters. *Language* 52. 121–30.

Klaeber, F. 1950. *Beowulf and the Fight at Finnsburg*, 2nd edn. Boston, Mass.: D. C. Heath.

Kuhn, Sherman M. 1970. On the consonantal phonemes of Old English. In *Philological essays: Studies in Old and Middle English language and literature in honor of Herbert Dean Meritt*, ed. by James L. Rosier, 18–49. The Hague: Mouton.

Kurath, Hans 1956. The loss of long consonants and the rise of voiced fricatives in Middle English. *Language* 32. 435–45. Reprinted in Lass 1969a, 142–53.

Lass, Roger ed. 1969a. *Approaches to English historical linguistics*. New York: Holt,

Rinehart and Winston.

Lass, Roger 1969b. Introduction to Lass 1969a, 3–5.

Lass, Roger 1976. On the phonological characterization of [ʔ] and [h]. Ch. 6 of *English phonology and phonological theory*. Cambridge: Cambridge University Press.

Lass, Roger 1983: Glottal stop and syllable structure in South African English; with a note on Germanic alliteration. MS.

Lass, Roger 1984. *Phonology: An introduction to basic concepts*. Cambridge: Cambridge University Press.

Lass, Roger and John M. Anderson 1975. *Old English phonology*. Cambridge: Cambridge University Press.

Luick, Karl 1914–1940. *Historische Grammatik der englischen Sprache, I*. Leipzig.

Martinet, André 1936. Neutralisation et archiphonème. *Travaux du cercle linguistique de Prague* **6**. 46–57.

Moulton, William G. 1954. The stops and spirants of early Germanic. *Language* **30**. 1–42.

Moulton, William G. 1972. The Proto-Germanic non-syllabics (consonants). In *Toward a grammar of Proto-Germanic*, ed. by Frans van Coetsem and Herbert L. Kufner, 141–73. Tübingen: Niemeyer.

Ó Dochartaigh, Cathair 1980. Aspects of Celtic lenition. In Anderson and Ewen 1980a, 103–37.

Pheifer, J. D. 1974. *Old English glosses in the Epinal-Erfurt glossary*. London: Oxford University Press.

Pilch, Herbert 1970. *Altenglische Grammatik*. München: Hueber.

Sledd, James 1953. Some questions of English phonology. *Language* **34**. 252–58.

Staun, Jørgen 1983. The Old English obstruent system and its history: A dependency account. *Studia Linguistica* **37**. 9–29.

Stockwell, Robert P. and C. W. Barritt 1961. Scribal practice: Some assumptions. *Language* **37**. 75–82. Reprinted in Lass 1969a, 133–41.

Sweet, Henry 1882. *Anglo-Saxon primer*. London: Oxford University Press.

Trubetzkoy, N. 1939. *Grundzüge der Phonologie*. Travaux du cercle linguistique de Prague 7.

Vachek, J. 1964. The elimination of the Modern English /h/-phoneme: Ch. 4 of On peripheral phonemes of Modern English. *Brno Studies in English* **4**. 9–21.

4

THAT: A RELATIVE PRONOUN? SOCIOLINGUISTICS AND SYNTACTIC ANALYSIS

Jim Miller

The analysis of English relative clauses is not straightforward. Particular controversy is caused by relative clauses introduced by *that*: is the latter word a pronoun or a conjunction/complementiser? Van der Auwera (1985) provides a critique of the many arguments that have been deployed in support of the various analyses and concludes that the relativiser *that* (henceforth *R-that*, in contradistinction to the complementiser *C-that*) is a highly pronominal relativiser. It is not, however, completely pronominal, as it has developed from a Middle English constituent that was not a pronoun.

The analysis of *that* as a complementiser/conjunction has much to recommend it, but an argument to that effect is not the main concern of this study. What is of concern is that Van der Auwera (henceforth VdA) does not take into account recent work on non-standard English demonstrating that standard written English differs greatly from all varieties of non-standard English with respect to all major areas of grammar, including relative clauses. VdA employs data from standard and non-standard English, from various geographical varieties of the latter and from spoken and written standard English. The problem is that he draws his data from different SYSTEMS and is comparing what cannot be compared.

The point is not new, but it has become very clear to linguists investigating spoken English and non-standard English — hence the presence of socio-linguistics in the title. Before examining VdA's account, let me make some remarks on sociolinguistics and on the reason for choosing Scottish English as an example of non-standard English.

The scope and quality of sociolinguistic research in Britain have changed considerably over the last fifteen years. Not only has there been sociolinguistic research in the strict sense of correlating social and linguistic variables, but researchers have collected and described syntactic data from non-standard varieties of English. The latter achievement is significant: it places new variables at the disposal of sociolinguists and reveals the extent of grammatical differences between (written) Standard English and other varieties. Just as importantly, it bears on the question of how syntactic analyses are established for a particular language and indeed on the question of whether one can write a grammar of a language (as opposed to describing one variety of a given language at a time).

The most detailed work has been carried out on Scottish English, partly because research into the modern language has been able to build on a long tradition of linguistic investigation: ranging from work on the language of mediaeval Scottish literature, as in the various publications last century and earlier this century of the Scottish History Society, to descriptions of modern dialects. Much of the modern work has been concerned with phonology and morphology, but many syntactic facts are to be found in the *Scottish National Dictionary* and there are two major grammatical descriptions that provide points of orientation: Murray (1873) and Wilson (1915).

As a result of recent work on the syntax of Scottish English and on a number of other varieties of English, one view now emerging is that the non-standard spoken varieties of English have much in common, in contradistinction to the standard written language. This fact is important, because most descriptions of English, including generative ones, are based on written English. When spoken language is taken into account, usually a few 'odd' examples are cited but there is no mention of the view that spoken and written English might have different grammatical systems.

It might be expected that, compared with the complexity of standard written English, the non-standard varieties would pose a simpler task of description. This is not so. With respect to Scottish English, one problem is lack of homogeneity. At the very least, we need to draw a distinction between Broad Scots and standard written English. Broad Scots is the language of the urban and rural working class. (For present purposes, I will ignore the existence of geographical varieties within Scottish English.) On the basis of various sources — a recent SSRC-funded investigation into the syntax of Scottish English, radio and TV documentaries, information from teachers of English in primary and secondary schools, an on-going investigation of Glasgow English (Macafee 1984) — it is possible to postulate a grammar of Broad Scots. The word 'postulate' is used advisedly. In the nature of things we cannot analyse all the spoken output of all speakers. We can only examine some of the output of some speakers and work out hypothetical generalisations that are subject to revision as more data is collected.

Broad Scots is one pole of a continuum with standard written English at the other pole. Educated Scots employ a mixture of the two: some constructions occur both in Broad Scots and in the speech of educated people, whereas others are shunned by educated speakers. Double negatives and double modals fall into the latter category. Rather than attempt to establish intermediate varieties, it is easier to regard Scottish speakers as drawing on the two extreme varieties, though many speakers are not in a position to draw on standard written English to any great extent.

Before examining VdA's arguments, we can usefully look at some facts from Broad Scots. The spoken data analysed by the SSRC-funded project mentioned above demonstrates that the speakers in the one hundred hours of informal conversation introduce relative clauses with *that* (where there is an introducing constituent). Regardless of whether the relative clause modifies a human or non-human, animate or inanimate noun, the relativiser is *that*. Where the relative clause has to do with possession, the construction is *that* + possessive pronoun:

the man that his arm was broken. Which does occur, but in clauses relating to an entire event or proposition: *Her father likes rock music which is really peculiar.* What is peculiar is not rock music but her father liking rock music.

As in all varieties of English, the relativiser can be omitted in examples as *the programme I watched.* In Broad Scots the relativiser can also be omitted in relative clauses modifying the NP in the existential construction THERE BE NP . . .: *There's a man in our street has a Jaguar.* Note also existential-like constructions introduced by NP HAVE . . .: *I had a witch fell down a trap* (spoken by a theatre manager). ((IV) below contains further comments on the omission of the relativiser.)

Far from being peculiar to Broad Scots, the system outlined above is typical of many geographical varieties of English, though other constructions occur in England: *he's a man as likes his beer, he's a man what likes his beer* and *he's a man likes his beer* (Exx. from Trudgill, 1974).

The facts from the conversations studied by the SSRC project match exactly the accounts of relative clauses in Murray (1873) and Wilson (1915). They jibe with the informal impressions of scholars working on Scottish English (cf. Romaine 1981) and of school teachers. Even more interesting, within Scotland the system is typical not just of Broad Scots but of the spoken language of many educated speakers: the construction with *that* + possessive pronoun is very frequent.

In writing, on the other hand, Scottish speakers favour the relative construction with *who, which, whose.* This is evident from essays written by secondary school pupils and from undergraduate assignments. Certain arbiters of style (e.g. Fowler and Fowler (1938: 89–91) prescribe the use of *that* and *wh* words thus: *that* for restrictive relative clauses, *who*, etc. for non-restrictive relative clauses. Be that as it may, the preferred written variant, restrictive or non-restrictive, is *who, which.*

We can now examine VdA's arguments. I. One argument in support of the view that *R-that* is not a pronoun is that prepositions cannot precede it but are stranded at the end of the relative clause: **the book in that the article was published/the book that the article was published in.* VdA (p. 151) suggests that *R-that* may be a pronoun but not a prototypical one. He comments that if *wh*-relativisers are to be characterised as allowing both preposition-stranding and preposition-movement — cf. *the book in which the article was published/the book which the article was published in* — then a difficulty is presented by the infinitive relatives in (1).

(1.a) I found an usher from whom to buy tickets
  b) **I found an usher whom to buy tickets from*

Two comments are appropriate. The first is that even (1a) is horrendous. The second is that the handling of infinitive relatives in terms of *wh* movement is peculiar to the Government and Binding model of Chomsky. In practice, infinitive relatives have no *wh* relativiser. Typical of spoken English, Broad Scots or otherwise, is: *an usher to buy tickets from.* (1a) should not be seen as part of the same system as the last example, which occurs in both spoken and written English; (1a), if it occurs at all, belongs to a highly formal variety which nobody learns from their parents' spoken language and which is not regularly used even in written English.

II. *R-that* is not sensitive to gender, but neither, observes VdA, is *whose* — and neither was *which* at one time. VdA argues (p. 153) that in any case *R-that* is not completely insensitive to gender. He cites studies by Malmberg (1947) and Quirk (1957) which show that relative clauses introduced by *that* typically modify a non-human antecedent. This may be true of written English, where there is in general a preference for the *wh* forms, but it is certainly not true of Broad Scots or the informal speech of educated speakers, and seems not to be true of spoken English in general.

III. The occurrence of shadow pronouns, as in *the book that I asked you to look for it*, has been used to support the analysis of *R-that* as a conjunction. VdA's riposte (p. 156) is that *wh* relatives have shadow pronouns. One of his sources, Geoghegan (1975), is not available to me at the time of writing, but his other source, Jespersen (1927), is. Geoghegan's examples, certainly those from Old and Middle English, must be from written texts, and Jespersen's examples are from dialogues in novels.

The imitation of spoken language in literature raises problems of interpretation: how accurate is the author's rendering of spoken language?; what social class does the fictional character belong to? Such examples fall into a different class from spontaneous conversation by real speakers. The data available to me suggest that the combination of *who* + shadow pronoun is untypical, because *who* is confined to written language and formal speech, varieties that are usually very carefully monitored by writer and speaker. The combination is not attested at all in the Scottish English data.

Suppose, however, that examples with *who* or *which* + shadow pronoun were indeed common among some speakers. VdA claims that nobody would use such examples as evidence that *which* and *who* are not pronominal. A number of examples in the SSRC corpus suggest, on the contrary, that *which* can function as a conjunction. The best example is (2).

(2)   you can leave at Christmas if your birthday's in December to February which I think is wrong like my birthday's March and I have to stay on to May which when I'm 16 in March I could be looking for a job.

The interesting feature is the second occurrence of *which*. It does not refer back to anything in the text, but can be seen as referring back to the entire preceding chunk of text. It functions like a conjunction, signalling a connection between the preceding text and following text, and it is widespread in Scottish English. (Although examples are not publicly available on tape, I have heard many occurrences of the 'conjunction' *which* in radio interviews.)

In spite of VdA's dismissal of such an analysis as preposterous, it is quite natural in the light of what we know about spoken and written language. It is common knowledge that clauses are more closely integrated in written than in spoken language. It is also common knowledge that the change from pronoun to conjunction is typical of Indo-European. (Cf. the *OED* entry for *that*.)

This use of *which* is far from new. I had myself noted occurrences of a 'conjunction' *which* in Mr Wegg's speech in *Our Mutual Friend*, but Kjellmer (1986) points out that the usage is found in Swift and had become so frequent by the nineteenth century that it served as a hallmark of non-standard speech in magazines such as *Punch*. Kjellmer's data confirm that this usage — like a number of other usages in spoken English — is not a mere accident of performance but rather a long-standing and enduring construction of the spoken language.

The upshot of the discussion is this. We record examples such as (3).

(3)　they sent it to my old address which I hadn't been there for two years

Is *which* a relative pronoun and is the occurrence of *there* an accident? Or is *which* a relativiser (but not a pronoun) introducing a relative clause? Or do we consider the two clauses as independent, with *which* functioning merely as a conjunction? The essential point is that the analysis of spoken language is far more subtle and problematic than VdA imagines: the analysis of *which* as a conjunction he dismisses as improbable; but it is quite plausible for spoken English.

IV. Both *R-that* and *C-that* (complementiser) are deletable, as in (4).

(4.a)　I know the man (that) you mentioned
　　b)　I know (that) Antwerp has a harbour

VdA (p. 160) observes that *R-that* and *C-that* delete under different conditions. *R-that* deletes freely when the relativised constituent is the object of the relative clause, as in (4a), but not when it is the subject of the relative clause. In the latter case, *R-that* deletes only in existential sentences, as in (5).

(5)　There is a man (that) wants to speak to you

VdA suggests that this zero relativisation is very restricted, serves a very specific focusing function and is typically colloquial. It is unclear whether VdA is being neutral or dismissive when he mentions the colloquial nature of the construction. It is indeed colloquial, which is grist to our mill: written and spoken English have different systems of relativisation. Just how restricted this zero relativisation is cannot be accurately stated at the moment: examples such as VdA's (38b),* *I met the woman loves John* do occur in spoken English, but their frequency is not known, nor is it clear to me whether zero relativisation is possible when the entire NP is in subject position, as in (6).

(6)　The woman loves John is very keen on dancing

Again, whether the structure is restricted depends on whether written or spoken language is under analysis.

VdA's comment on the focusing function is incorrect. The structure could express contrastive focus if contrastive stress were placed on *man* in (5). Without the contrastive stress the construction is merely existential, serving to introduce an entity into the universe of discourse. In this existential construction, zero

E

relativisation is the norm in all spoken varieties of Scottish English and in many other spoken varieties of English. It may indeed be the norm in spoken English as a whole.

V. VdA (p. 154) counters the argument that *R-that* is not a pronoun because it does not display the case contrasts typical of English pronouns, as in *he/him/his, who/whom/whose*, etc. He mentions the loss of *whom*, which does not affect the pronominal status of *who*. But, as stated in III, it is possible that the relativiser *who* could lose its pronominal status, though this change seems more appropriate to *which*. Since *who* is still confined to human nouns, it is not appropriate for the linking of pieces of inanimate text.

VdA suggests that *whose* could be regarded as a suppletive genitive of *R-that*. This suggestion does not apply to Broad Scots, where *whose* does not occur as a relative pronoun. More generally, *whose* is rare in many geographical varieties of English. It is, of course, found in the spoken language of educated people, but here we immediately meet the problem of whether such speakers have developed an intermediate variety of English or whether they merely draw more heavily on standard written English.

VdA adds to his counter-argument by referring to the Scots relativiser *that's*, which he describes as having a case marking. Once more there are problems of analysis. Is *that's* to be analysed as a genitive form or as a coalescence of *that + his/its*? Whatever the answer, *that's* no longer occurs, at least in recently recorded data. What does occur is *that* + full possessive pronoun. In these circumstances, if *that's* did occur it would probably be regarded as deriving from *that + his/its*.

VI. VdA, and other linguists, refer to restrictive and non-restrictive relatives. *That* does occur in non-restrictive relatives, though *who* is typical in written English. In informal spoken English non-restrictive relatives with *who* or *that* are so rare that they could be regarded as non-existent. The typical way of presenting the parenthetical information that is conveyed in written English by non-restrictive relative clauses is to use a clause introduced by *and* or zero. Cf. (7).

(7)   the boy I was talking to last night — (and) he actually works in the yard — was saying it's going to be closed down.

Conclusion

It would be foolish to suggest that confining one's attention to Broad Scots or to formal written English will cleanse the data of vagueness. Clear-cut data do not come the linguist's way very frequently. However, the analysis of *R-that* as a complementiser is attractive for Broad Scots, and the analysis of *wh* words as pronouns is attractive for formal written English. Difficulties appear wherever speakers draw on two varieties. (It is worthwhile drawing attention to the work of Romaine (1981), who demonstrates that the tension between the use of *that* and *wh* words was present in Scottish English as long ago as the sixteenth century, and that relative clauses in sixteenth-century informal Scottish English possessed the same characteristics as those mentioned above.)

One last comment in connection with different varieties of English. In some varieties — in southern England — *as* introduces both relative clauses and verb complement clauses, as in (8).

(8.a)   They say as he's lost his nerve
   b)   He's a man as likes his beer

VdA is inconsistent in his treatment of cross-variety or cross-language data, sometimes appealing to it (p. 152) and sometimes dismissing it (p. 162). Of course the facts of southern varieties of English do not prove anything about other varieties. But the fact that in each variety one and the same item can introduce both relative clauses and verb complement clauses does make more plausible the analysis of *R-that* as conjunction or complementiser.

It is time to reassert a commonplace of traditional philological descriptions of languages: different varieties of English (or German or Classical Greek) are employed in different contexts. The analyst must state whether the description relates to a geographical variety as recorded among manual workers in pubs, in the poetry of Douglas Dunn, the prose of Bernard Levin or examples in the writings of generative linguists. With the exception of Klima (1964), the commonplace has been lost in generative work. This is regrettable, because the distinctions bear, not just on analyses of English, but on the general issue of explanatory adequacy and language acquisition. As linguists digest the work on non-standard varieties of English, their approach not just to specific analytical problems but also to the general issue should become less dogmatic.

REFERENCES

Fowler, H. W. and Fowler, F. G. 1938. *The King's English.* Oxford: Clarendon Press.

Geoghegan, S. G. 1975. Relative clauses in Old, Middle and New English. *Ohio State University Working Papers in Linguistics* 18. 30–71.

Jespersen, O. 1927. *A Modern English grammar on historical principles.* Vol.III. Heidelberg: Carl Winter.

Kjellmer, G. 1986. Conjunctional/adverbial *which* in substandard English. Paper read at the International Conference on Historical Dialectology, Blażejewko, 7th–10th May.

Klima, E. S. 1964. Relatedness between grammatical systems. *Language* 40. 1–20.

Macafee, C. 1984. *Glasgow.* Varieties of English around the World, 3. Amsterdam: John Benjamin.

Malmberg, B. 1947. Till fragan om who eller that efter personliga korrelat. *M. Språk* 41. 197–216.

Murray, J. 1873. *The Dialect of the Southern Counties of Scotland.* London.

Quirk, R. 1957. Relative clauses in educated spoken English. *English Studies* 38. 97–109.

Romaine, S. 1981. Syntactic complexity, relativisation and stylistic levels in Middle Scots. *Folia Linguistica Historica* 2. 71–97.

Trudgill, P. 1983. *Sociolinguistics,* Harmondsworth: Pelican.

Van der Auwera, J. 1985. Relative *that* — a centennial dispute. *Journal of Linguistics* 21. 149–79.

Wilson, Sir James 1915. *Lowland Scotch as spoken in the Lower Strathearn District of Perthshire.* Oxford: OUP.

5

THE NOT-SO-SCOTTISH VOWEL LENGTH RULE*

Alex Agutter

1 Introduction

1.1 Background

Vowel length differences have been observed in Scots dialects over a long period. Earlier studies relating to specific dialects, including the Scots-influenced dialects of the Belfast area (Patterson 1860; Dieth 1932; Wettstein 1942; Zai 1942) and the soon-to-be-published phonological data from the Linguistic Survey of Scotland, provided information from which Aitken (1962, 1975, 1981, 1984a, b) has induced the Scottish Vowel Length Rule (SVLR). The importance of this rule is twofold. First, by structuring the data in terms of a historical-phonological rule, it provides a framework in which dialectally disparate vowel-length data can be viewed coherently. Second, it is of significance for historical phonologists because it emphasises that vowel length in Scots, unlike that in other dialects of English, is phonetic not phonemic (see section 2.1.2), suggesting a more advanced stage of simplification of the vowel inventory than is found in other dialects of English (Lass 1974, 1976).

The continued operation of SVLR in Modern Scots, including for so-called Standard Scots or Scottish Standard English (SSE) speakers, is claimed by Abercrombie (1979), Aitken (1979, 1981, 1984a, b), McClure (1977) and Wells (1982). Its influence, though not its complete operation, is observed in Belfast accents by Milroy (1981) and Harris (1985). Of these studies, only that of McClure (1977) is based on machine measurement of vowel length data. However, it is clear from the accounts given of SVLR that it is considered by its proponents to describe objectively-measurable vowel length differences. Indeed, as vowel length according to this rule need never be lexically determined in Scots but depends entirely on phonetic context, it follows that perceptually significant vowel quantity differences must be objectively measurable in different phonetic contexts.

1.2 Formulation of the SVLR

The general form of the rule can be summarised as follows. Stressed vowels are long

---

* I am grateful to Roger Lass and John Anderson for their comments on this paper.

— before a morpheme boundary
— before /r⁺, v⁺, ð⁺, ʒ⁺, z⁺ / (where ⁺ indicates a morpheme boundary)
— in hiatus
and non-long elsewhere.

As Aitken (1981) makes clear in the most detailed account of the operation of SVLR to date, there are exceptions and modifications to this basic formulation. Four vowels are normally excluded from the rule. The reflexes of Early Scots /i/ and /u/ (Present-day Scots /ɪ/ and /ʌ/) are non-long irrespective of phonetic context. The diphthongal reflex of Early Scots /ai/ and the various reflexes of Early Scots /au/ (Present-day Scots /ai/; and /a/ or /ɔ/) are usually long irrespective of context. In addition, Aitken comments on a number of dialect-specific amendments to the rule, especially in relation to peripheral parts of the Scots-speaking area. Harris (1985) discusses the partial operation of the rule in Belfast partly in terms of Belfast's peripheral position in the Scots dialect area.

Provided such amendments are borne in mind, it is clear that SVLR gives rise to predictions about relative vowel length of the same vowel in different phonetic contexts, and that these predictions can be treated by objective measurement. For example, the vowel in *teethe* should be measurably longer than the vowel in *teeth*. Aitken's (1981) formulation of SVLR includes a statement of which vowels are affected by the rule in terms of their ancestor phonemes in Early Scots. Although it is not clear that historical development is crucial in the operation of the rule in Present-day SSE I have assumed that for true comparability potential minimal pairs must not only have the same modern reflex phoneme but also an identical phoneme in Early Scots. It is obviously important to bear these issues in mind when words are being selected for an experimental study. Also, although SVLR predicts relative lengths of the same vowel in different phonetic contexts, it does not necessarily make predictions about the relative lengths of different SVLR-affected vowels in the same phonetic context; nor does it predict absolute vowel durations (Agutter 1988).

In the following section, I describe an empirical study in which some SVLR-affected and some SVLR-nonaffected vowels were measured in a variety of SVLR long and non-long contexts.

2 Methods

2.1 Linguistic material investigated

2.1.1 Vowels. Five phonemes were selected to illustrate the range of vowels reported to be affected and non-affected by SVLR according to the account given in Aitken (1981). One, /ɪ/, is always short and is not affected by SVLR; one, /ɔ/, is generally long and not affected by SVLR; and three, /ai/, /i/, and /au/ (from Early Scots /u:/), are reported to be affected by SVLR. /ɪ/ is also regarded as a short vowel in RP (contrasting with /i/) and /ɔ/ is regarded as a long vowel in RP (contrasting with /ɒ/: N.B. this contrast does not occur in a typical SSE accent: Abercrombie 1979). One would expect general agreement between RP and SSE

F

accents for these two vowels: /ɪ/ should be short in both and /ɔ/ should be long in both. The other three vowels /ai/, /i/ and /au/ should show context-dependent length differences as specified by SVLR in SSE accents. Context-dependent vowel length differences in RP are discussed below.

The other main criterion in selection was this. For each of the vowels studied, the ancestral vowel in Early Scots was the same for all of the monosyllables used.

2.1.2 Phonetic contexts. The phonetic contexts selected included six that are designated long by SVLR: –+, /–+d/, /–r⁺/, /–v⁺/, /–ð⁺/, /–z⁺/; and seven that are designated non-long by SVLR: /–d⁺/, /–b⁺/, /–n⁺/, /–t⁺/, /–p⁺/, /–s⁺/, /–f⁺/. Some phonetic contexts are well known to affect vowel length in American and RP accents of English. For example, according to Chen (1970), American accents of English have a vowel length hierarchy as follows: longest vowels in open syllables; next longest, preceding voiced consonants; shortest, preceding voiceless consonants. This is broadly in agreement with what Gimson (1972: 96–98) says of vowel length in RP. Since all the SVLR long contexts are also long contexts for these other accents of English, it seemed reasonable to predict that the measured vowel lengths would not differ significantly in these long contexts between the accents studied. Among the SVLR non-long contexts selected, however, are three (/b⁺/, /d⁺/ and /n⁺/) which, as voiced consonants, are predicted as long for accents of English other than Scots. It can therefore be predicted that these three contexts will provide noticeable contrasts between the vowel lengths of RP and SSE speakers. The other four SVLR non-long contexts are voiceless consonants, and would therefore be predicted as non-long for RP as well. It was assumed that vowel duration is not significantly affected by preceding consonants (Peterson and Lehiste 1960).

Only monosyllables in English were chosen. The monosyllables selected, and their relationships to the vowels and the contexts discussed above, are shown in Table 1.

TABLE 1

The monosyllables used in this study, shown here in a vowel × context matrix.

Context	/ai/	/i/	/au/	/ɔ/	/ɪ/
–++	Sigh	Tea	Cow	Saw	
/–+d/	Sighed	Tee'd	Cowed	Sawed	
/–t/	Sight	Beet	Tout	Naught	Bit
/–d/	Side	Feed	Dowd	Bawd	Bid
/–r/	Dire	Beer	Hour		Sir
/–n/	Dine	Keen	Town	Dawn	Sin
/–v/	Dive	Peeve		Mauve	Give
/–ð/	Tithe	Teethe	Mouthe		
/–z/	Rise	Freeze	Rouse	Pause	Liz
/–p/	Type	Keep		Gawp	Dip
/–b/	Jibe			Daub	Dib
/–s/	Vice	Geese	Louse		Kiss
/–f/	Fife	Beef			Tiff

2.1.3 Linguistic frames. The monosyllables selected were read in the same invariant frame sentence as that used by McClure (1977): "I say WORD sometimes". An invariant frame sentence was used to minimise variation in intonation patterns between the different monosyllables. Variation in speed of speech can be caused by either increasing facility of reading the examples or, conversely, increasing fatigue of the informant. Such variation could obviously introduce serious errors into measurements of vowel length. Two controls were used to prevent this: not all the informants read the sentence-list in the same order; and the duration of the frame sentence itself could be checked.

2.2 Informants

Six informants, male and female, aged 18–23 years, were recorded individually in a soundproofed recording studio. The informants comprised two speakers (one male, one female) of RP and four speakers (two male, two female) of SSE. All six informants were students, and all would be designated middle-class by other commonly-applied criteria such as father's occupation, type and extent of schooling, etc. All the SSE speakers had resided in Edinburgh all their lives. The RP speakers were from different parts of the UK. None of the six informants knew the purpose of the investigation until they were de-briefed at the end of the recording session.

2.3 Measurement of vowel lengths

The recorded sentence-list from each informant was analysed using a Digital Sona-Graph 7800 and Sona-Graph Printer 7900 (Kay Elemetrics Corp., Pine Brook, New Jersey).[1] Vowel length was measured to the nearest 1 centisecond (csec) from the printed sound spectrograms. Aspiration was considered to be part of the consonant and was not included in vowel duration (Chen 1970). Triplicate measurements of the vowel in the same monosyllable from the same informant were found to agree to +/- 1 csec.

2.4 Analysis of results

2.4.1 Dependence of vowel length on phonetic context: calculation of length index. For each of the six informants, the length of each vowel in each context was recorded. In addition, the overall average vowel length was calculated to the nearest 0.1 csec for each informant. These data are presented in Table 2a, and were used to calculate the length index of each context. The calculation was performed as follows.

(a) For a particular group of informants (RP, SSE, or all six combined) the average duration (the v-con value) of each vowel in each context was calculated to the nearest 0.1 csec. For instance, the appropriate v-con value for /ai/ in the context /–t$^+$/ for all six speakers is the average of the six values in the row corresponding to *sight* in Table 2a.

(b) For each of the five vowels, all the relevant v-con values were averaged to give the v-tot value. For instance, the v-tot value for /ai/ over all six informants is in effect the average of the 77 numbers in the first 13 rows of Table 2a.

(c) Each v-con was divided by the corresponding v-tot. For each context, up to five of these ratios was generated. The (v-con/v-tot) values for each context were averaged. Such an average is the length index of the particular context. Clearly, a

TABLE 2a

Vowel lengths (csec) for each informant for each monosyllable. The average vowel length for each informant is given at the end of the Table. Key: V = vowel. Con = phonetic context.

MONO-SYLLABLE	V	Con	RP				SSE	
Sigh	/ai/	−+	26	25	24	23	28	29
Sighed		−+d	24	28	26	25	30	27
Sight		−t	18	15	12	16	16	14
Side		−d	22	22	18	22	24	21
Dire		−r	20	22	18	24	24	27
Dine		−n	19	21	17	19	23	17
Dive		−v	30	22	26	25	34	32
Tithe		−ð	32	24	24	28	—	29
Rise		−z	30	23	26	28	30	28
Type		−p	15	14	15	15	14	10
Jibe		−b	24	20	20	24	30	23
Vice		−s	14	13	15	17	17	12
Fife		−f	17	14	15	15	19	15
Tea	/i/	−+	14	14	22	14	26	20
Tee'd		−+d	18	17	20	17	20	18
Beet		−t	13	12	12	10	10	8
Feed		−d	11	16	15	10	12	7
Beer		−r	20	20	22	16	16	16
Keen		−n	17	11	8	8	9	6
Peeve		−v	22	16	16	16	22	20
Teethe		−ð	12	15	19	16	19	—
Freeze		−z	24	21	26	21	22	20
Keep		−p	7	9	8	6	6	8
Geese		−s	14	12	10	10	9	7
Beef		−f	9	11	11	10	6	8
Cow	/au/	−+	23	25	23	21	22	25
Cowed		−+d	23	24	22	23	25	26
Tout		−t	15	13	17	15	16	10
Dowd		−d	27	25	20	23	29	26
Hour		−r	31	26	13	21	17	17
Town		−n	18	18	16	15	14	13
Mouthe		−ð	17	18	25	17	—	—
Rouse		−z	26	22	17	22	29	—
Louse		−s	19	19	14	18	15	14
Saw	/ɔ/	−+	21	24	26	20	22	25
Sawed		−+d	22	24	22	20	21	18
Naught		−t	16	12	19	12	18	16
Bawd		−d	23	21	20	18	23	19
Dawn		−n	17	16	24	19	22	22
Mauve		−v	19	—	23	—	24	20
Pause		−z	21	22	22	19	23	22
Gawp		−p	20	14	16	13	16	12
Daub		−b	23	20	21	19	20	19
Bit	/ɪ/	−t	10	11	9	7	6	5
Bid		−d	16	10	9	9	9	8

TABLE 2a continued

MONO-SYLLABLE	V	Con	RP			SSE		
Sir		−r	13	13	14	12	11	9
Sin		−n	10	6	8	8	7	5
Give		−v	15	13	15	10	14	8
Liz		−z	13	11	12	12	12	10
Dip		−p	14	12	7	7	7	5
Dib		−b	12	12	9	8	8	7
Kiss		−s	12	10	9	9	7	7
Tiff		−f	10	10	10	—	7	—
AVERAGE LENGTH:			18.6	17.1	17.1	16.3	17.8	16.1

length index greater than 1 characterises a phenomenologically long context; an index of less than one characterises a short (non-long) context.

(d) Table 2b gives the (v-con/v-tot) values and the length indices of all the contexts used calculated over all six informants.

TABLE 2b

The (v–con/v–tot) values and the length indices (L) for each of the contexts investigated, determined over all six informants studied. The values are not markedly different for the RP and the SSE informants calculated separately (see sections 3.1 and 4.1 of text).

Context	/ai/	/i/	/au/	/ɔ/	/ɪ/	L
−+	1.19	1.28	1.16	1.16	—	1.20
−+d	1.24	1.28	1.19	1.10	—	1.20
−r	1.04	1.28	1.04	—	1.22	1.14
−v	1.31	1.31	—	1.08	1.28	1.25
−ð	1.27	1.13	0.97	—	1.19	1.15
−z	1.27	1.56	1.09	1.08	1.19	1.24
−d	1.00	0.83	1.25	1.04	1.04	1.03
−b	1.09	—	—	1.02	0.95	1.02
−n	0.89	0.69	0.79	1.01	0.74	0.85
−t	0.70	0.76	0.72	0.78	0.82	0.76
−p	0.64	0.51	—	0.76	0.82	0.68
−s	0.68	0.71	0.83	—	0.92	0.78
−f	0.69	0.64	—	—	0.95	0.76

On the basis of the information in Table 2b, conclusions were drawn about the context dependence of vowel lengths. Using data of the kind shown in Table 2b, differences between RP and SSE accents in respect of the context dependence of vowel length were inferred.

2.4.2 Context independent differences between lengths of vowel phonemes. Average vowel length can vary widely. For the male RP speaker in this study it was 18.6 csec; for a male SSE speaker it was 16.1 csec (see Table 2a). The informant in McClure's (1977) study had an average vowel length of 21.7 csec, and I have recorded data from a Northern Ireland speaker for whom the value was 13.0 csec (Agutter 1988). Lodge's (1984: ch.4) informants had average vowel lengths of 16.4 csec and 16.1 csec (see §3.3). The overall range of vowel lengths also varied between individuals: from 28 csec for a male SSE speaker to 19 csec for a female SSE speaker (see Table 2a). McClure's (1977) range of vowel lengths was 34 csec; the ranges for Lodge's (1984) informants were 21 csec and 28 csec. This shows that valid comparisons of vowel length are possible only when allowance is made for the great variation between individual speakers. Such allowance is implicit in the calculation of length indices described above. For context-independent length measurements, the appropriate allowance was made as follows.

(a) The average length of a particular vowel for a particular informant was calculated.

(b) This was multiplied by the ratio 13.O/A, where A = overall average vowel length for that informant (from Table 2a). It was by means of this weighting technique that allowance was made for individual variations in this study. (13.0 is an arbitrary average vowel length in csec: Agutter 1988.)

(c) These weighted average values were recorded (see Table 3a), and the mean RP and SSE lengths for each vowel were calculated and recorded in the same table.

2.5   Comparison with previous studies

The raw data from McClure (1977) that concerned the vowels and the contexts used in the present study were analysed as in section 2.4.2, and the results are presented in Table 3b.

Lodge (1984), who marked vowel length by perception rather than by machine measurement, reported that he did not find any consistent application of SVLR in the speech of his two Edinburgh informants. Although it was not possible to match Lodge's data with those in Tables 2 and 3 directly, selected items from Lodge's recorded interviews were treated as follows. Words illustrating the five vowels used in the present study, in as many of the phonetic contexts as could be found in suitable stressed positions, were subjected to spectrographic measurement and were analysed in the manner described above. The results are presented in Table 4.

Lodge (1984) does not mark many instances of vowel length for the five vowels used in this study. However, spectrographic measurements of other vowels in his recorded interviews give results that are largely consistent with his marking of vowel length (results not shown).

3 Results

3.1   Context-dependence of vowel length

The raw vowel-length data are given in Table 2a, and the length-indices of the various contexts are given in Table 2b.

The contexts /–+/, /–+d/, /–r⁺/, /–v⁺/, /–ð⁺/ and /–z⁺/ are generally long, the contexts /–n⁺/, /–t⁺/, /–p⁺/, /–s⁺/ and /–f⁺/ are generally non-long, and /–d⁺/ and /–b⁺/ are intermediate in length, for both RP and SSE. When length indices were calculated for RP and SSE informants separately, the differences between the accents were few, slight, and not related to SVLR predictions (data not shown). For example, there is some indication that RP speakers have longer vowels than SSE speakers in the context /–s⁺/. None of these findings was affected when allowance was made for idiolectal variations in average vowel length (see §2.4.2).

Some vowel phonemes show a greater length than others in particular phonetic contexts. For instance, /–d⁺/ is a long context for /au/ but is not noticeably long for /ai/ or /i/. This and similar observations on the data in Table 2 are equally true of both accents. McClure (1977) also found that some vowel phonemes showed greater length than others in particular phonetic contexts.

It is also noteworthy that the two reportedly SVLR-insensitive vowels, /ɪ/ and /ɔ/, show a similar context-dependence of length to the three reportedly SVLR-sensitive vowels /ai/, /i/ and /au/. Again, this is true for both the RP and the SSE informants.

3.2 Context-independent vowel length differences

Vowel length differences can indeed be observed between the two accents, but these are context-independent (Table 3a). These differences are consistent with Aitken's (1981: 149–150) observations regarding /ɪ/ and /ɔ/: namely, /ɪ/ is the shortest of the vowels for both accents, but is noticeably shorter in SSE than in RP: /ɔ/ is the longest of the monophthongs studied in both accents, but is noticeably longer in SSE than in RP. The data in Table 3a also show that /ai/ is markedly longer than /au/ in SSE; in RP, where the length difference between these diphthongs is less marked, /au/ is longer than /ai/. The data from McClure (1977) are consistent with the SSE data in Table 3a in all these respects (Table 3b). The results in Table 3 therefore show that the informants in this study who represented SSE speakers are not unduly Anglicised. First, they have characteristically different vowel length patterns, e.g. for /ɔ/ and /ɪ/. Second, these patterns are very similar to those found by McClure (1977) for a non-Anglicised Scots speaker.

TABLE 3a

Dependence on accent of average lengths of each of the five vowels studied. Key: V = vowel; M = male; F = female; A = overall weighted average for accent group. Other abbreviations have the meanings described in the text.

V	RP					SSE		
	M	F	A	F	F	M	M	A
/ai/	15.6	15.4	15.5	15.0	17.2	17.6	17.6	16.9
/i/	10.7	11.0	10.9	12.0	10.2	10.8	10.1	10.8
/au/	15.9	16.0	16.0	14.1	15.8	15.2	15.1	15.1
/ɔ/	14.1	14.5	14.3	16.3	14.0	15.3	15.5	15.3
/ɪ/	8.7	8.2	8.5	7.8	7.3	6.4	5.7	6.8

TABLE 3b

The results given by McClure (1977) corrected for individual variation by the same technique as described for Table 3(a). The average SSE values from Table 3(a) are repeated for comparison.

Vowel	Average from Table 3(a)	McClure (1977)
/ai/	16.9	17.8
/i/	10.8	10.7
/au/	15.1	15.7
/ɔ/	15.3	14.2
/ɪ/	6.8	4.7

3.3   Vowel length in conversation

The results given so far all pertain to pre-selected words spoken in frame sentences. While this allows good comparability of results it does not necessarily reflect the patterns of vowel length to be found in connected speech. Table 4 shows the data selected from Lodge (1984). There are serious difficulties comparing these data with the frame sentence format data: these difficulties are discussed in §4.3 below. Nevertheless, it is clear that they too show phonetic context-dependent vowel length. In Table 4 $/-+/$, $/-r^+/$, $/-d^+/$ and $/-n^+/$ are long contexts; while not only $/-t^+/$, $/-f^+/$, $/-s^+/$ and $/-p^+/$, but also $/-v^+/$ and $/-z^+/$, are short.

TABLE 4

Data from Lodge (1984) that pertain to the vowels and the contexts used in the present study. Lodge interviewed two adult male informants, G and H, from the Edinburgh area. In some cases, two or more measurements of the same vowel in the same context were obtainable from the same informant: these replicates are shown below.

Context	Informant G					Informant H				
	au	ai	i	I	ɔ	au	ai	i	I	ɔ
-+			14				31	19		
							30			
r	16	28		14		27		9	4	
								13		
ə										4
v				6			20	12		
							17			
z	16					25	18	10	3	
d		17	23				22			
		27					24			
		22								
n	23	17		11		28	23			
	16									
s	19							12		
p		16	13	8			16			
t	14	13						12		11
f		16				17		5		

Context-independent vowel length patterns in Table 4 are consistent with those given for SSE speakers in §3.2 above with the exception of /ɔ/ which is so under-represented in these data as to make meaningful comparison impossible. However, although the pattern is consistent, the actual average values for each phoneme are very different in Tables 4 and 3b.

4 Discussion

4.1   Context dependence of vowel length
It is clear from the results given in this paper that the context-dependence of vowel length predicted by SVLR does occur in SSE accents. However, it is also clear that it is not confined to SSE accents, but can also be found at least among some RP speakers. The results permitted three broad groups of contexts to be distinguished for all speakers, as noted in §3.1.

This investigation, then, supports the view that SVLR applies, but does not support the view that it characterises anything phonetically distinctive of Scots. Thus while the findings are broadly in line with those of McClure (1977), the data in Table 2 imply that this broad agreement would have been maintained with a study using a single RP informant rather than a single Scots informant.

In two important respects, the data are inconsistent with SVLR. First, as noted above, phonetic contexts fall into three, not two, phenomenologically distinct classes in terms of vowel length. Second, the two vowels investigated that are claimed to be excluded from SVLR, /ɪ/ and /ɔ/, showed the same pattern of context dependence of length as did the three vowels to which SVLR is said to apply. Thus, the characterisation of /ɪ/ as short in all contexts in Scots, while not incorrect, should not be taken to mean that it has an invariable length.

The implication of these results is that while SVLR describes vowel length patterns reasonably correctly, it is too restrictive as a description of phonetic behaviour both in its geographical scope and in the range of vowels to which it applies. It seems as though all vowels may be subject to context-dependent length variation, but that this variation interacts with an independent dimension of inherent vowel length (John M. Anderson, personal communication).

4.2   The status of SVLR
SVLR correctly describes vowel length patterns in SSE, but this is not important in differentiating SSE phonetically from other accents of English. Apart from /ai/,[3] vowel phonemes in Scots do not show quality differences correlating with length differences. In RP, however, length is associated with particular vowel phonemes and is inextricably linked to vowel quality differences. This composite factor of length + quality is seen as having phonemic importance. Phonetic context-dependent vowel length, on the other hand, is not considered important in the phonological patterns of RP. Scots accents do not show the vowel quality correlations with vowel length heard in RP, and context-dependent vowel length in Scots thus takes on a more important role.

Vowel length as described in SVLR is phonetic in Scots as in RP. The crucial difference, then, between Scots and RP as regards vowel length is not that the former has SVLR and the latter does not. If the data presented in this paper are correct, both accents have the characteristics of SVLR. The difference is that Scots only has SVLR: it has no phonemes that contrast in terms of both length and quality in the way that RP has.[2]

Two caveats must be entered in relation to this claim. First, Aitken (1981), McClure (1977) and the evidence of the present paper suggest that some vowel phonemes in Scots may be associated with vowel length. However, there is no evidence to indicate that this is true of all vowel phonemes in Scots. Second, the quality distinctions characteristically associated with differences of vowel length in RP but previously unknown in Scots dialects are to be found in the speech of a number of SSE speakers (Abercrombie, 1979). If these two caveats are indicative of changes in progress in SSE, then it may be that Scots accents are reverting to a more redundant phonological system.

4.3　Comparability with vowel length in conversation

The results in Table 4 from analyses of the interviews recorded by Lodge (1984) reveal some inconsistencies with those in Tables 2a and 2b. The easiest inconsistency to account for is that of $/-s^+/$. In Lodge's data, this had a mid to long rather than a short rating, but there were too few instances for this value to be reliable. Other inconsistencies that require explanation are as follows: $/-d^+/$ and $/-n^+/$ are long contexts in Lodge's data, while $/-v^+/$ and $/-z^+/$ are short. The most likely explanation for these differences seems to me to lie in the more variable stress patterns possible in conversation than in frame sentences. Although the average vowel lengths of Lodge's speakers and their range of vowel lengths were comparable to those found in more controlled experimental conditions (§2.4.2), this does not imply that specific vowels in specific contexts will behave in similar ways on all occasions.

Lodge (1984: 93–94) states that his data are not entirely consistent with SVLR. This is true in at least the senses discussed here, and it is unclear whether these would be resolved if only equivalently-stressed items of exactly SVLR context were to be studied in a conversational setting, or whether SVLR simply does not operate exactly in conversation.

4.4　Machine measurement versus perceptual judgment

In §2, we saw that the average vowel lengths and vowel length ranges of individual informants are extremely variable, so much so that one speaker's long vowel might have exactly the same duration as another speaker's short vowel. It follows that perceptual judgment of vowel length cannot be reliable unless the researcher has an extended sample of the speech of the informant. Inferences should not be drawn from the speech of a single informant to the accent of a whole group of speakers. Given the complexities of vowel length patterns, it seems desirable that perceptual judgments of vowel length should be corroborated by objectively measured data.

On the other hand, machine measurement can identify differences which are not and may never be perceptually important, or even perceptible in normal language use. For instance, the male informants in the present study had a slightly wider range of vowel lengths than the female informants. It seems improbable that this is an important clue to identifying the sexes of the speakers from their speech; it is doubtful whether the difference is even perceptible.

Another point indicating a need for caution is this. Machine measurement certainly goes some way to overcoming the implicit tendency of a non-naive investigator to discover what he is looking for. However, it is still important for the informants to be unaware of the object of the study, regardless of the degree of objectivity of the vowel length measurement, if the results are to be objective overall (Agutter 1988).

In relation to the SVLR, the evidence cited in the literature is almost entirely based on perceptual judgment: no large-scale machine-measurement study has ever been undertaken. Such a large-scale investigation of SVLR is needed to resolve the doubts raised by Lodge's (1984) study and the present one about the descriptive adequacy of the rule.

NOTES

1. I wish to acknowledge the help of the Department of Linguistics, University of Edinburgh, in making the sound spectrograph and recording studio available to me. I also wish to thank J. Dodds for his technical assistance.
2. There is one exception to the statement that vowel length in Scots is unaccompanied by vowel quality differences. The vowel /ai/ of RP generally occurs in Scots as [aːe] when vowel duration is long, but as [ʌi] when vowel duration is non-long. (In RP /ai/ does not show such marked quality variation.) This phenomenon has sometimes been noticed independently of the SVLR (Noske, Schinke and Smith 1982). However, there is evidence in Lodge (1984: 89) and in my own studies (unpublished) that this quality distinction does not necessarily occur as predicted by SVLR. This quality distinction associated with vowel length is of particular importance: it is exceptional because it is a quality difference associated with a *phonetic* length difference, irrespective of whether this quality difference is treated as being phonemic in Scots. See Aitken (1981: 141–144) and Harris (1985: 27–28).

REFERENCES

Abercrombie, D. 1979. The accents of Standard English in Scotland. In A. J. Aitken and T. McArthur (eds.) *Languages of Scotland*. Edinburgh: Chambers.

Agutter, Alex 1988. The dangers of dialect parochialism: the Scottish Vowel Length Rule. In J. Fisiak (ed.) *Historical Dialectology*. Berlin: Mouton de Gruyter.

Aitken, A. J. 1962. Vowel length in modern Scots. Unpublished mimeograph. University of Edinburgh.

Aitken, A. J. 1975. The Scottish Vowel Length Rule. Unpublished mimeograph. University of Edinburgh.

Aitken, A. J. 1979. Scottish speech: a historical view with special reference to the Standard English of Scotland. In A. J. Aitken and T. McArthur (eds.) *Languages of Scotland*. Edinburgh: Chambers.

Aitken, A. J. 1981. The Scottish Vowel Length Rule. In M. Benskin and M. L. Samuels (eds.) *So Meny People, Longages and Tongs*. Edinburgh: Benskin and Samuels.

Aitken, A. J. 1984a. Scottish dialects and accents. In P. Trudgill (ed.) 94–114.

Aitken, A. J. 1984b. Scots and English in Scotland. In P. Trudgill (ed.) 517–532.

Chen, M. 1970. Vowel length variation as a function of the voicing of the consonant environment. *Phonetica* **22.** 129–159.

Dieth, E. 1932. *A grammar of the Buchan dialect.* Cambridge: Cambridge University Press.

Gimson, A. C. 1972. *An introduction to the pronunication of English,* 2nd edition. London: Edward Arnold.

Harris, J. 1985. *Phonological variation and change: studies in Hiberno-English.* Cambridge: Cambridge University Press.

Lass, R. 1974. Linguistic Orthogenesis? Scots vowel quantity and the English Length Conspiracy. In J. M. Anderson and C. Jones (eds.) *Historical linguistics,* vol.2, 311–343. Amsterdam: North-Holland.

Lass, R. 1976. *English phonology and phonological theory.* Cambridge: Cambridge University Press.

Lodge, K. 1984. *Studies in the phonology of Colloquial English.* London: Croom Helm.

McClure, J. D. 1977. Vowel duration in a Scottish accent. *J. Internat. Phonet. Assoc.* **7.** 10–16.

Milroy, J. 1980. *Accents of English: Belfast.* Edinburgh: Blackwell.

Noske, R. G., J. Schinke and N. S. H. Smith 1982. The question of rule ordering. *J. Linguist.* **18.** 389–408.

Patterson, D. 1860. *The provincialisms of Belfast and the surrounding districts pointed out and corrected.* Belfast: Mayne.

Peterson, G. E. and Lehiste, I. 1960. Duration of syllable nuclei in English. *J. Acoustic Soc. Am.* **31.** 1296–1303.

Trudgill, P. (ed.) 1984. *Language in the British Isles.* Cambridge: Cambridge University Press.

Wells, J. C. 1982. *Accents of English II: the British Isles.* Cambridge: Cambridge University Press.

Wettstein, P. 1942. *The phonology of a Berwickshire Dialect.* Zurich.

Zai, R. 1942. *The phonology of the Morebattle dialect.* Lucerne: Raeber.

6

STYLISTICS AND THE GHOST STORY: PUNCTUATION, REVISIONS, AND MEANING IN *THE TURN OF THE SCREW*

Norman Macleod

The following discussion of Henry James's *The Turn of the Screw* concentrates on the detailed analysis of linguistic expressions, and on the minute examination of the stylistic consequences of particular linguistic arrangements. But in the development of this microscopically stylistic discussion of exquisite linguistic examples taken from this most problematic of texts, there can be discerned — running in and out of the details of the more general discussion — the threads of two occasionally overlapping themes which ought, perhaps, to be given an emphasis of their own quite apart from how they connect with whatever else it is that is going to be said about the language of this text. These themes concern the significance of punctuation in establishing or obscuring meaning, and the value of authorial revisions as stylistic evidence. It should not be understood from this 'trailing' that these topics matter more than anything else that is going to be said here: but, correspondingly and in an unexpected way, they matter as much as anything else that is going to be said, and giving them this kind of initial prominence, while running the risk of drawing to them too much attention or an attention that will not be continuously maintained later, will ensure that they are not simply seen and dismissed as what they might otherwise be very easily taken to be — the evidential and rather-to-be-expected flotsam and jetsam of any attempt to grapple with the language of James. James (it might be said) is simply the kind of pernickety and fastidious writer who takes the business of writing far above the level of the utilitarian and into the realm of the meticulous, and inevitably with such a writer there is going to be significance in how he points and alters the words on the page. But there is more to it than that. Details of punctuation and fine points of revision are not simply either evidence of James's extraordinary care or the by-product of the exercise of such care: chippings and shavings that now strew the floor beneath the master's work-bench, but that have nothing any longer intrinsically to do with the finished work displayed above. With James, the study of his writing embraces every detail and extends to become a study of him writing and re-writing. In the case of *The Turn of the Screw*, particularly, punctuations and revisions lead us to understand things about the text of the story that we would otherwise not be able to see so easily.

Punctuation in *The Turn of the Screw* is not a means of pointing and clarifying meaning, but can be a source of contrivances which obscure or cancel it: and revisions, rather than refining some sense, already broached but only imperfectly grasped, seem instead to make meaning more diffuse and intangible, and less rather than more capable of being perceivable. In the case of the famously controversial text of *The Turn of the Screw*, the evidence of punctuation and revisions reveals, not an author elucidating the particular meaning he strives for in his text, but an author intent on establishing a text that cannot be interpreted in a definite way.

The significance of punctuation in *The Turn of the Screw* (and perhaps also the paradoxical nature of this significance) seems to be supported by a comment made by James himself. This comment comes in a letter (unpublished, and now in Yale University Library) which James sent to his agent J. B. Pinker in September, 1914, giving authorisation for the English publisher, Martin Secker, to publish *The Turn of the Screw* in London as the first volume of *The Uniform Tales of Henry James*. In his Norton Critical edition of *The Turn of the Screw*, Robert Kimbrough (James 1966: 89) reminds us that this edition of Secker's (which appeared in 1915) was to be the fifth authorised publication of *The Turn of the Screw*: after serialisation in *Collier's Weekly* in 1898, there followed — also in 1898 — English and American book editions incorporating *The Turn of the Screw* as the first of two tales, and then in 1908 came Scribner's New York edition where *The Turn of the Screw* was included with other tales in volume XII. In his note on the textual history of *The Turn of the Screw* (the source of the details given above). Kimbrough (James 1966: 89) quotes from James's letter to Pinker showing that authorisation for Secker's edition of 1915 was — as James put it — on the 'distinct understanding, please, that he conform *literatim* and punctuation to [the New York edition] text — to the last comma or rather, more essentially, no-comma'.

James's demand, with its insistence on the importance of the established punctuation, is clear. But what is to be made of James's additional — and, it might seem, supererogatory — quibble, 'or rather, more essentially, no-comma' and its final, striking nonce-hyphenation? The more one thinks about it, the less straightforward James's meaning seems to be — a situation that is not all that unusual where *The Turn of the Screw* is concerned. It is easy to be inattentive to the hyphen, or to ignore it, and take the expression as a simple reference to the absence of punctuation with the force — given the context — of giving advice not to introduce commas where they do not appear. But any such intention or meaning would surely be more obviously expressed with a simple 'no comma', without a hyphen. And besides, why bother at all to be so quaintly explicit? The preceding advice to 'adhere to that authentic punctuation' would ordinarily be taken as covering all possibilities — as advice both to keep the punctuation that was there and not to introduce any that wasn't. Characteristically the embellishment turns the expression of James's advice into something that goes beyond the simply utilitarian and direct, and can only securely be made sense of if we treat the hyphenated form 'no-comma' as specially intended by the scrupulous James. That must mean taking it, not as an alternative to the preceding 'comma' — contrasting the places where punctuation is absent with those others where it is present — but as refining and specifying a narrower meaning in contrast with that standardly introduced by the earlier 'comma', and indicating that the 'comma' James is referring to has a special, unusual, or even indeed negative function not usually associated with this punctuation mark as it is ordinarily referred to.

Where commentators have alluded to James's nonce usage of 'no-comma', they have taken it straightforwardly. For instance, E. A. Sheppard (1974) takes it as advising care lest commas be inserted. Sheppard argues (unconvincingly, to my mind) that James's reliance on dictation as a working method in his later career led him to omit commas and this forced him to revise earlier heavily-punctuated works (such as *The Turn of the Screw* when put into the New York edition), so as to make them uniform with his later dictating practice. From this perspective, Sheppard (1974: 254) explains James's 'no-comma' with the remark: 'Moreover, commas once discarded, their chance insertion by an over zealous compositor becomes a danger to be obviated — this is the point of James's letter ...' Sheppard (1974: 254) associates this conclusion with an unjustifiable — indeed, a really quite unlikely — suggestion of what the effect would be of James's bringing the punctuation of texts being prepared for the New York edition (among them *The Turn of the Screw*) up to date with the dictating practice of his late period — that is, by making it lighter:

> The effect is to free the reader visually, but to impose on him instead an aural discipline: he must hear 'in his head' the sentences unroll and their cadences will assist his interpretation. The record of the 'stream of consciousness' is therefore unaffected, *since the reader still has, mentally, to supply the grammatical checks and pauses formerly ensured by the printer* (italics added).

All of this is unconvincing, not only since it can be shown that James *adds* commas to *The Turn of the Screw* in 1908 at points where they were not included earlier, but also because (much more significantly) his *deletions* of commas have demonstrable semantic effects, something which makes the business of 'the reader mentally supplying grammatical checks and pauses' absurd. Above all, it is unconvincing since it is part of an argument that assumes that earlier punctuation by comma had no lasting significance and could be harmlessly effaced. If James later felt free to cancel commas so liberally, why had he earlier bothered to introduce them so liberally?

James's 'no-comma' can be perfectly understood as a comment indicating the nature of his comma punctuations as refined in the 1908 text of *The Turn of the Screw* — that they can be ambiguous, that they can be false lights, punctuation marks that work by confusing rather than clarifying, insertions that have two or more functions from which one single function can never be extricated, with — as a result — a consistent ambivalence in the text; for this especial reason, namely that semantic ambiguities in the text depend on ambiguities of punctuation, a close attention to the facts of punctuation is important for how we understand *The Turn of the Screw*.

The same goes for James's revisions of the text between 1898 and 1908. These provide virtually laboratory notes of the working-out of his semantic intentions, consistently showing him working towards the achievement of a text permeated by ambiguity of a striking kind. A usual view of James's revisions — as summarised by Cranfill and Clark (1965: 396), quoting Edel (1948) — is 'that the changes betrayed James's determination "to alter the nature of the governess' testimony from that of a report of things observed, perceived, recalled, to things *felt*" '. While essentially correct about the lexical facts of James's revisions (he replaces *perceive* by *feel, reflect* by *feel, appear to me* by *affected me*, and so on) this view is incomplete since it ignores syntactic and semantic developments that accompany, or appear as consequences of, these lexical alterations: paying attention to these matters of syntax and semantics, as well as to more concrete changes brought about by simple alterations in vocabulary, it can be shown that the overall consequence of James's revisions is to increase the special ambiguous nature of the text as a text — so that we have no regularly firm or clear understanding on such key issues as whether the text conveys the governess's concurrent or subsequent understanding of the events she narrates, whether statements have the status of objective observation or subjective impression, and so on. To say that James strives to increase the ambiguity of the text on such matters is not to imply that he fully achieves his aim — there are things that escape him, some point matter to him more than others, and he is — as the original need to revise shows — all the time working towards some ever more complete refinement.

The highlighted contentions of this study then (alongside its more normally stylistic concerns) are clear: that the punctuation of, and the authorial revisions incorporated in, the standard 1908 text are extremely important to an interpretation and appreciation of *The Turn of the Screw*, this being evidence which is hardly ever attended to or considered in the large body of critical interpretation that has grown up around this work, or which — when it is considered — is not attended to so as to bring out all the relevant linguistic issues bearing on the semantic consequences of James's deliberate punctuations and considered revisions. A failure to attend to elementary but nevertheless significant linguistic matters such as these (and others) characterises the large majority of those myriad interpretative commentaries that have accumulated around one or other of the polarised readings that define the critical debate about *The Turn of the Screw*: that the governess is sick, and a victim of her own deranged hallucinations, or that there really are ghosts and the governess is the innocent victim of supernatural visitations. Not always but sometimes, critics who avoid advocating one or other of these 'either-or' readings, and instead emphasise the duality, ambiguity, or uninterpretability of the text, are critics who pay attention to structural and/or linguistic aspects of the text (early on, Costello (1960), more recently — and more strikingly perhaps — Brooke-Rose (1981)). This study sees itself as a contribution to that tradition, where linguistic structure gets argued about before meaning is taken for granted.

The urge to justify one or other reading of *The Turn of the Screw* (even if this co-exists with a recognition that the story is ambiguous — which, as Krook

(1973) has reminded us, was essentially the attitude taken by Edmund Wilson (1960) in his famous attempt to support a Freudian reading) draws attention away from the question of what James's purpose was in deliberately constructing an ambiguous story capable of being read in two (or a variety of) conflicting ways. The difficulty is that attempts to achieve a settled or single reading of *The Turn of the Screw* must assume that alternative or secondary readings are somehow fallacious, or — if tenable — are still not readings intended by the author. Consequently, any such assumption does not permit into consideration a question that comes to the fore once the ambiguity of the text is recognised or allowed as being deliberate, and which becomes the over-riding question for any study taken up with linguistic or stylistic matters. That is the question, 'What was James trying to do or construct in making this story ambiguous?' Unfortunately, this very interesting question has hardly been considered in the huge literature on *The Turn of the Screw*: throughout most of the critical debate, the abiding question has been one that is of no interest because it is spurious, namely 'Which reading of the story is correct, or at least the one the author intended?' But the real interest of *The Turn of the Screw* is not the question of its interpretation (how to interpret it?) but rather of its interpretability (can it be interpreted?). Important evidence that leads us to see this question as central rests on semantic and other aspects of the language of the text.

Much of the following discussion will centre on a detailed examination of some aspects of the language of a passage containing one of the key episodes in *The Turn of the Screw*. The passage is the following, from the close of chapter IX. The text quoted is from the edition prepared by Robert Kimbrough (James 1966: 40–41), which follows in general the New York edition of 1908. In the extract, I have italicised certain forms which are different in 1908 from their equivalents in 1898, and after the extract a list correlates these italicised later forms (1908) with their earlier variants (1898). This is the extract:

> Then, with all the marks of a deliberation that must have seemed magnificent had there been anyone to admire it, I laid down my book, rose to *my feet and*, taking a candle, went straight out of the room and, from the passage, on which my light made little impression, noiselessly closed and locked the door.
>
> I can say now neither what determined nor what guided me, but I went straight along the lobby, holding my candle high, till I came within sight of the tall window that presided over the great turn of the staircase. At this point I precipitately found myself aware of three things. They were practically simultaneous, yet they had flashes of succession. My candle, under a bold flourish, went out, and I perceived, by the uncovered window, that the yielding dusk of earliest morning rendered it unnecessary. Without it, the next instant, *I knew that there was a figure* on the stair. I speak of sequences, but I required no lapse of seconds to stiffen myself for a third encounter with Quint. The apparition had reached the landing halfway up and was therefore on the spot nearest the window, *where, at sight of me*, it stopped short and fixed me exactly as it had fixed me from the tower and from the garden. He knew me as well as I knew him; and so, in *the cold faint twilight*, with a glimmer in the high glass and another on the polish of the oak stair below, we faced each other in our common intensity. He was absolutely, on this occasion, *a living detestable dangerous presence*. But that was not the wonder of wonders; I reserve this

distinction for quite another circumstance: the circumstance that dread had unmistakably quitted me and that there was nothing in me *unable to* meet and measure him.

1898		1908
'my feet, and'	:	comma *deleted* > 'my feet and'
'I saw that there was someone'	:	*deleted* > 'I knew that there was a figure'
'where at sight of me'	:	comma *inserted* > 'where, at sight of me'
'the cold, faint twilight'	:	comma *deleted* > 'the cold faint twilight'
'a living, detestable, dangerous presence	:	commas *deleted* > 'a living detestable dangerous presence'
'there that didn't'	:	*deleted* > 'unable to'

In compiling this list of revisions I have collated the text edited by Kimbrough (James 1966) with an edition of the text deriving from the 1898 edition (James 1962).

When we examine the above passage in detail, we find that it has startling semantic characteristics: or rather, to speak more accurately, very many of the individual sentences and expressions in the passage — and every one of these the kind that matter to the questions of interpretation raised about *The Turn of the Screw* — are expressions for which it is impossible to establish settled interpretations, not simply because they are ambiguous in the usual sense (so that we cannot decide whether the meaning is this or that), but rather because it is difficult to perceive any particular separate meaning (or meanings) at all in these expressions. The expressions do not come overburdened with several establishable competing meanings. Instead, they are impoverished semantically, not making several different kinds of sense, but not clearly making a particular sense at all.

We can begin to illustrate this matter by considering the opening sentence of the second paragraph, concentrating first of all on the later portion of this adversative sentence (after *but*): *I can say now neither what determined nor what guided me, but I went straight along the lobby, holding my candle high, till I came within sight of the tall window that presided over the great turn of the staircase.* Let us, first of all, consider the following English sentences:

(i)   John walked along the road until he came to a pub.
(ii) John walked along the road, until he came to a pub.
(iii) John walked along the road, carrying an open map in his hand, until he came to a pub.

Sentence (i) associates its main and subordinate clause in a relationship of purpose — John is walking along the road so as to find a pub. Sentence (ii) is different — John's coming to a pub and stopping there is a *result* of John's walking along the road, but that is not why he did so: it merely came about as a consequence. Another difference between (i) and (ii) relates to the consciousness in which two separate propositions are correlated through the conjunction *until*. In sentence (i), it is the consciousness of the character spoken about, John: in sentence (ii), it is that of the narrator or present speaker of the sentence. An important formal correlate of these various differences between (i) and (ii) as written sentences is the absence or presence of a comma punctuation (and in the case of the spoken language, what that punctuation tries to represent in writing — differences of continuous or interrupted intonational patterns).

The interpretation of sentences like (i) and (ii) is clear enough. But when we come to consider a written sentence like (iii), we encounter an interesting difficulty of interpretation — namely, that it is impossible to tell whether the relationship between the main clause and the subordinate clause introduced by *until* is like that of (i) or that of (ii): that is, one cannot decide, for a written form like (iii), whether it is the speaker or the person spoken about who sees the connection between the two notions correlated in the sentence — what the connection between them is or, indeed, whether one event is the purposeful or simply the consequential outcome of the other.

This uncertainty about (iii) arises because of an interesting and transparent fact of its structure. Because of the presence in the sentence of the inserted (or transposed) adverbial phrase *carrying an open map in his hand,* necessarily marked off by comma punctuation (partly signalling its transposition from a perhaps more normal location at the end or the front of the whole sentence), it becomes impossible to tell whether the commas surrounding this phrase are also commas separating the main from the subordinate clause, or not. Putting this another way, we cannot be sure whether the apparent separation of the main clause and the subordinate *until*-clause is only an accidental consequence of the punctuation necessarily accompanying the transposed adverbial, or whether — without the adverbial — they would still have been marked as separate by an intervening comma. To put it briefly, it is a feature of (iii) that the relationship of the main and subordinate clause — whether like that in (i), or like that in (ii) — remains unclear.

Now the point of this extended discussion of these three constructed sentences is that the character of (iii) is exactly like that found in the second portion of the sentence in the text: ... *but I went straight along the lobby, holding my candle high, till I came within sight of the tall window that presided over the great turn of the staircase.* This sequence is essentially like (iii). Leaving aside the first portion of the whole sentence, which raises no difficulty for our present argument and to which we will return, in the latter portion of the sentence the relationship between a main clause *I went straight along the lobby* and a subordinate temporal clause *till I came within sight of the tall window* ... — a relationship that would be clearly indicated by the presence or absence of a comma between *lobby* and *till* — is obscured by the presence of the inserted phrase *holding my candle high.* That inserted phrase is necessarily surrounded by punctuation (because of its position) and that leaves us uncertain whether, without the inserted phrase, there would still be a separation, marked by a comma, between the main and subordinate clause, or not. This amounts to saying that we cannot be clear whether the conjunction of events reported in the sentence is one constituted in the consciousness of the person spoken about (the governess at the time of the visitation) or that of the person now speaking (the governess as the narrator at the time of the narration). Furthermore, that uncertainty is mingled with another one: whichever it is — governess as narrator or experiencer of the events — it is also unclear whether the correlation of these events, in whichever consciousness it exists, is seen as a purposeful one or simply a consequential one. In the end, we just cannot say whether the governess is describing something she did with foresight and purposefully, or simply talking with hindsight of something she became aware of consequentially.

So far we have ignored the earlier portion of the whole sentence, saying nothing at all about the sequence *I can say now neither what determined nor what guided me,* . . . either in its own terms or in terms of how it coheres with what follows. These prefatory remarks have a different status from the later remainder of the sentence in that they clearly seem to constitute a narrative statement about the narrator's present state of mind (*I can say now* . . .) while the remainder (after *but*) is a statement about the person spoken about's previous state of mind and activities, possibly (or not) complicated by involving judgements deriving from the later (and different) knowledge of the narrator at the time of the narrative. Because the first part of the sentence is about the time of the narrating (*now*), while the rest is not, or not simply that, the first part of the sentence is adversatively conjoined (*but*) to the later part. *But*, here, has the force of 'but to go on with my story'.

Unfortunately, even this prefatory piece of apparently straightforwardly current narrative reflection turns out to have its own intricacies and uncertainties, and they too revolve around an intermingling of the time of the narrative (*now*) and the time of the experienced events (*then*). In fact, the whole sequence *I can say now neither what determined nor what guided me* is exceptionally ambivalent linguistically. At first sight, the sentence seems to locate the stated uncertainty in the speaker's present state of mind, as an uncertainty over what in particular it was that impelled the person to act at the earlier time spoken about, the implication being that there is no uncertainty in the speaker's mind that the action being recalled was precipitate rather than considered, that she was a passive victim of events and not a purposeful agent of deliberate and conscious actions. Now if that were to be clearly and undeniably established, then all our earlier reservations about the interpretability of the remainder of the sentence might become dubious, since they would be at odds with the apparently sterling clarity of the remark prefacing the main body of the sentence. The speaker, being also the person being spoken about, would have to be taken as the final authority on her own state of mind, then as well as now, and could not be seen as making retrospective statements not exactly in keeping with her current judgements.

It is not the case, however, that the most obvious sense of the introductory part of the sentence is its only possible sense, or indeed its real sense (if it can be said to have one). As well as having a reading for the clauses *neither what determined nor what guided me* indicating doubt about what it was that impelled the person involved to act (though not doubt that the person involved *was impelled* to act) and about the exact nature of the impulsion (determination or guidance), the sequence also has a reading where the doubt expressed concerns the question of whether the person involved acted deliberately (from an internal compulsion) or acted without prior purpose (by an external impulsion) — in essence, a doubt as to whether the person involved acted or was acted upon. This is because, on one reading, the clause mentions two (*determined, guided*) of a large set of possibilities that occur as possible precise characterisations of the external impulsion to act: on this reading the initial sequence is equivalent to a sequence with a negative main verb phrase (*I can not say now either what determined me or what guided me*) where the binary set of *either-or* options mentions only the first pair of a larger set and could be added to by other *or* options: *I can not say now either what determined me, or what guided me, or what* . . . (with the additions all mentioning near-synonyms of *determine* and *guide*). The speaker has a definite idea but searches for a precise and exact word to express it. On this reading, where the negative element is idiomatically transportable between a subordinate and main clause position, the sequence in the text *I can say now neither what determined nor what guided me* could allow additional *nor*-clauses, with all the *nor*-clauses being separately punctuated. Here the speaker has a definite idea but cannot word it precisely and exactly and expresses that inability in a legitimately idiomatic way, saying that she cannot express that she was impelled to act because she cannot find the precise word for the exact nature of the impulsion. Normally where a sequence of several clauses is linked in a *neither-nor* correlation (with the sense of looking for the right word for a confirmed idea) each segment would be separately punctuated by a comma: *I can say now neither what determined me, nor what guided me, nor what impelled me, nor what drove me,* . . . . Now the sentence in the text, on this interpretation of listing lexical alternatives that could connect with the expression of a confirmed idea, escapes from this convention of punctuation by another convention. Because the expression in the text mentions only two options (only one being introduced by *nor*) there is no need for the punctuation of a comma before the *nor*-clause. And it is this absence of punctuation which allows the sequence as it stands to have a second reading, one where the two clauses in the *neither-nor* conjunction exhaust the binary set of possibilities, the two possibilities being diametrically-opposed differences of kind (with both kinds mentioned), rather than gradually-opposed differences of degree (with just two degrees mentioned). On this reading the sequence is not equivalent to *I can not now say either what determined me or what guided me*. The negativity of the sentence, on this reading, is firmly located with the adverbial conjunction (*neither . . . nor . . .*) and the whole expression indicates, not an inability to speak with exactitude of something that is sufficiently clear mentally, but rather provides the reason lying behind an inability to speak with certainty and clarity. That is, not only is there a reading on the lines of 'I can't be sure of the right word for it, whether something determined or guided me, or whatever, but what I did was something I was impelled to do — the motivation came from outside of me' (the first and accessible reading), there is also a second, covert sense, on the lines of 'I cannot be sure whether the impulsion came from outside me, or was a motivation of my own'. For this second reading to hold, allowed for as it is structurally by the fact that the *either-or* correlation involves only two mentioned possibilities, there must be a genuine semantic distinction (as well as the genuine lexical distinction of which the first, more prominent, sense partakes) between *determined* and *guide* in *what determined me* and *what guided me*. And there is: while *what guided me* can only indicate *a process that affected me*, the alternative *what determined me* (while it can have just such a sense) can also indicate *a process that affected me and which I caused*. When the two verbs are both glossed with the simpler, earlier sense of *a process that affected me*, then any opposition between them is a lexical one between two near-synonymous verbs: but when *determine* is glossed with the second more complex sense of *a process that affected me and which I caused*, then it is opposed semantically to *guide* (which can only ever take the simpler sense). These various claims are borne out by the oppositions of the following paradigm: while there are expressions where the first-person pronoun is the object of both the verb *determine* and the verb *guide (something determined me to do it; something guided me to do it)* it is only with *determine* that we find an equivalent expression with the first-person pronoun as the subject of the verb in an intransitive clause — the canonical form for describing a process where the person involved is both *causer* and *affected* in relation to the process. Thus we have *I determined to* $\genfrac{}{}{0pt}{}{(act)}{(go)}$ but not **I guided to* $\genfrac{}{}{0pt}{}{(act)}{(go)}$. The two relationships which the pronoun *I* can hold to *determine* (object — *something determined me ...*; subject — *I determined ...*) are neutralised in the nominalisation *what determined me*, the two relationships made covert under a structure which is superficially indistinguishable from that of *what guided me*, where there is no covert subject relationship involving *me*. *What guided me* has only one reading, while *what determined me* has two, and this possibility that these syntactic equivalents can be semantically dissimilar gives the whole sequence in which they occur at least two distinct readings. The first reading of the whole sequence indicates certainty as to the nature of the person spoken about's involvement (passive and affected, prompted from without) and uncertainty about the exact kind of external cause that affected her; and the opposite, second reading is one where the uncertainty concerns the person spoken about's involvement (expressing the options that this was passive and affected — prompted from without, *or* agentive and with the participant both causer and affected — a self-directed action prompted from within).

Now this is exactly the uncertainty of interpretation, as we have seen, posed by the remainder of the sentence. Far from clearing up this uncertainty, as its apparent announcement might seem to do, the opening sequence compounds it by appearing to locate the prime cause externally, but only in a form of words which can raise the possibility that the prime cause was internal. One further piece of evidence bearing on the unified non-interpretability characteristic of the whole sentence concerns the location of the expression of negation in the first sequence. An additional reason why this sequence can be taken in either of the ways suggested is that the negation is placed, rather unidiomatically, in the complex co-ordination of *neither what determined nor what guided me*, rather than, more straightforwardly, with the superordinate main verb, as in *I can not $\frac{(now\ say)}{(say\ now)}$ either what determined me or what guided me, but* .... Such an alternative form is slightly more idiomatic than what is in the text, in the same way as 'negative raised' forms like *I don't think the US will agree, I don't believe he is coming, I don't suppose you saw him* are idiomatically established alongside their more stilted equivalents, *I think the US will not agree, I believe he isn't coming, I suppose you didn't see him*. Between such pairs there is a very subtle, not always operative, difference of meaning.

To say *I don't believe he is coming* is to suggest that the person spoken about is not coming, but with the speaker hedging his bets: this is very much a suggestion, or some kind of attenuated statement, rather than an expression of belief or disbelief. The rhetorical meaning is something like 'He isn't coming — but don't quote me!' By contrast, the form without negative raising *I believe he isn't coming*, is very much a literal statement of belief, amounting almost to a strong assurance — based on the speaker's belief — that the person spoken about is not coming. In this case, the rhetorical meaning is something like 'He isn't coming, believe me!' As Lakoff (1969: 140–1), following and acknowledging observations first made by Dwight Bolinger, points out, the negation of the subordinate clause (albeit the location of the proposition that is being negated or which is under speculative consideration) is in some way weaker or less certain in a sentence like *I don't believe he is coming* than in a sentence like *I believe he isn't coming*: pairs of sentences like these are *not* synonymous.

When the governess writes *I can say now neither what determined nor what guided me* (rather than the alternative with negative raising) she makes more likely an interpretation where what is at issue is the precise nature of external motivation rather than whether motivation was external or not: *I can say now neither ... nor ...* looks very like saying 'I can't choose the right word for what I clearly recognised or felt'. But although that reading is strongly prompted, the other is not excluded — it is simply not focused on. What is crucial here is that the verb used is *say*, a verb of verbal description rather than a verb of mental description like *believe*. Just as there is a difference of meaning between *I believe ... NEG* and *I NEG believe* (only the former is a statement of belief, while the latter is not a statement of non-belief or of disbelief but an idiomatic way of hedging the force of an accompanying statement), so forms like *I can say now ... NEG* and *I can NEG say now* involve different meanings of *say*. In the former, *say* speaks of an absence of linguistic precision, in the latter of an absence of knowledge. But as is usual in such cases, while the latter meaning cannot encompass the former, the former can the latter — and the expression associated with it can convey the encompassed meaning. Hence the possibility that *I can say now ... NEG* can be used to convey the complementary meaning belonging to *I can NEG say now* ...; just as, in ordinary language, *I believe* ... *NEG* may overlap with *I NEG believe.*

We have gone into considerable detail on just one elaborate sentence from the passage chosen from *The Turn of the Screw.* If our discussion has shown anything characteristic of the sentence it is its complexity of interpretation, a complexity that verges on non-interpretability, so that we are left with a sentence behind whose apparently convincing statement there is a tangle of conflicting possibilities. Not quite a tangle, actually: the real trouble with the sentence is two-fold. First, one can never be sure whether the governess is drawing on retrospective understanding as narrator or re-creatively talking only of her earlier experiences: the *now* and *then* dimensions of the narrative are inextricably intermingled. And second, related to the first matter, there is no way of knowing what assumptions and presuppositions the governess brings to what she talks about: expressions which seem to assume a perspective and to offer a reflection have the quality of being reflections which destroy or remove the assumed perspective. And this, as I now want to proceed to show, is not an isolated set of features of this single sentence: if it were, it might be accidental, or a trivial distortion; if one can show that it isn't, one may be pointing to a possibly deliberate tactic of the author's, and to a certainly significant feature of the text in a crucial and typical sample.

This self-defeating or tail-biting semantic quality turns up elsewhere in the passage — for instance, in the sentence: *He knew me as well as I knew him.* The comparative conjunction *as well* relates two clauses that identify identical processes (*know*) and identical participants (*I, he*). The function of *as well as* is to predicate a relationship of degree 'to an extent X' between the conjoined clauses. Thus the meaning of *He knew me as well as* ... is to make a statement involving (i) an assertion ('He knew me to an extent x') and (ii) a presupposition ('the extent x = the extent asserted by what follows *as well as*'). But since, then, the meaning of ... *as well as I knew him* is to make a statement involving (i) an assertion ('the extent x = the extent presupposed by what precedes *as well as*') and (ii) a presupposition ('To that extent x I knew him'), the whole sentence emerges, first of all, as trivially and self-justifyingly true, and in the second place, as nonsensically involving an endless regression of dependence between its first and second parts, presupposing what it asserts and asserting what it presupposes. We can compare it with sentences like *I see what I see, I am as tall as I am, He loved me as much as I loved him,* and so on, sentences which seem to tell us something but which on examination turn out to tell us nothing apart from the fact that they are telling us ... *that.*

Let us next consider this sentence from the text: *Without it, the next instant, I saw that there was someone on the stair* (revised in 1908 to ... *I knew that there was a figure* ...). What is the relationship between *Without it* and the main clause *I saw* ...? 'Because I was without it, I saw' — raising one interpretation for *see*? Or, 'Despite being without it, I saw' — raising another, more literal interpretation for *see*? We cannot tell (and the same holds when *see* becomes *know*, and *someone* becomes *a figure*): these distinct interpretations would be associated with different punctuations for *Without it* (and what these punctuations would signal, different structural relationships). There is a difference between *Without it, I saw* and *Without it I saw*, and the question of punctuation is obscured by the commas which have to be there anyway around the inserted adverbial *the next instant: Without it, the next instant, I saw* .... We can not work out just what it is the governess is telling us — that unhampered by the light of the candle she saw clearly something that the light had obscured to her, or that what she saw did not need the light to make it visible. The governess may be saying that what she saw was inescapable even in the absence of light, or that the lack of light made possible the condition of its being seen.

It is worth noticing here, in connection with this particular sentence, how James's revisions (*I saw/knew that there was someone/a figure on the stair*), while of course altering things lexically, are also alterations which complement the already-present ambivalence surrounding *Without it*. The cognitive verb *know* (replacing the verb of perception, *see*) not only has a literal, mental-descriptive sense ('be in possession of knowledge') but also has a more idiomatic sense of insistent assurance of the truth of what follows ('just know'): *I knew that there was a figure on the stair* can mean 'I was in possession of the knowledge that there was a figure on the stair' or 'There was a figure on the stair — I just knew it!'. And these two senses correlate with those available to the ambivalently-punctuated *Without it*, so that putting both parts together the whole can mean (at least) either (i) 'Because I was without it I just knew (maybe now I realise that I was foolish) that there was a figure on the stair', or (ii) 'Even though I was without it I cognised the fact that there was a figure on the stair'. The introduction of *know* introduces a verb more clearly differentiable into senses complementary to other ambivalences than was the verb *see*, as well as introducing a verb which, lexically, talks of something cognitive rather than something perceptual. The revisions, making it a matter of cognition not perception, and a matter of shape not body, make things more abstract and more fitting to reports of sensings achieved either despite or because of the *absence* of a physical, visual aid.

Other revisions in the passage are similarly effective. The deletions of commas at (i) ... *the cold, faint twilight* ... and (ii) ... *a living, detestable, dangerous presence* are more than merely tidying actions dictated by new standards of housekeeping. The meanings of these noun phrases where they occur are different according to whether these adjective sequences are punctuated or not. Thus the phased adjectives of *a living detestable dangerous presence*, while they are (individually) subjective, evaluative forms (just as is the listed alternative *a living, detestable, dangerous presence*), take on a semantic characteristic, which is not there in the punctuated series, of suggesting that these subjective or impressionistic evaluations which are reported are exactly right — that they capture the descriptive, objective essence of the vaguely-identified thing (*presence*) to which the adjectives are applied. Similarly in the related case of *the cold faint twilight*: where *the cold, faint twilight* merely attributes coldness and faintness to the twilight as the subjective evaluations of the speaker, the unpunctuated *the cold faint twilight* goes further. The later form suggests —

without of course cancelling the subjective dimension — that *cold* and *faint* are literally and objectively accurate as qualities predicated of *the twilight*. The coldness felt in the ambient environment, and the faintness perceived from the twilight, are both equated as properties belonging to the twilight. In cases such as these, the deletion of commas is highly significant, having semantic consequences, and being more than merely a factor in the house- or period-styling of the later text. Furthermore, the semantic ambivalence introduced by these deletions (*the cold faint twilight* and *a living detestable dangerous presence* seem both objective and subjective, where their punctuated equivalents are only subjective) is exactly in keeping with other semantically uncertain or vacuous characteristics of the text.

There are yet other instances of well-achieved semantic ambiguity; in a sentence we have already considered, the first of the second paragraph, there is a feature we have not yet considered associated with the noun phrase and the qualifying relative clause at the end of the sentence: . . ., *till I came within sight of the tall window that presided over the great turn of the staircase*. The head noun phrase is definite (*the tall window*) and the relative clause (*that presided* . . .), not marked off by commas and introduced by the relative pronoun *that*, is restrictive. There is a very important complexity in the form in the text, unlike the only possible alternative, formed with an indefinite noun phrase (*a tall window that presided* . . .). With such an alternative the narrator would have been clearly seen to be speaking *now*, with retrospection, recalling a state of affairs *then* where the knowledge *then* possessed by the narrator was different from that *now* possessed. The sense of a statement . . . *till I came within sight of a tall window that presided* . . . would have been that knowledge of the tall window's location arose only from the experience described and was not something known by the narrator prior to that experience. Thus, a narrator saying . . . *till I came within sight of a tall window that presided* . . . would have been talking of an earlier experience from the later vantage point of knowledge she has at the time she narrates. Such a narrator would be clearly allowing the reader to see, and distinguish, the two perspectives of the narrative — the time of the experience (*then*) and the time of the narration (*now*).

But that is not the form James has written. Instead, he has used a definite article (*the tall window that presided* . . .), and that makes all the difference. Such a form can suit not only a situation like that just envisaged above, where the narrator imports later understanding into the narration of an earlier experience, but also one where the narrator, simply talking from the *then*-perspective of her earlier experience, indicates something she already knew then — indeed, something she already knew before the experience arose. The form in the text is thus ambiguous, and in a way that no alternative would have been — and, moreover, ambiguous in a way that conspires with other ambivalences, producing an overall uncertainty over whether the governess's narrative imports later perspective or is restricted solely to the perspective bearing on the earlier experience. Additionally, in connection with this particular example we should note how the ambivalence involved in the phrase . . . *the tall window that presided* ... (whether the governess already knew about the window or discovered it only on her walk) cooperates with uncertainties we have already located in earlier parts of the sentence, and particularly the general question of whether the governess is motivated internally or externally, and whether her experience is purposeful or consequential.

The overall character consciously achieved in James's text is also illustrated in the opening sentence of the above extract: *Then, with all the marks of a deliberation that must have seemed magnificent had there been anyone to admire it, I laid down my book* ... Consider the introductory word *Then*: is this form operative (in the sequential link it makes) in the form of the narrative, or in the content of the story — that is, is it used to introduce what is said next in the narrative or to introduce what happened next in the events being narrated? To answer that question, we have to decide whether *Then* is conjunctive or adverbial (in discourse-semantic terms, whether it is continuous or initiating in relation to what has preceded), and *that* depends on whether *Then* is unpunctuated (*Then I laid down my book*) or punctuated (*Then, I laid down my book*). But this issue is again one that is obscured by the intervention of a phrase that itself requires separation by commas — and, moreover, one whose considerable length tends to take attention away from the trickiness of its own location (*Then, with all the marks of a deliberation that must have seemed magnificent had there been anyone to admire it, I laid down my book,* ...). *Then* as a conjunctive would have added what it introduced to the content of what preceded, making the link one in the story of what happened *then; Then* as an adverb would link what followed as a statement to the statements that have preceded, making the link this time one in the story being constructed and told *now*; but this issue is exactly the kind of thing that is kept unclear in the governess's narrative. The governess speaks of 'deliberation' in her actions, but the locus of 'deliberation' is in the narrative that tells of these actions — *I laid down my book, rose to my feet, and, taking a candle, went straight out of the room and, from the passage, on which my light made little impression, noiselessly closed and locked the door.* There is a great deal that could be said about this sentence: here, it will have to be sufficient to note that the various punctilious interpolations (and their associated commas) force a heightening of the spoken-for quality of 'deliberation' (a 'deliberation', moreover, which the governess self-assesses as if capable of objective self-observation — this is something which guarantees a perception of deliberateness, rather than its necessary existence). But the actions brought together in this series as deliberate are naturally consequential actions. Usually, a series like this would be introduced and punctuated as follows, giving a quality of inevitability rather than 'deliberation' to the narrative sequence: *Then I laid down my book, rose to my feet, (and) went straight out of the room and closed and locked the door.* Crucially, in such a given sequence, introductory *Then* is unpunctuated and the last clausal conjunct is unpunctuated (as — inspection will show — it clearly is in James's text).

Where a report of a sequence of events is not naturally given, the opposite is the case — *Then* is punctuated, and so also is the last clausal conjunct. Thus: *Then, I looked out the window, put on my coat, (and) combed my hair, and switched off the gas*. In James's text, a report of a series of events occurring in a determinate sequence is given a quality of claimed-for 'deliberation' which makes the series of events appear not to be determinate, but considered and determined by the agent. This quality is achieved by the use of interpolations and associated punctuation so that the claimed 'deliberation' is, in fact, imported and staged in the narrative report rather than belonging necessarily to the experience described.

The governess uses a similar tactic later in the passage. She tells us that *I precipitately found myself aware of three things* and, before telling us of these three things, explains: *They were practically simultaneous, yet they had flashes of succession*. In the previous example, we saw that the governess contrived a quality in her narrative which inevitably bore out a quality she claimed for the experience being described. Here the opposite situation seems to hold: the governess seems to admit as a property of the experience being described a quality which a narrative of that experience is bound to have by virtue of being a narrative — sequentiality rather than simultaneity. The governess talks of becoming *aware of three things* as if they were simultaneous — 'precipitately', as she says. But to talk of these three things she must do so in sequence, and so she qualifies the sense of simultaneity — *They were practically simultaneous, yet they had flashes of succession*. The governess seems to want to make her narrative iconic of what it purports. The narrative, not clearly associated with either the time of experience or the time of narration, intermingles experience and narration in other ways. Either the narrative takes on arrangements which bear out qualities purported or claimed for the experience or, alternatively, aspects attributed to the experience seem to anticipate or prepare for inevitable properties of the narrative.

There are two major lines of thought on the significance of James's revisions to *The Turn of the Screw*. The view of Leon Edel (1948), supported in their study of the revisions by Cranfill and Clark (1965), and also subscribed to in his critical edition of the text by Robert Kimbrough (James, 1966), is that the revisions serve — as Edel (1948) puts it — 'to alter the nature of the governess's testimony from that of a report of things observed, perceived, recalled, to things *felt*.' E. A. Sheppard (1974) and David Timms (1976) have, independently and in different ways, dissented from this view, arguing essentially that there is no shift from 'seeing' to 'feeling' in the governess's testimony. Putting the matter as summarily as that does not cover all the details of the arguments of Sheppard and Timms, but the essence of their position is that they are not prepared to see at all as much significance in James's revisions as others do.

It seems to me that James's revisions are highly significant, and that what is important about them is something not at all suggested by either of the positions indicated above (that the tale becomes a record of 'feeling', or that it remains a record of 'seeing'). Instead, the revisions seem to me to show us the construction in the text of a quality that brings it nearer and nearer to being consistently ambiguous. The achievement of this ambiguity means that the text has to be read in an inclusive way, being so constructed that what it reports embodies both objective and subjective dimensions, and with additional uncertainty prompted by an intermingling of the narrative layers of *discours* and *recit*: when these layers become intermingled the reader cannot always separate the *then* of the events being described and the *now* of their being narrated: the thesis of what is said and the situation of its saying intermingle.

The kind of evidence that is most consistently exploited by those critics who speak of the revisions as making the text more a 'report [of] . . . things felt', as establishing the tone of '*felt* trouble' (James's own characterisation in the Preface to *The Turn of the Screw*), consists of revisions of the following type: the changing of *I perceived* to *I felt, I now reflect* (or *I now recollect*) to *I now feel, Mrs. Gross appeared to me* to *Mrs. Gross affected me, I saw that* to *I knew that, I saw* and *I believed* to *I felt, I see* to *I know, it appeared to me* to *it struck me*, and so on. For the most part, critics are prepared, in the manner I have just followed, to cite the facts of revisions thus baldly, out of context and even bereft of the remainder of the sentence within which a particular example falls. Their attitude is that these revisions matter lexically, rather than for instance syntactically or semantically, that the revisions are substitutions of word for word and that no syntactic (or, apart from differences of word meaning, semantic) consequences follow therefrom. But this is wrong. As well as substituting a word that is subjectively expressive (of an emotion or state of mind) for a word that is more objective and descriptive (making some kind of tie between the observing mind and an external reality) when he replaces *perceive, reflect, appear to, see, believe*, etc. by *feel, affect, know, strike*, and so on, James is making — at least simultaneously: I would say this is what he really is striving for — changes affecting the semantics and syntax of the sentence (and hence of the passage, and the whole text) in which the word is involved: replacing a word which reports something *then* of the event, rather than something *now* of the later narrative (*perceived*) by a word (*felt*) which is ambiguous between exactly these senses — whether what is now described as 'felt' is the mental *gestalt now* taken towards an earlier event in recalling it, or whether that 'felt' state of mind was consciously apprehended *then* at the moment now being talked of: similarly with the replacement of *it appeared to me* with *it struck me*. Considering the two versions of the sentence involving this revision:

1898   Yet it appeared to me (1908: it struck me) that we were all, at Bly, sufficiently sacrificed to make that venial.

a lot more than a lexical objective-to-subjective move depends on the revision. The 1898 sentence conveys a sense that the idea that appeared to the narrator (*that we were all . . . that venial*) was an idea consciously grasped, in the words she now uses to characterise it, at the time she is speaking of: this sense of the sentence is quite clear, and this clarity is involved with the fact that, with a present tense form of the verb (*Yet it appears to me that we were all . . . that venial*), this sentence form would express an idea now being formulated and grasped for the first time just as it is being spoken of. By contrast while a form like: *Yet it strikes me that we were all . . . that venial* is like the *it appears* form in now conveying an idea just as it is being formulated and grasped, the past tense 1908 form *Yet it struck me that*

... is quite different in its implications from the unambiguous 1898 antecedent *Yet it appeared to me that* .... And it is different precisely because it is ambiguous between a reading where *strike* is performing a 'mental descriptive' function (now characterising a state of mind as it was *then* apprehended) or is carrying a 'parenthetical' function (hinting to the reader what the state of mind was, by *now* characterising that state of mind as it is *now* apprehended); so that the sentence is ambiguous between the following readings:

(i)   'I was consciously aware *then* of thinking that we were all etc. and I *then* grasped this thought as striking me *then* ...

or

(ii)   I must have been aware *then* of thinking that we were all etc. — since I grasp this thought as a thought that struck me *then* ...

And there is another aspect to the ambiguity of the 1908 form, related to — if not dependent on — this earlier ambiguity. It is that, following the introductory clause *It struck me* ..., the subordinate clause following *that* can represent either the recollection of the very verbal form which that earlier thought originally took or can represent a recasting, at this present moment of speaking, into this new form of words, of a thought which in its earlier manifestation might have been differently formulated. Many of James's most crucial revisions between 1898 and 1908 consist of the replacement of a 'mental descriptive' verb by a verb which is capable of being both 'mental descriptive' and 'parenthetical' and which, when used in a past tense, makes a text ambivalent on two important parameters: these being whether the mental configurations being described and ascribed to an earlier time are conceptions taken from that earlier time or perceptions only now arrived at; and whether, even allowing that the thoughts are old rather than new, the words describing the recollected idea are themselves recollected (as part of the whole recollection) or are freshly chosen stylisations of the present, constituting not merely the return to an old idea but the taking of a new stance towards that old idea. Precisely those verbs which can be 'parenthetical' or 'mental descriptive' permit, in the past tense, this ambivalence: and it is a regular feature of James's textual revisions to replace an unambiguously 'mental descriptive' verb by such an ambiguous verb. The difference can be very, very subtle — as indeed in the opposition between *appear* and *seem*, and involves an interaction between the potential sense of the verb and its tense. Thus, *it strikes me* and *it appears to me* in the present tense are equivalent, both expressing subjective attitudes the speaker now holds, as he speaks, to the accompanying proposition. But in the past tense a difference is discernible. While *It appeared to me* and *It struck me* both also express subjective attitudes of the speaker towards the accompanying proposition or report, *it appeared to me* strongly suggests that this attitude is recalled from the earlier time spoken about and *it struck me* is ambiguous between that possibility and the alternative, that the attitude only comes to the speaker's mind now at the moment of speaking. *It struck me* can not only mean what it says but can also be equivalent to *it strikes me: it appeared to me* is more restricted, and is not so easily taken as equivalent to *it appears to me*. A confirmation of this distinction between the past tense forms *it struck me* and *it appeared to me* is provided by their negative forms, where the semantic dissimilarity is less covert. Thus if we take a sentence like *It didn't appear to me that he was tired* we see that *appear* is a negative-raising verb like *think* (and many others) since the meaning of the sentence involves the implication *he wasn't tired*. Putting the same point another way, we can say that *It didn't appear to me that he was tired* is a near synonym (though not an exact synonym) of *It appeared to me that he wasn't tired*. This is not at all so with *It didn't strike me that he was tired*, which has no equivalence in meaning with *It struck me that he wasn't tired*. Similarly, *It didn't strike me that he was tired* does not carry the implication *he wasn't tired*: indeed, it carries the opposite implication, *he was tired*, as something found out only later by the speaker.

Absences of correspondences of this kind between *appear to* and *strike* reveal the essential semantic dissimilarity exploited by James in revising *it appeared to me ...* to *It struck me ...*, and reveal moreover a subtlety in James's linguistic sense that has sometimes escaped critical attention. The most uncomprehending of responses to James's revisions is that of E. A. Sheppard (1974: 260-1), for whom many of James's revisions — 'unnecessary, or inept, or both' — simply arise because James, 'the multiplier of words' in his late period ('that late and garrulous stage'), exhibited a 'perfectionist's obsessional tinkering with his work'. 'What conceivable gain,' Sheppard asks about what is simply the last of an extended list of examples, 'is there in altering ... "I fancy my smile was pale" to "I imagine my smile was pale" (ch. xxiii)?' (1974: 260). One answer to Sheppard, concerning this example and the kind it represents, would be to consider the syntax and semantics of the interchanged verbs *fancy* and *imagine*.

Both *fancy* and *imagine* can function as *parenthetical* verbs, making them less part of the statements they accompany and more like hints to the reader as to how to take the rest of the statement. In this use the function of *I fancy* and *I imagine* is closer to that of a sentence adverbial than to that of a normal main clause. Alternatively, and slightly less typically, these verbs can be verbs of *mental description*. Here, the clauses are to be truly taken as main clauses, contributing descriptions or reports of mental states, namely of fancying and imagining; they are *not*, this time, adverbial-like 'stage directions' qualifying the commitment of the speaker to the rest of the statement. There is, then, with verbs like *fancy* and *imagine* an ambiguity — which is there with either verb, and with all verbs of this class. But there is also a difference between these verbs, which has to be taken account of before discounting the verbs as entirely interchangeable. The difference shows up in various syntactic ways, whose annotation is originally due to Dwight Bolinger (1968-9). First of all, only *imagine* allows an anaphoric nominal replacement for its subordinate clause, as shown by the following paradigm.

| *I fancy he'll come round* | : | **Why do you fancy that?* |
| *I imagine he'll come round* | : | *Why do you imagine that?* |

Again, there is the following paradigm, which also distinguishes the verbs:

> He isn't coming, I imagine.
> He isn't coming, I fancy.
> He isn't coming, I don't imagine.
> *He isn't coming, I don't fancy.

Only *imagine* permits the postpositioning of a negative main clause following an already negative subordinate clause. Furthermore, a sentence like *I don't imagine he is coming* (with the implication *he is not coming*) is much more idiomatic than a form like ?*I don't fancy he is coming*, which does not have an implication *he is not coming*, and which indeed sounds, not parenthetical at all, but much more like a negation or denial of a mental state of fancying. All of these (and other) characteristics correspond with the fact that *fancy* more than *imagine* always seems to retain some link with its basic lexical meaning, while *imagine* seems always to fill (and to be much more idiomatic in) a 'stage-directing' parenthetical function. When we look back to James's revision (changing *I fancy my smile was pale* to *I imagine my smile was pale*) we see the greater complexity associated with *imagine* over *fancy*. *I fancy my smile was pale* makes the basic observation *my smile was pale* read much more as (or indeed as only) the product of present reflective musing described by *fancy*. But *I imagine my smile was pale* can involve either the analogue of that meaning (*my smile was pale* is the product of current mental picturing described by *imagine*) or can mean that present doubt or hesitation (*imagine* now being equivalent to 'suppose' or even something like 'hazard') is involved in how the speaker now recollects or formulates what the speaker offers as being, at the time spoken of, a fact — *my smile was pale*. Bringing in an ambiguity where a descriptive report (*my smile was pale*) becomes uncertainly established as a product either of the situation of narrating or of the narrated thesis is exactly the kind of ambiguity James seems frequently to seek for in the construction of his ambiguous tale. The gain in altering *I fancy my smile was pale* to *I imagine my smile was pale* is one which is to be judged, as with so very many other of James's revisions, in semantic and syntactic terms rather than in basically lexical terms. The tangible, demonstrable, actual change is lexical: but a goodly part of the purpose and effect of such a change is to be found in its more widespread syntactic and semantic consequences.

Here is one other instance, deriving from observations of Sheppard's (1974: 257–8), of a set of changes which make more complex what was earlier more straightforward:

> *1898* I had so perfectly expected that (1908: deleted) the return of the others (1908: my pupils) would be marked (1908: to be marked) by a demonstration that I was freshly upset at having to take into account that they were dumb about my absence (1908: at having to find them merely dumb and discreet about my desertion).

This is the kind of altering that Sheppard chooses to regard as merely 'simplification of expression' (257), and which he annotates by saying (with an implication of its being insignificant) that 'The formal connective *That* (for noun or relative clause) is often avoided' (257).

There is more to the above instance than that. With accompanying changes of wording (*the others* > *my pupils*, and so on), what James does is turn a formally-marked, fully-tensed noun clause into a non-tensed accusative-and-infinitive form. Effectively *I had so expected that such-and-such would be marked by so-and-so that I this-and-that ...* becomes *I had expected such-and-such to be marked by so-and-so that I this-and-that ....* Similarly, a clausal closing sequence *(at having) to take into account that they were, etc.* becomes the infinitival equivalent (*(at having) to find them* [to be] etc.).

These are formal changes with far-reaching semantic effects. There is a considerable difference of meaning between the sentence 'I had so perfectly expected that the return of the others would be marked by a demonstration that ...' and 'I had so perfectly expected the return of my pupils to be marked by a demonstration that ...'. In the first form, the speaker is speaking of an expectation which she had in mind prior to the return: that is, before the return, she was in a particular state of mind and was aware of what that state of mind was — *an expectation that.* The second form is ambiguous, bearing exactly that sense, or the opposite sense, namely that it was after the return, and noticing the absence of a demonstration, that she became aware of — and consciously formed the notion of — having expected a demonstration. This is exactly an ambiguity in keeping with what is plausibly James's general tactic in revising: the revised sentence could refer either to a predisposition of which she was already aware at the time spoken of, or to a predisposition recognised as already there unconsciously, but of which she became aware only retrospectively — even perhaps, now, at the very moment of putting the whole idea into words. The root of the distinction exploited here is in the different semantics associated with a finite *that*-clause, and a non-finite accusative-and-infinitive as complements of the same main verb (*I had expected that it would be marked ...* versus *I expected it to be marked ...*).

At the very least, the difference between a noun clause complement and an accusative-and-infinitive complement rests on the potentiality of independent propositional status being available only to the noun clause complement: that is, part of the difference between an expression *I believe (that) he is sound* and *I believe him to be sound* involves the fact that the complement of the former (*he is sound*) can stand, propositionally, on its own. It is this more apparent propositionality, perhaps, which makes a main clause complement more appropriate where the idea referred to has some antecedent linguistic status, or where it does not have any expression other than the mental or the verbal. Thus, when I muse abstractedly at the Travellers' Club one evening and you ask what I am doing, I may reply *I'm pretending that I'm in Antarctica.* But that reply, while still possible, would be less apt than the alternative (*I'm pretending to be in Antarctica*) when you put your question, having come upon me, in midwinter — all kapok and snowboots — pulling a sledge around my garden. In this case, when I'm not talking about something that exists solely as my idea, a complement framed as an accusative-and-infinitive seems more appropriate than a noun clause. Similarly, when I discover that I have been misled by the reports of others, I can complain *You can't rely on references nowadays. I thought that he was capable of everything.* But it seems to be only my own previous, and privately-held, judgements which are dismissed when I complain *Peter turned out to be a dud, and I thought him to be capable of everything.* A verb like *believe*, which seems to have two senses ((i) express or indicate a view; (ii) assent to or underline a view) shows one or other sense more prominently according to the type of the following complement. In a sentence like *I believe (that) he is sound* I am likely to be adjudicating on earlier evidence, or passing on someone's earlier report, or — if expressing my own view — expressing it as a considered one. But with *I believe him to be sound* I could be deciding my view as I formulate it, or taking a line different from others, or bringing the issue up to see what others think. In the latter case *believe* is more assertive than in the former case.

Considerations like these point to the kind of difference that James may have been responding to as he turned an original noun-clause form into an accusative-and-infinitive form. A form on the lines of *I had expected that it would be marked* ... places the estimate, and the narrator's sense of it, too firmly within the thesis — that aspect of the text associated with the description of earlier experiences and states of mind: an alternative on the lines of *I had expected it to be marked* ... effectively removes the clarity of that association — now what is being said could belong either in thesis, or could instead be taken as being associated with the current situation of narrating, making what is now said merely the current expression of retrospective estimates of earlier experiences and states of mind.

In his structuring, arranging, and revising of the text of *The Turn of the Screw*, James seems constantly to be trying to make us uncertain about the status of what the governess writes, making it always more rather than less difficult — if not, in fact, finally impossible — for us to ascribe statements either to the narrated thesis or to the discourse situation, so that the two fundamental levels of the text — what is narrated and the narration itself, *histoire* and *discours*, the story and its telling — remain inextricably interrelated. What is important about that is that we can not then perceive, in a continually separate way, the different involvements of the governess in the story — as protagonist and as narrator — and because of that, we can never be sure, in a wide variety of ways, of the status of what we are being told. *The Turn of the Screw* is a 'ghost' story in more than just the usual sense.

REFERENCES

Bolinger, Dwight L. 1968–9. Postposed main phrases: an English rule for the Romance subjunctive. *Canadian Journal of Linguistics* **14**. 3–30.

Brooke-Rose, Christine 1981. *A rhetoric of the unreal: studies in narrative and structure, especially of the fantastic.* Cambridge: Cambridge University Press.

Costello, Donald P. 1960. The Structure of *The Turn of the Screw*. *Modern Language Notes* **75**. 312–321.

Cranfill, Thomas and Robert L. Clark, Jr. 1965. James's revisions of *The Turn of the Screw*. *Nineteenth-Century Fiction* **19**. 394–398.

Edel, Leon 1948. Introduction, in *The Ghostly Tales of Henry James*, edited by Leon Edel. New Brunswick, N.J.: Rutgers University Press. v–xxxii.

James, Henry 1962. *The Turn of the Screw and other short novels*, with a foreword by Willard Thorpe. London: New English Library Ltd.

James, Henry 1966. *The Turn of the Screw*, edited by Robert Kimbrough. New York: W. W. Norton & Company.

Krook, Dorothea 1973. The madness of art: further reflections on the ambiguity of Henry James. *The Hebrew University Studies in Literature* **1**. 25–38.

Lakoff, Robin T. 1968. A syntactic argument for negative transportation. In Robert I. Binnick, Alice Davidson, Georgia M. Green, & Jerry L. Morgan, eds. *Papers from the 5th Regional Meeting of the Chicago Linguistic Society, April 18–19, 1969*. Chicago, IL: Chicago Linguistic Society.

Sheppard, E. A. 1974. *Henry James and The Turn of the Screw*. Auckland and London: Auckland University Press & Oxford University Press.

Timms, David 1976. The governess's feelings and the argument from textual revision of *The Turn of the Screw*. *The Yearbook of English Studies* **6**. 194–201.

Wilson, Edmund 1960. The ambiguity of Henry James. In Gerald Willen, ed. *A casebook on Henry James's The Turn of the Screw*. New York: Thomas Y. Crowell Co.

7
THE DISCUSSION OF PROSE STYLE:
AN EXAMPLE FROM *DAVID COPPERFIELD*

Norman Macleod

This study is an attempt to illustrate a linguistically-based approach to the discussion of prose style. The discussion of prose style in the classroom faces two particular difficulties (quite apart from whatever residual anxieties students may have about linguistic analysis being too objective and too unfeeling to be applied to literary topics, and to the discussion of literary issues). First of all, such discussion involves giving very close attention to the text concerned, or to a sample from it in the form of a passage, and such concentration can come up against the tendency of students to ignore questions relating to the form of a text, and to see reading as simply the business of getting at, and keeping hold of, the paraphraseable content of the text. (Behind this bias lies a long schooling where questions of historical background or of authorial personality and belief and the like have always been made more prominent than any concern with the text as an object and a structure). This predisposition to set the text aside and to focus on what it says is compounded, in the particular case of prose, with a second, overlying inclination which makes more difficult still the eradication of the earlier, more fundamental prejudice. As well as the notion that the language of a text is simply a transparent and inert medium serving to facilitate the apprehension of a more interesting content, there also exists — in the case of prose — a readiness to regard the language as also provisional and accidental, so that the text is not the essential *echt* record in the way that the text of a poem is, but simply and accidentally the one out of many perhaps available that has come to be written down. Novels and other extended works of prose are not, on this student view, 'loose and baggy monsters': it is simply that they come wearing a poorly cut and ill-fitting, possibly hand-me-down, form.

Stylistics, in looking at the linguistic organisation of passages of prose, can inculcate valuable lessons countering the general view that language is a dismissible means which, in the case of prose, is also a doubly-dismissible accidental means. What follows is an illustration of one such stylistic undertaking — a discussion of a well-designed and largely self-contained extract which seeks to demonstrate the central necessity to the passage of the linguistic form it takes. This extract comprises the last three paragraphs of chapter VII of Dickens's *David Copperfield*. In this chapter, David has narrated his experiences during his 'first half' (or term) at Salem House, the school run by Mr. Creakle, to which David has been sent by Mr. Murdstone. These three closing paragraphs are a coda-like retrospective summary, looking over what the preceding narrative has left out, and introducing the climax of the chapter — David's anticipation of (and experience of) returning home for his first holidays from school. (Paragraphs are labelled and lines numbered for reference.)

Extract from DAVID COPPERFIELD

A. The rest of the half-year is a jumble in my recollection   1
of the daily strife and struggle of our lives, of the waning
summer and the changing season, of the frosty mornings when
we were rung out of bed, and the cold, cold smell of the dark
nights when we were rung into bed, of the evening schoolroom   5
dimly lighted and indifferently warmed, and the morning
schoolroom which was nothing but a great shivering-machine,
of the alternation of boiled beef with roast beef, and boiled
mutton with roast mutton, of clods of bread-and-butter,
dog's-eared lesson-books, cracked slates, tear-blotted copy-   10
books, canings, rulerings, hair-cuttings, rainy Sundays, suet
puddings, and a dirty atmosphere of ink surrounding all.

B. I well remember, though, how the distant idea of the
holidays, after seeming for an immense time to be a stationary
speck, began to come towards us, and to grow and grow. How,   15
from counting months, we came to weeks, and then to days, and
how I then began to be afraid that I should not be sent for,
and when I learnt from Steerforth that I *had* been sent for
and was certainly to go home, had dim forebodings that I
might break my leg first. How the breaking-up day changed   20
its place fast at last, from the week after next to next
week, this week, the day after tomorrow, tomorrow, today,
tonight — when I was inside the Yarmouth mail, and going home.

C. I had many a broken sleep inside the Yarmouth mail, and
many an incoherent dream of all these things. But when I   25
awoke at intervals, the ground outside the window was not the
playground of Salem House, and the sound in my ears was not
the sound of Mr. Creakle giving it to Traddles, but was the
sound of the coachman touching up the horses.   29

The 'feel' or 'flavour' or effect of these paragraphs — more or less self-contained as they are — can be summed up in various impressionistic terms. We might variously suggest or observe about the passage:

— that it is distanced at first, but that it becomes progressively more immediate and actual; allied to this is an uncertainty about the first-handness of the earlier recollections, which seem to read with a vicarious or 'read-about' rather than lived quality;

— that it is cool and detached, becoming involved, involving, and emotional;

— that it seems to be amused, ironic, knowing, and that it later takes on solemnity, innocence, trustingness, spontaneity;

— that it sounds more adult at first, more adolescent and juvenile later;

— that it shows a concern with time — with the passage of time — which becomes more and more apparent, while the earlier part is (or has a feeling of being) spatial and static, rather than temporal and dynamic;

— that it is at first unconvincing, literary, clichéd, contrived, reading more like an exercise done by someone who has read lots of school-stories rather than been at school, with lots of unnatural things in the language, and that it becomes more natural — less 'scripted' — although still with hints of melodrama.

There are other progressions and oppositions to be discerned in the passage, and which will occur variously and independently to individual readers of the passage. But whatever single or particular impressions of the passage are most striking for individual readers, it is likely that they will all form a constellation (as do those above) around a sense that the passage moves from being more objective, managed, and 'worked-at', to being more sentimental, spontaneous, and natural. At a more general level, there is perhaps one other thing to notice: it is that the distinct qualities registered in the earlier and later sections of the passage (quite apart from how these qualities are apprehended) are not confined to just these sections. The properties of the passage are fluid rather than sectional, and qualities that become predominant later on are minimally anticipated from very early on, just as marked features from the beginning continue to resonate, however mutedly, until the end of the passage.

With observations such as the above (or others like them and related to them) in mind, we can go on to ask whether there are similar linguistic distinctions separating or distinguishing the earlier and later stages of the passage, so that effects we have identified impressionistically are to be understood as products or consequences of features of language, and specifically of differences in linguistic structure and organisation identifiable at different stages of the passage. We are not going to be surprised if an equation of this kind, between effect and structure, can be identified; but we are going to be satisfied, the more direct, the more complete, and the more inevitable are the details of whatever links we can find between these two levels.

No one can help but notice that the whole of the first paragraph of the passage consists of one sentence. What is not perhaps so obvious, but what is more striking when it is observed — and moreover is significant as a clue to how the language of the first stage of the extract is working — is that this one-sentence paragraph comprises one clause as well. Various apparently clausal instances, identified as such because they contain finite main verbs — for instance, *when we were rung out of bed* (3–4) — are not really independently-functioning clauses, but embedded or rank-shifted clauses, occurring not as a fully-functioning part of the structure of a sentence, but as an element of the structure of a unit smaller than a clause, namely a phrase. In the particular instance just mentioned, the sequence *when we were rung out of bed* — while having the form of a clause — does not fulfil the usual function of a clause by being directly part of the structure of an instance of the higher unit of sentence. Instead, *when we were rung out of bed* is part of the structure of the noun phrase *the frosty mornings when we were rung out of bed* (3–4), that noun phrase itself being coordinated, into a noun-phrase complex, with the similarly-structured noun phrase which follows it (*the frosty mornings ..., and the cold, cold smell of the dark nights when we were rung into bed* (3–5), with this whole complex then being itself embedded inside the structure of a prepositional phrase (*of the frosty mornings ..., and the cold, cold smell ... when we were rung into bed* (3–5). This lengthy prepositional phrase is itself an appositional part — with the various other *of*-phrases and, latterly, other forms — of a larger noun phrase *a jumble in my recollection of the daily ..., of the waning ..., of the frosty ... rung into bed, of the evening ...*, etc. (1–5). Now this one example points to something pervasive in the first paragraph-sentence-clause: the predominance of noun phrases (and, associated with these, of prepositional phrases), so that the paragraph has a distinctly phrasal rather than predicational construction, and a character that is much more distinctly nominal (or 'nouny') than it is verbal (or 'verby'). Indeed, we see here the motivation for the paragraph being written as a single-clause sentence, since all but one of its potential predications (and similarly for the associated 'verby' forms) are attenuated by losing their usual function of establishing clausal predications.

If we examine the whole of the first paragraph from beginning to end, paying close attention to the structural function of its various constituent syntactic forms, we see that we have a paragraph made up of one sentence, which in turn consists of one clause, the structure of which is

The rest of the half-year   is   a jumble in ... ink surrounding all
      S   V   C

Taking it from the beginning, we have first of all the opening (and subject) noun phrase *The rest of the half-year*; this is followed by a finite main-verb form, a form of the copular verb *to be*, present tense *is*. And that, in fact, is the only instance of a main verb standing as the predicate of a clause which is, in turn, directly part of the structure of a sentence; the complement of the verb *is* turns out to be the whole of the complex interdependence of noun phrases (and associated with these, prepositional phrases) extending from *a jumble in ...* (1) down to *... ink surrounding all* (12), a complex that involves subordination, apposition, and conjunction — and other relationships — in its linking of a series of noun and prepositional phrases. Wherever we look for verbs within this complex phrasal sequence, we find (after the first *is*) no finite verbs involved in separate or independent or normally-functioning clauses, but instead either (1) representatives or derivatives of verbs, but where the original or fundamental 'verby' quality has been lost, or (2) verbs but not in finite forms, or (3) finite verbs but only within clauses that have lost their clausal status through being rank-shifted to an intra-phrasal structural role. Thus, if we go through the passage we find

(a)   deverbal nominal forms — nouns derived from verbs — like *jumble* (1), *recollection* (1), *strife* (2), *struggle* (2), *smell* (4), *alternation* (8)

(b)   a special variety of the type categorised under (a), namely gerundive nominalisations where a noun form transparently derives from some antecedent verb form (*canings* (11), *rulerings* (11)) or plausibly from some fuller verb-centred clausal form (*hair-cuttings* (11), *shivering-machine* (7))*

(c)   non-finite participles (both present and past) functioning adjectivally, and hence standing in a more substantive function that masks their characteristic 'verbiness': *waning* (2), *changing* (3), *lighted* (6), *warmed* (6), *dog's-eared* (10), *cracked* (10), *tear-blotted* (10); and associated with these, deverbal adjectives no longer apprehended as participles, such as *boiled* (8), *roast* (9)

(d)   verbs in clauses acting, usually as qualifiers, within noun phrases, and not standing separately as clauses functioning directly within the structure of sentences: *the frosty mornings when we were rung out of bed* (3–4) *the dark nights when we were rung into bed* (5) *the morning schoolroom which was nothing but a great shivering-machine* (7) (The adjectival or relative clause here is significantly defining, and hence is part of the structure of the associated noun phrase: had it been non-defining, or non-restrictive, it would have been interpolated, rather than structured, within the associated noun phrase). Also in this category can be included the noun phrase *a dirty atmosphere of ink surrounding all* (12), where the non-finite participial remnant of some fuller clause (*surrounding all*) occurs as part of the structure of the fuller noun phrase.

There is, as can be seen from the above variety of attenuated or non-predicational verb forms, potentially a good deal of verbal activity in this paragraph, but none of this 'verbiness' comes to the usual kind of predicational fruition. Verbs are mutilated, disguised, suppressed, in some way no longer functioning in recognisable ways as verbs, so that we look in vain (except for the single, early case of *is*) for finite verbs providing the predicational centre of independent (or at least separate, properly-functioning) clauses. The overall effect of this characteristic of the paragraph (along with all the various other factors involved in the distinctive organisation of the paragraph — for instance, the way various noun phrases are specific and definite) is to make its style 'nouny' or nominal.

The interesting linguistic property of nominality has been discussed by Michael Halliday in *Grammar, Society and the Noun*, his inaugural lecture on becoming, in the mid-sixties, Professor of General Linguistics at University College, London (Halliday, 1967). Quoting a typical expression from scientific English as an example (*The conversion of hydrogen to helium in the interiors of stars is the source of energy for their immense output of light and heat*), Halliday goes on to make remarks that will be immediately seen as apposite to the opening paragraph of our *David Copperfield* extract, just as the equative structure of Halliday's example parallels the structure-as-a-clause of the paragraph:

---

*   The verbs *to cane* and *to ruler* — which underlie the gerunds *canings* and *rulerings* — are themselves derivative, being verbs developed from the still more 'basic' noun forms *cane* and *ruler*.

This represents perhaps the most nominalized form of communication; and the prevalence of clauses of this type is I think one of the diagnostic features of what is referred to as a 'nominal style'. The clause is structured into two nominalized segments, containing between them all the lexical items, and the one is then equated with the other. The process is thus reduced to one of simple equation. But this clause type is no more than an extreme form of the very general pattern whereby a cluster of assorted nominals is linked each to the other by a verb whose function is little more than that of glue: it holds them together. What we have been calling the 'process' is then merely a relation among objects, the elements that designate processes being, along with everything else, nominalized. In Whorf's terminology, such processes are 'objectified': that is patterned on (some aspect of) the outer world rather than on our subjective experience of them as processes. In this case the model is the outer world of concrete objects (including, . . ., persons, so that this 'objectifying' includes 'personifying') (Halliday 1967: 22)

It seems to me, when we go back to the opening paragraph of the *David Copperfield* extract, that it is in the nominality of this paragraph, present to such an excess that the whole paragraph amounts to one heavily-nominalised clause of a dozen lines, with verbality reduced to the simple minimum of the equative *be* gluing the two nominal sides of the clause together, that we find a source for our feeling that the quality of the earlier part of the extract is detached, impersonal, distanced, cool, general, amused and so on. Of course, there are other properties that contribute other effects to the paragraph: thus there is the increasing randomness, or unpredictability, of the stray and non-specific details of things recollected, from *the daily strife and struggle* (2) to *suet puddings* (12), and through the various intervening recollections. This, I think, introduces, as a subtexture so to speak, counterpointing the major effects, qualities that anticipate properties that emerge in full only later. Near the end, the paragraph becomes more linear, and more loosely-structured.

In contrast to the opening paragraph, the remaining two paragraphs exhibit a fairly normal verbality: that is to say, the two later paragraphs rely on clausal kinds of statements, they are concerned with processes and relations, actions and events, rather than with objectifications, entities and things. One important indication of this, apart from the ideational evidence (what is said, or talked about) and the lexico-semantic evidence (what the words used mean), is that the main complementiser linking subordinate or dependent clause forms to the preceding main (or understood main) clause *I well remember* is the form *how*. To see the effect of this, just read the whole paragraph substituting *that* for each instance of *how*. With the *that* forms, the series of statements are very much more propositional, and the subordinate clauses conjoined in that way are more like nouns in that they name or represent (albeit abstract) entities or facts. It is because *how* is used, not *that*, that we have a feeling of growing involvement in the events and actions that are spoken of as being remembered. And, of course, the statements of the third paragraph are offered, as the narration becomes less contrived, without any need for a connective introducing them and linking them to some dominating overall general statement — and so they are more immediate still.

Now, so far, we have distinguished paragraph A from paragraphs B and C in that it is nominal where they are verbal, its only clause being an equative statement, not a normally clausal statement of process as are the many, or at least several, clauses of B and C. Conversely we can show that there is a linking feature encompassing A and B which distinguishes them from C on its own. Both of the first two paragraphs involve some reference to the mental acts of recollection or of remembering:

> ... is a jumble in my recollection of ... (1)
> I well remember, though, how ... (13)

In A it is in a *nominal and phrasal form (my recollection)*, in B the mental process is reported by a *verb* in a *clause* (*I well remember*). Both these forms dominate and characterise the grasp of the references (to things and happenings) that follow. Thus all of lines 2–12 are headed by *my recollection*. This means that *The rest of the half-year* is characterised as being the equivalent of *a jumble* in the speaker's *recollection* of these various things. The things are not spoken of as being jumbled in his recollection. But because of how these things (which characterise the half-year) are recollected the half-year is perceived as a jumble. It is the contrast with this vagueness and absence of clarity that motivates the concessive contrast (*though*) and the intensifying positive emphatic (*well*) which accompany *I* ... *remember* ... at the start of B. In contrast to A and B, C is not prefaced or framed by any reference to memory: instead, what is recollected is directly reported without explicit indication that it is recollected — something which, since it *is* recollected, lessens, in fact removes, any sense of there being a recollection, so that what is spoken of is seen with immediacy, directly, more subjectively, emotively, realistically, and so on. To see that this sort of thing matters, just notice what happens to B, how more like C it becomes, when it is read without the prefatory clause *I well remember, though*, and, of course, without any of the subsequent *how* conjunctions.

> The distant idea ... to grow and grow. From counting months ...

Still concentrating on B and C we can see differences between these paragraphs in how the sentences that make them up go together. Thus, in B, there is a crescendo-like growth, from sentence to following sentence, of the amount of conjunction and apposition within sentences. Thus, the second sentence of the paragraph (lines 15–20) is one made up of, basically, a series of conjuncts where each conjunct could stand on its own as a sentence — and where indeed, there is little or no apparent reason for their being brought conjunctively together within one sentence. And the third (and final) sentence (lines 20–23) marks its own stage of development, since what contributes to the extension of the sentence is not a conjunction of potentially independent sentences but an appositioning of various more and more specific (that is, referring to shorter periods of time) temporal adverbials. Notice how the restricted (and much less obvious) extension of the basic first sentence of the paragraph (lines 13–15) consists simply of a conjunction of two semantically overlapping verb phrases, the second of these involving a repetitive conjunction of verbs. These various features of this paragraph give it its easily-felt sense of forward-driving narration. And this underlies the quality of involved, subjective, immediate, concrete narrative which this paragraph contributes to the passage. Notice how the vocabulary of the paragraph is basically one of process of alteration: *began to come towards us, grow and grow, began to be afraid, had dim forebodings, changed*, and how — associated with that lexical emphasis — an explicit and narrowing sense of time becomes more and more prominent, until it dominates the climactic point of the paragraph: ... *from counting months, we came to weeks, and then to days* ... (16); *How the breaking-up day changed its place ... from the week after next to next week, this week, the day after tomorrow, tomorrow, today, tonight* — (20–23).

The narrative quality of C is different again — and this quality is prefaced in the closing remarks of B — *when I was inside the Yarmouth mail, and going home* (23). One of the things we can see as distinctive about C is that it has less in common with B than with A, this being something that can explain our sense that features or effects that are discernible early in the passage do not disappear but continue to resonate more mutedly until the end, just as the effects predominant at the end are hinted at or slightly anticipated from the start. The quality of C is clearest if we look, first of all, at something which distinguishes C from B.

B is virtually about nothing but the passage of time — a passage seen (indeed, felt) and registered in the narrative as increasingly speedy. One single idea, going home for the holidays, made explicit in those words at the close of the paragraph, but earlier referred to in different ways (*the distant idea of the holidays, being sent for, the breaking-up day*) — this single idea is related in B to a varying and altering but insistent reiteration of the passage of time. This is quite unlike A, for there, one aspect of the half-year's being a 'jumble in ... recollection' is that a sense of time (*daily strife, summer and changing season, mornings, nights*) already grasped only in general terms, without the specificity of either *days and weeks* or *tomorrow, today, tonight* is forgotten entirely about in the latter half of the paragraph, so that what is recalled is a whole series of things but without them being in any way related to time. In a way, while B fixes on one encompassing exclusive eventuality in relation to the passage of time, with the passage of time given in detail, A details a number of eventualities but the only temporal point made is that they occurred during 'the rest of the half-year'. This is the only sense one is given in A of when the things referred to happened, and it does not involve — as the temporal references in B do — any real sense of time passing, of any progress from any one point to the next in 'the rest of the half-year'. In A, there is a sense of a lot of things happening, or as having occurred, but we are never told when; in B, we are given every indication of when, but have no real sense of anything happening: the only thing that happens is the passage of time. This, of course, is connected with the idea of how the only thing that mattered was the idea of getting away from school, so that everything else that happened at school both obscured that idea, and was only fleetingly grasped and understood because of the obsession with that one idea.

Looked at against this perspective, C — while it shares features with both A and B — is more like A. Thus the narrative is not of specific incident associated with a sense of the real and detailed passage of time, but one which generalises over several occurrences of incidents in one reportive mention (*I had many a broken sleep inside the Yarmouth mail*) and where these are associated not with specific periods or moments of time but with a sense, derived rather than known directly, that time is passing, or has passed (*at intervals*). In this, C is like A; both these paragraphs generalise one mention over several occurrences and do not involve a direct sense of periods or moments of time, and thus they are both distinguished from B.

There is something else that makes C resemble A. It is that it relies, in a different way but there is an essential relation, on objectifying and nominalised forms of statement. Instead of saying things like *I couldn't (any longer) hear Mr. Creakle giving it to Traddles* or *I thought I heard Mr. Creakle giving it to Traddles*, or whatever, we get the statements of lines 26–29, where reports of processes of audition are not given in an ego-centric subjective form (*I heard* and so on), but in the more nominal and more objective form *the sound in my ears was not the sound ... but was the sound ...* (27–29), and so on. Similarly, what is seen is reported without making explicit a process of visualisation: *the ground outside the window was not the playground of Salem House* (26–27). Partly this tactic in the report is motivated by a desire to make things that are said explicit and emphatic as to the unexpectedness of what was seen and heard. But that is not entirely the explanation of these roundabout forms of statement, since the notion of surprise or unexpectedness that they encode could still have been expressed in suitable and alternative ways: there are options like *I thought for a split second that what I could see was ...* or *I could not make out where we were, but at least I knew that it wasn't ....*. What the options used in the text also achieve is an objectivity in giving grammatical record to perceptions whose lexical framing still betrays an underlying subjectivity. (David describes what is there in terms of its not being what he expected, and what he has become used to: for instance, sounds perceived in half-wakefulness are assimilated to the pressing paradigm of school experience — the whipping of the horses is momentarily taken as a school caning).

This negative, objective, and nominal style captures best the sense of disorientation, of what you see and hear not really being what you expected, of the novel thing you hear being momentarily misinterpreted as the familiar and the customary, of a mental struggle to reassert understanding over more primitive or more instinctive sense — all these things that are characteristic of waking up in a new place, and away from a place that you still have not got used to being relieved to be away from, are expressed strikingly in an objectifying, nominal style. There are various features that could be brought together as showing the first paragraph written in the voice and from the perception of the all-knowing adult, the second with the voice and perception of the excited boy, the third the voice and perception of the child: and maybe the features here are among the tactics that create this voice. Other things in the third paragraph point to it: the identification partly by denial, partly by contrast (*was not ... was not ... but was ...*).

There are other things that can be said about C, and that can be correlated or contrasted with features elsewhere in A and B. C has none of the rhetorical, well-made-paragraph contrivance of both the paragraphs that have gone before. Instead of one whole elaborate paragraph-long sentence, or three highly cohesive sentences, linked by intricate lexical connections, and tied in dependence on the returned-to opening statement by a reiterative single conjunction, we find — in C — a sequence of sentences and clauses with no rational plan determining which things go together in one sentence, or why two things are separated between two different sentences. The main linkage between clauses is now by conjunction, but the distribution of coordinative and adversative conjunction between and within sentences seems quite capricious. Thus, the second sentence of C begins with a *But* that might have been better placed as linking within one sentence (rather than separating into two) what follows it and what has preceded. Then, further into this second sentence, there are two other conjunctions — first an *and*, and then a second *but* — which make for both the looseness (too many conjunctions) and the disharmony (the two clashing and contradictory uses of *but*) which lie behind the jarring, unliterary quality of the second sentence (and major part) of C. (The sentence jars on the page as a piece of writing that we read silently, and against the context of the previous fluent and highly-contrived paragraphs: but this is surely the quality Dickens sought — what we have in the third paragraph are sentences characteristic of the loosely-coordinative, circumlocutory-but-not-quite-fluent style of natural, unreflective *speech*).

Without in any sense suggesting that no more remains to be said, in linguistic terms, about this passage, we can still usefully summarise here what has already been argued for in sufficient detail for at least the general tendency of our claim to be clear — that there are various ways in which the three paragraphs that make up the passage relate to, and differ from, each other in terms of language, and that these varying linguistic properties demonstrably correlate with — are, indeed, the source of — different effects and qualities that can be impressionistic-ally recognised (and indeed would be difficult not to recognise in some or other terms) whenever the passage is read. Even very summarily, the interdependence of structure and effect seems clear, since the stages that impression would identify turn out to be distinguished linguistically as well.

Paragraph A is markedly nominal, consisting of just one equative clause, characterising its subject in terms of another description, and making explicit mention in the form of a noun phrase of an act of recall by the writer. It generalises, and has a contrived, rhetorical quality, bringing together many instances in one referential mention. It is static, making mention of one particular and extensive period of time (this reference being the grammatical subject), but associates no specific event with a single, particular temporal instance.

Paragraph B is verbal and clausally predicational, with separate sentences, but with these all linked grammatically in a reiterated dependence back to the first main clause — which constitutes an explicit mention of an act of recall (stated as a clause whose verb describes the recall) by the writer. The paragraph is general rather than specific, and while still contrived and organised reads more naturally than A. There is a strong sense that the only thing that happens is the passage of time, with various specific references to — and a continuing strong sense of — the passage of time all explicitly connected to one specific event — the coming of the holidays. Where time was in A an undifferentiated unity, in B it comes across as a continuous and uninterrupted series of stages picked out in relation to a unifying or linking event.

Paragraph C is verbal and clausally predicational, but with mental processes described objectively, and with the division of clauses between and into sentences seemingly capricious rather than contrived — giving a natural rather than rhetorical quality to the paragraph. Events and observations are introduced directly, without explicit mention of an act of recall by the writer. Details are now specific and unlike the varying lexical links of earlier paragraphs there are now closely-located lexical repetitions. Several instances are generalised (or implied) in one singular mention; now it is references to time, perceived as separate and discontinuous intervals of consciousness, that are rendered plurally and non-specifically. Each time is now associated with its own characteristic occurrence.

There is one other general set of observations that can be made (or at least hinted at) briefly. The overall narrative structure of *David Copperfield*, as is natural in a fiction which purports to be the writer's retrospective autobiography, is one of the movement from the beginning (with the birth of the hero) to the present moment of his life (when the hero is writing his story), with the forward movement of the story always bringing closer together the two temporal dimensions of the book — the time of the experience being narrated and the time of the narrative itself. These two are at their most distant when the book opens, becoming progressively closer until they finally coincide at the end, in the final retrospective chapter. It is a relevant observation about the passage we have been looking at that its changing structural quality involves a similar progressive coalescing of the temporal poles of narration and experience: the climactic point of the passage (line 20 — *How the breaking-up day changed its place at last, from the week after next to next week, this week, the day after tomorrow, tomorrow, today, tonight* —) is made apparent in two ways: it is here that the growing awareness of time becomes most insistent (*the week after next to next week, this week, the day after tomorrow, tomorrow, today, tonight* —), and the final point of this insistence involves terms (*today, tonight* —) that encompass in their reference both the time that is being talked about, when what is described happened in the past, and the time of its being narrated, when what is described is brought back to consciousness and is now recreated in words on the page. This narrowing of the temporal dimensions of the passage provides a local analogue of the structure that operates globally in the whole book. And the narrative and climactic merging into just one experience and one statement of the writer's past life and present story (and, in association with that, other emergent qualities of the passage that we noted at the start) is in step with what the best criticism recognises as the hero's educative experience in *David Copperfield*. As Robin Gilmour (1975: 31) has observed:

The characteristic narrative movement in *David Copperfield* is a return from a secure present ('advanced in fame and fortune') to a less secure but more vital and complex past ... For in *David Copperfield* the past exists in dynamic and subversive relationship to the present: it is both something which David outgrows, the background to his success, and also an inner landscape to which he returns compulsively, where the experience of loss and defeat can still be felt and thus modify the position of security towards which the novel tends. And in so far as the past is invoked in its full complexity, the rhythm of memory in *David Copperfield* becomes something more than simple nostalgia: it is an imaginative process which, mediating between different states of being, complicates and enriches the book's total perspective.

In this study, we have concentrated very much on the internal connections of one passage, viewing the passage as virtually a self-contained piece, and illustrating the possibilities for the discussion of prose style in an extract: but when such an extract comes from a complex and significant work of fiction, discussion of the style and structure of the extracted passage can be suggestively extended outwards towards the overall design and process of the whole of the rest of the work. In this way, the different undertakings of linguistic analysis and literary appreciation can be brought closer together.

REFERENCES

Gilmour, Robin 1975. Memory in *David Copperfield. The Dickensian* **71**. 30–42.
Halliday, M. A. K. 1967. *Grammar, society and the noun: An inaugural lecture delivered at University College London, 24 November 1966*. London: H. K. Lewis, for University College, London.